The Message of Revelation

I Saw Heaven Opened

Michael Wilcock

Vicar of St Nicholas' Church, Durham

Inter-Varsity Press
Leicester, England
Downers Grove, Illinois, U.S.A.

Inter-Varsity Press

38 De Montfort Street, Leicester LE1 7GP, England

Box 1400, Downers Grove, Illinois 60515, U.S.A.

© *Michael Wilcock 1975. Originally published under the title* I Saw Heaven Opened.

Unless otherwise stated, quotations from the Bible are from the Revised Standard Version, copyrighted 1946, 1952, © *1971, 1973, by the Division of Christian Education of the National Council of the Churches of Christ in the USA, and used by permission.*

Inter-Varsity Press, England, is the publishing division of the Universities and Colleges Christian Fellowship (formerly the Inter-Varsity Fellowship), a student movement linking Christian Unions in universities and colleges throughout the United Kingdom and the Republic of Ireland, and a member movement of the International Fellowship of Evangelical Students. For information about local and national activities write to UCCF, 38 De Montfort Street, Leicester LE1 7GP.

InterVarsity Press, U.S.A., is the book-publishing division of Inter-Varsity Christian Fellowship, a student movement active on campus at hundreds of universities, colleges and schools of nursing. For information about local and regional activities, write IVCF, 233 Langdon St., Madison, WI 53703.

Distributed in Canada through InterVarsity Press, 860 Denison St., Unit 3, Markham, Ontario L3R 4H1, Canada.

Text set in Great Britain

Printed in Great Britain by Richard Clay (The Chaucer Press) Ltd, Bungay, Suffolk

UK ISBN 0-85110-739-7 *(paperback)*

USA ISBN 0-87784-293-0 *(paperback)*

USA ISBN 0-87784-925-0 *(set of The Bible Speaks Today, paperback)*

17	16	15	14	13	12	11	10	9	8	7	6	5
98	97	96	95	94	93	92	91	90	89			

To Mary and Ruth

General preface

The Bible Speaks Today describes a series of both Old Testament and New Testament expositions, which are characterized by a threefold ideal: to expound the biblical text with accuracy, to relate it to contemporary life, and to be readable.

These books are, therefore, not 'commentaries', for the commentary seeks rather to elucidate the text than to apply it, and tends to be a work rather of reference than of literature. Nor, on the other hand, do they contain the kind of 'sermons' which attempt to be contemporary and readable, without taking Scripture seriously enough.

The contributors to this series are all united in their convictions that God still speaks through what he has spoken, and that nothing is more necessary for the life, health and growth of Christians than that they should hear what the Spirit is saying to them through his ancient—yet ever modern—Word.

J. A. MOTYER
J. R. W. STOTT
Series Editors

CONTENTS

ACKNOWLEDGMENT

The biblical text in this publication is from the Revised Standard Version New Testament, Second Edition copyright © 1971, by the Division of Christian Education, National Council of the Churches of Christ in the United States of America, and used by permission.

PREFACE

MOST readers of the Bible have a love–hate relationship with the last of its sixty-six books. Revelation is full of mysteries, in the modern sense of the word as well as in the special biblical sense of it, and like all mysteries they alternately repel and attract. Certainly friends in my own congregation at St Faith's, Maidstone, have expressed both the exasperation of 'I can't understand a word of it!' and the curiosity of 'Do let's have a shot at it!' This double reaction, together with an earlier study I had done on the subject of predictive prophecy, and the exhilarating memory of my own previous dips into Revelation (further along the shore than the much-frequented chapters 2 and 3, though still only in the shallows), resulted in a series of Bible studies at our midweek church meeting.

Whatever others may have gained from this series, the thing which impressed the one leading it was its inadequacy! I realized afresh that even after those weeks of exploration, 'depths all unfathomed lay beyond'. We had begun to wade, where till then most of us had merely paddled; but now I felt that the least one could do in face of such profundities was to try to learn to swim.

This exposition is the result of such an attempt. It may be further removed from its spoken origins, more 'bookish', than some of the other contributions to the twin series *The Bible Speaks Today* and *The Voice of the Old Testament*, for the simple reason that it has to treat—though with no great pretensions to scholarship—problems which belong rather to the lecture room than to the pulpit. It has, on the other hand, tried to bring out a quality which shines on every page of Revelation, and which belongs very much to the pulpit, because it should be a part of the living experience of the church. That is the appeal to the imagination. The truths of Revelation are indeed matters for the mind to grasp; but they are presented to us in a riotous procession ot symbols, with the panoply of music and colour and texture, and even taste and smell. It is a great thing that one's intellect should be captive to the Word of God. But in how many Christian people has the imagination never yet been harnessed for the service of Christ? That, I believe, is something which a renewed appreciation of John's great vision can scarcely fail to achieve.

MICHAEL WILCOCK

St Faith's Vicarage,
Maidstone,
Kent

CHIEF ABBREVIATIONS

AG   *A Greek–English Lexicon of the New Testament and Other Early Christian Literature* by William F. Arndt and F. Wilbur Gingrich (University of Chicago Press and Cambridge University Press, 1957).

AV   *The Authorized* (King James') *Version* of the Bible (1611).

Caird   *The Revelation of St John the Divine* by G. B. Caird (A. and C. Black, 1966).

Farrer   *The Revelation of St John the Divine* by Austin Farrer (Oxford University Press, 1964).

Glasson   *The Revelation of John* by T. F. Glasson (*The Cambridge Bible Commentary on the New English Bible*, Cambridge University Press, 1965).

JB   *The Jerusalem Bible* (Darton, Longman and Todd, 1966).

JBP   *The New Testament in Modern English* by J. B. Phillips (Collins, 1958).

Kiddle   *The Revelation of St John* by Martin Kiddle (*The Moffatt New Testament Commentary*, Hodder and Stoughton, 1940).

Knox   *The New Testament of our Lord and Saviour Jesus Christ* translated by Ronald Knox (Burns, Oates and Washbourne, 1946).

Maycock   *The Apocalypse* by A. L. Maycock (Dacre Press, n.d.).

Morris   *The Revelation of St John* by Leon Morris (*Tyndale New Testament Commentaries*, Inter-Varsity Press, 1969).

NEB   *The New English Bible* (New Testament, 1961; Old Testament, 1970).

RSV   *The Revised Standard Version* of the Bible (New Testament, 1946; Old Testament, 1952; revised edition, 1971).

RV   *The Revised Version* of the Bible (1885).

Swete   *The Apocalypse of St John* by H. B. Swete (Macmillan, third edition, 1911).

Walvoord *The Revelation of Jesus Christ* by John F. Walvoord (Marshall, Morgan and Scott, 1966).

THE STRUCTURE OF THE DRAMA

INTRODUCTION

THE books in the present series are intended to be 'expositions' of Scripture. The danger of attempting to write something of this kind, neither a commentary nor a volume of sermons, is of course that one may fall between two stools and produce a book which is negative and unsatisfying. But so far as the Revelation to John is concerned, there is certainly room for positive exposition which takes a course between the academic and the sermonic, and tries to combine exegesis (what the text says) with application (what is says *to us*). For the literature on Revelation is in one respect unique. No part of the Bible has had written about it so many commentaries—indeed 'a great multitude which no man could number'—and so few books which the ordinary Christian of average intelligence can actually sit down and *read*, to find John's message grappled with and applied to his present needs.

This volume attempts to be one of the latter. Whether it succeeds or not is for the reader to say. The writer has to confess that he often found himself wondering if he had bitten off more than he could chew, let alone digest! The sheer length and difficulty of Revelation, compared with other parts of the Scripture being expounded in this series, bring special problems. Its twenty-two chapters will have to be treated more sketchily than would be the case with the shorter Letters of the New Testament, if the length of the exposition is to be kept within bounds, and that means that one will inevitably do less than justice to some of their riddles. The difficulty of the book means that the balance between explanation and application has to be weighted on the side of the former, so that there is a higher proportion of exegesis than with other books: the bones will tend to show more. However, although the reader may not find every word interpreted, it is hoped that he will become sufficiently conversant with the language to be able to catch the drift of the argument; and although there has to be a good deal of explanation, this has been concentrated in the short 'essays' at the beginning of each Scene of the drama, so that it does not clutter the text itself too much.

The analysis of the book as a drama in eight Scenes is an example of this. It is an important matter, because some of the unnecessary difficulties of Revelation arise from the traditional divisions into chapters and verses, which are useful but often misleading. A clear analysis of John's visions, arrived at by an attempt to put oneself in his place and see things as he saw them, is a great aid to understanding what he is about. The reasons for the one adopted here are gathered together in the introductory essay to Scene 4 (pp. 110–115).

Another valuable aid—indeed the most valuable—is Scripture itself. Of the sixty-six books, perhaps Revelation above all is dependent on the rest for its proper interpretation. Hence Glasson's judicious observation: 'The marginal references in the Revised Version of the Bible . . . are often as enlightening as any commentary.'[1] The importance of this basic tool is referred to again in connection with the Prologue (p. 30). Indeed, all that follows is written in the conviction that the real, central, message of Revelation can be understood without the help of any 'background knowledge' drawn from beyond the limits of the Bible itself.

Nevertheless, certain questions inevitably arise concerning the book's background, and even if they are not considered essential to a grasp of its main message, they deserve at least a brief treatment here.

The style of the book

'Revelation' and its alternative title 'Apocalypse' come from the Latin and Greek words for 'unveiling'. The latter gave its name to a whole class of Jewish religious writings which appeared chiefly between 200 BC and AD 100, and which is known as 'apocalyptic literature' or simply 'apocalyptic'. It is generally

[1] Glasson, p. 125.

agreed that the Bible contains examples of this, particularly in the books of Daniel and Revelation.

A comparison between Revelation and non-biblical books of this type does indeed show many similarities. Truths which could not be discovered by normal investigation (matters of the future, for example, or of the spiritual realm) are unveiled, usually through the agency of angels, in lurid colours and with a wealth of bizarre symbolism—stars and mountains, monsters and demons, and complex number schemes.

This sort of thing is obvious enough in John's book. But there are other features notable by their absence. Where the apocalyptists often attached their 'visions' to some famous name of a past age, as if it were Enoch or Ezra describing what he had seen, Revelation claims to be by 'John', which even if a pseudonym is still not one in the apocalyptic style. It also claims to be a 'prophecy' (1:3), and expects the activity of God and the moral response of man to be a part of present-day life, as the old prophets (unlike the apocalyptists) did.

Yet at a deeper level there are important similarities. The soil which nourished 'Enoch' and 'Ezra' and the rest was a Jewish community very conscious of its precarious position in a world of big, unfriendly powers. Its voice was the voice of the oppressed minority, vainly protesting its rightness and comforting itself with the prospect of eventual vindication. The apocalyptists, like John, saw everything in stark contrasts of black and white. They were at once extreme pessimists, for whom things were so bad that only God could ever put them right, and extreme optimists, looking forward to the time when he was going to do just that.

This attitude, along with much of the conventional style of apocalyptic writing, was John's when he wrote Revelation. 'The God of the spirits of the prophets' brought together the man and the method, and the result was a work designed (in this case with divine effectiveness) to remind another oppressed minority, the Christian church, how things really stand in the spiritual realm.[1]

[1] On the whole subject, see L. Morris, *Apocalyptic* (Inter-Varsity Press, 1973).

The circumstances of the book

To the Christian churches in seven of the towns of Asia Minor Revelation was sent as a circular letter, to be read aloud in their meetings as a message directed to the real needs of real first-century people. The churches had been established long enough to display between them a full range of spiritual conditions, from tenacious devotion to decadent laxity. The message was consequently twofold. It brought encouragement, in the true apocalyptic manner, to Christians who were under great pressure, assuring them that their enemies would in the end be destroyed and God would be triumphant. On the other hand, in the style not of apocalyptic but of prophecy, it challenged them to combat even within themselves the subtle forces of evil, for Satan must be overcome and Christ given his rightful place here and now in their own spiritual and moral lives.

The Roman Empire, powerful in many senses, exercised one particular power which became a cause of great trials to the early Christians. The growing practice of 'emperor worship' meant that an increasing number of them were required publicly to make the fateful choice between Caesar and Christ. Every age has its equivalent test of a Christian's true allegiance; for them it meant actual persecution and the threat of martyrdom.

In this respect the situation in the churches of Revelation is a pointer to the date of the book: it must have been late enough for them to be well established, but early enough for them to have felt only the first squalls of the storm of persecution which was in due course to burst upon them.

Some scholars combine these factors with calculations based on the statements of 13:18 or 17:10, to place the writing of the book at the end of Nero's reign (AD 54–68), or, less convincingly, in Vespasian's (AD 69–79). Most evidence, however, seems to favour a date in the latter part of the reign of Domitian (AD 81–96).[1]

This would mean that if the traditional view of authorship is correct, and the book was written by the apostle John, he would have been in his eighties when the vision of Patmos was given

[1] For a survey of the evidence, see D. Guthrie, *New Testament Introduction* (Inter-Varsity Press, 1970), pp. 949–961.

him. There is nothing intrinsically unlikely in that; another great visionary, Moses, had his first dazzling sight of God's glory at the age of eighty (Acts 7:23, 24). But there are other reasons why doubt has been cast on the apostolic authorship. The arguments turn on the relationship between the five books attributed to John (the Gospel, three Letters, and the Revelation), and the possible existence of a second, and even a third, person of the same name. Guthrie concludes fifteen pages of discussion on the subject with these words: 'To extract a conclusive or even satisfactory result from all this mass of conjecture seems impossible. The most certain line of evidence is the early tradition ... At least, if this is the true solution it at once explains the rise of the tradition, which none of the others satisfactorily does. But many prefer to leave the authorship an open question.'[1] At all events, the 'John' of Revelation makes the clear apostolic claim that though he may have written the book, its real author is none other than Jesus Christ. 'No book in the Scriptures opens in such solemn terms; none makes so uncompromising a statement of its own direct inspiration.'[2]

The interpretation of the book

But what—and this is the most important question—what does it all *mean*? The innumerable attempts to explain it may be classified in various ways. Opinions about its structure are legion: so far as that is concerned, Luther's comment has a wry accuracy—that 'everyone thinks of the book whatever his spirit imparts'.[3] Opinions about its historical references are broadly of four kinds: the preterist view, that it describes in veiled language events of John's own time, and nothing more; the futurist, that it is largely a prophecy of events still to come; the historicist, that it is a chart of the whole of history from Christ's first coming to his second, and beyond; and the idealist, that between messages for the first century and prophecies of the far future it deals chiefly with principles which are always valid in Christian experience. Opinions also divide over the particular

[1] Guthrie, *op. cit.*, pp. 948 f.
[2] Maycock, p. 20.
[3] Quoted by Kiddle, p. xxi.

matter of the 'millennium', the thousand-year period described in chapter 20; premillennialism, postmillennialism, and amillennialism will be considered in the introductory essay to Scene 7 (pp. 175–182).

It is impossible for a commentator to avoid plumping for one or another of these views, unless he waters his comments down to the point where they cease to be nourishing. This exposition accordingly opts for a particular kind of interpretation, as will quickly become apparent to the connoisseur who has a nose for such things; and it does so not from preconceived ideas, but because a straightforward reading of the text seems to point that way. It does try to avoid, however, the exasperating use of the adverbs 'clearly' and 'obviously' in statements which those with other views might think not at all clear or obvious!

The use of the book

The conviction that Revelation really is meant to *reveal* truth, and not to obscure it, and that its treasures really do lie on the surface if one looks for them in the right light, is by no means the same as a belief that its meaning will be spelt out for us verbally, with logic and precision. Of course God does not despise verbal communication; after all, 'the Word' was the name he gave to his own Son. But his words, his declarations and arguments and reasonings, have all been spoken by the time he brings John to Patmos. What he has in store for his last unveiling is a word of a different sort: an acted word, a word dramatized, painted, set to music—a word you can see and feel and taste. In fact, it is a sacrament.

It is no use reading Revelation as though it were a Paul-type theological treatise in a slightly different idiom, or a Luke-style history projected into the future. You might as well analyse the rainbow—or the wine of communion or the water of baptism. Logical analysis is not what they are for. They are meant to be used and enjoyed.

We of the late twentieth century, we of all people, should understand this. We live in a post-literate age, which, tiring of words, is beginning to talk again in pictures. So television replaces radio, and the noun 'image' comes back into use with a dozen modern connotations. Well, God knew all about it long ago; and when his children have had enough of reciting systematic theology, he gives them a gorgeous picture-book to look at, which is in a different way just as educational.

Pictures, potent images of Christian truth, to use as we use the sacraments—that is what we are given in Revelation. Do you remember the spell 'for the refreshment of the spirit' which Lucy Pevensie found in the Book of Magic? When the book was closed, the spell (which was a story) began to fade from her mind, until all she could remember was that 'it was about a cup and a sword and a tree and a green hill'.[1] It is the images that stick. John's pages are studded with them, for the same purpose: that our imagination, as well as our mind, should grasp the key concepts of the faith. So till the bridegroom returns—till the city descends from the sky, and the day of the wedding-feast dawns—we do this, in remembrance of him.

[1] C. S. Lewis, *The Voyage of the Dawn Treader* (Bles, 1952), p. 144.

1:1-8

THE PROLOGUE

THE RELEVANCE OF THE BOOK OF REVELATION

'COME up hither', says the mysterious voice (Rev. 4:1); and John is transported into regions so strange and remote that many Christians hesitate to explore them with him. The Gospels and Letters are territory which is more familiar and more accessible; can this extraordinary book at the end of the Bible, belonging (in more senses than one) to a different world, have anything to do with the practicalities of life in the twentieth century?

From the outset, however, the book of Revelation claims to have been written not for the benefit of a minority in the church, but for all; and not for its own age alone, but for the church in all ages. Like the rest of the Bible, it speaks today.

a. Relevance claimed in the Title

Luke's two-volume history (his Gospel, and the book of Acts) was compiled for a person whom he calls Theophilus (Lk. 1:3, Acts 1:1). Nevertheless we have no doubt that what he wrote for Theophilus is relevant for readers in any age. Paul's Letters were written to particular Christians living in the Roman Empire. Nevertheless we take it that what he wrote to them applies equally to us. These writings were meant specifically for first-century readers, but we do not hesitate to accept them as relevant to modern Christians also. How much more ought we to accept the relevance of those parts of the New Testament which are actually addressed to Christian people in general?

And the Title (1:1-3) tells us that this book is of such a kind. It is the Revelation of Jesus Christ given by God to his servants. If I am one of those who serve him, then this book is for me, however irrelevant its contents may seem when I first glance through it. It behoves me therefore to persevere in reading it, so that I may receive the blessing its author promises me (1:3).

b. Relevance claimed in the Greeting

Although in the Title John tells us that his message is for Christ's servants in general, in the Greeting (1:4-8) he says he is writing in particular to the seven churches of Asia. What he sends them is more than the short letters contained in chapters 2 and 3. The entire book is his letter, and his final 'yours sincerely' comes in its very last verse (22:21). So the address in the Title ('to his [Christ's] servants') and that in the Greeting ('to the seven churches that are in Asia') are both headings to Revelation as a whole. What John is writing is *in form* a letter to a group of first-century Christians, but *in fact* a message to all Christians without distinction. Its beginning and ending place it in the same category as the Letters of Peter and Paul, of James and Jude, written in the first instance to situations in the early church, yet containing apostolic truth intended by God for the church in all ages. Revelation is no mere appendix to the collection of letters which makes up the bulk of the New Testament. It is in fact the last and grandest of those letters. As comprehensive as Romans, as lofty as Ephesians, as practical as James or Philemon, this 'Letter to the Asians' is as relevant to the modern world as any of them.

c. Relevance claimed in the opening Scene

We leave the Prologue (1:1-8), and steal a preview of Scene 1 of the great drama, where we see the risen Christ dictating to John his letters to the seven churches. To the church in Pergamum he says: 'I have a few things against you: you have some there who hold the teaching of Balaam' (2:14). To the church in Thyatira he says: 'I have this against you, that you tolerate the woman Jezebel' (2:20). What do we learn from these references?

It was in the time of Moses, probably in the thirteenth century BC, that Balaam misled God's people by his false teaching. Thirteen hundred years later, however, that teaching is still very much alive, misleading God's people at Pergamum. It was in the ninth century BC that Jezebel, Ahab's queen, was causing similar trouble in Israel. But 900 years later, in Thyatira, we find not merely her teaching but the lady herself once more in evidence!

Christ is not of course speaking of the reincarnation of a person, but of the repetition of a pattern. Bible history is full of such repetitions. Thus the preaching of Jesus repeats the pattern of the preaching of Jonah (Mt. 12:39 ff.), and the lifting up of Jesus on the cross is like the lifting up of the bronze snake by Moses (Jn. 3:14). John the Baptist not only resembles, but in a sense actually is, the prophet Elijah, who lived centuries earlier (Mt. 11:14).

The Letter to the Hebrews, rooted as it is in the Old Testament, provides many examples. God's message coming with urgency through the mouth of David, 'Today . . . hear his voice', was an equally urgent message when the Hebrew Christians read it 1,000 years after David, and when Moses' contemporaries heard it 300 years before him (Heb. 3:7—4:10). Going back further still, the oath God made to Abraham has undiminished force for us (Heb. 6:13–18). And it was in the remotest past of human history that Abel expressed his faith by the sacrifice he offered to God, but even now 'he being dead yet speaketh' (Heb. 11:4, AV). Just as in every generation the evil influence of Balaam and Jezebel is likely to reappear, so God in his mercy is constantly repeating the great truths of salvation; they are 'new every morning' (La. 3:23).

So we must give the fullest meaning to the present tenses of these verbs. The immediacy of Hebrews 3:7, which may be translated 'the Holy Spirit *is saying* "Today . . . hear his voice" ', is matched by that of the seven-times-repeated command of Revelation 2 and 3, which we could similarly translate, 'Hear what the Spirit *is saying* to the churches.' What we have here is a restatement of those truths of the spiritual world which were as real in the days of John as they had been in the days of Jezebel, and which are no less relevant today. The promise of blessing with which Revelation opens and closes (1:3; 22:7) is for all, even today, who will study and heed its teaching.

d. An important consequence

If this is so, there follows a conclusion of some importance.

Before we even reach the second verse, three major questions have been raised, which have long exercised the minds of critics and commentators. The name 'Revelation' (Greek *apokalypsis*) not only tells us that this is to be an 'unveiling' of great truths about Jesus Christ, but also links it with the particular type of Jewish religious literature called 'apocalyptic'. The question then arises, how far did John mean his book to be read as an example of apocalyptic, and therefore how much does one need to know about apocalyptic before one can understand the book properly? John himself is the second question. Is he in fact John the apostle, the son of Zebedee, and the author also of a Gospel and three Letters; or does that traditional view have fatal weaknesses, which mean that the author must have been someone quite different, but having the same name and similar authority? The third question concerns the 'servants' to whom the book is addressed. Would it not help us to understand the book if we could know exactly who they were, and what were the situations and the needs to which John was writing?

The fact that questions like these have been dealt with in very summary fashion in the Introduction does not mean that they are unimportant. But a warning is necessary. When the reader first encounters what seems to him to be the obscurity of Revelation, he may say, 'If only I had more specialized knowledge of Jewish literature, or Roman history, or Greek philosophy, these mysteries would become clear to me.' And this, I believe, is misleading. For the number of God's servants who are equipped with that kind of learning will always be comparatively small—not many wise are called (1 Cor. 1:26)—whereas the message of Revelation is addressed, as we have seen, to all his servants without distinction. Its chief value must therefore be of such a kind that Christians with no special academic resources can nevertheless appreciate it.

This is not to belittle the value of biblical research, still less to exalt anti-intellectualism; the study of Scripture demands the fullest possible use of the Christian's mind. But it is to assert that the prime requirement for the understanding of these great mysteries is a knowledge, such as John himself had, of the Word of God and the Witness of Jesus (Rev. 1:2, 9). For the majority of those who have set out to explore John's book, that Word and that Witness have had to be the only illumination: the Bible in their hands, and the Spirit in their hearts. It is by the focusing of this beam down the centre of their path, rather than by the sidelights which critical study sheds on its rough edges and dark corners, that 'the wayfaring men, though fools, shall not err therein' (Is. 35:8, AV).

I. THE TITLE (1:1-3)

The revelation of Jesus Christ, which God gave him to show to his servants what must soon take place; and he made it known by sending his angel to his servant John, ²who bore witness to the word of God and to the testimony (or *'witness'*—the word is parallel to that used at the beginning of the verse) *of Jesus Christ, even to all that he saw.*

³Blessed is he who reads aloud the words of the prophecy, and blessed are those who hear, and who keep what is written therein; for the time is near.

It is not John's revelation—he is merely the reporter of it— but Jesus Christ's; and even Jesus is not its originator, for he receives it (as John's Gospel also frequently tells us) from his Father. Through the five stages of its transmission, from Father to Son to angel to writer to readers, it comes with undiminished clarity as the Word of God and the Witness of Jesus. That phrase describes here what John was about to be shown on the island of Patmos. In verse 9, on the other hand, where it occurs again, it refers not to the object but to the cause of his coming there. Already God had spoken to him, already Christ had testified to the truth of that word, and it was because John would not and could not deny this Christian experience that he was sent into exile. And now he was again to receive the Word and the Witness, a genuine message from God, which in due course was to be read aloud in church meetings like other inspired scripture (verse 3).[1] It would in a sense be nothing new; simply a recapitulation of the Christian faith he possessed already. But it was to be

---

[1] See pp. 110f.

the last time that God would repeat the patterns of truth, and he
was to do so with devastating power and in unforgettable
splendour.

These verses discourage 'futurist' views of Revelation. Certainly the book deals with much that still lies in the future. But
notice that John was shown 'what must soon take place'. This is
a phrase taken from pre-Christian apocalyptic and subtly changed.
The revelation to Daniel concerned what was to happen 'in the
latter days' (Dn. 2:28). But the early church believed that when
the Christian era began, the last days had actually begun also
(Acts 2:16 f.; 3:24). It is true that the word for 'soon' could also
be translated 'suddenly' (it is ambiguous, like the English
'quickly'); and it could therefore be held to mean that when the
prophesied events did happen, they would happen speedily, but
that they might not begin to happen till long after John's time.
On this view the greater part of Revelation might still, even today,
be unfulfilled. 'Suddenly', however, sounds most unnatural in
the context of verse 1; and the verse as it stands is certainly not
referring to the far future. When we find Daniel's 'what will be
in the latter days' replaced by John's 'what must *soon* take place',
the object is rather the opposite—to bring events which were once
distantly future into the immediate present; so that it is in this
sense that 'the time is near'.

Time for what? we may ask. Time for the end of time, and all
its associated events? Time for the beginning of a long series of
happenings which will eventually usher in the end? Time for
some immediate crisis of trouble or persecution, which will be a
kind of foreshadowing of the end? John is not told immediately.

But it is worth pointing out what Daniel had in mind when he
spoke of the events of the latter days. It was the dream of
Nebuchadnezzar, in which that king had been shown, in the
shape of a great statue, a succession of world empires beginning
from his own. In the days of the last of those empires, explains
Daniel, 'the God of heaven will set up a kingdom which shall
never be destroyed' (Dn. 2:44).

And now John has seen the latter days arrive. The setting up of
God's kingdom has begun with the coming of Christ; and the
promise that 'it shall break in pieces all these kingdoms and
bring them to an end, and it shall stand for ever' (Dn. 2:44), is

already starting to be fulfilled. The fulfilment is a process, not a crisis; and a lengthy one, not a sudden one, we may observe—for though events at its climax will move swiftly enough, the process itself will occupy the whole of the gospel age, from the inauguration of the kingdom (12:10) to its final triumph (11:15). If this that Daniel has foreseen for the latter days is what the angel is now bringing into John's immediate purview, then 'the time is near' indeed. As soon as his letter reaches its destination in the churches of Asia, they will be able to say, 'These things are happening *now*.' Such immediacy it has always had for attentive readers, and so it can reveal to us in our own twentieth-century world the present reality of the conflict between the kingdom of the world and the kingdom of our Lord.

2. THE GREETING (1:4–8)

John to the seven churches that are in Asia:

Grace to you and peace from him who is and who was and who is to come, and from the seven spirits who are before his throne, ⁵and from Jesus Christ the faithful witness, the first-born of the dead, and the ruler of kings on earth.

To him who loves us and has freed us from our sins by his blood ⁶and made us a kingdom, priests to his God and Father, to him be glory and dominion for ever and ever. Amen. ⁷Behold, he is coming with the clouds, and every eye will see him, every one who pierced him; and all tribes of the earth will wail on account of him. Even so. Amen.

⁸'I am the Alpha and the Omega,' says the Lord God, who is and who was and who is to come, the Almighty.

At least ten churches had been established in the Roman province of Asia by the time John was writing, so there must have been some reason for his choice of seven of them. For the moment we simply note that both the number of the churches, whose symbolic meaning we shall consider later,[1] and the order in which they are addressed, which is as likely to be a matter of stylized symmetry as one of mere geography, seem to indicate that his message is for the church in general.

[1] See pp. 62f.

John opens with the greeting found in most of the New Testament Letters. But just as the readership he has in view is particularly broad, so his description of the senders is particularly lofty. Grace and peace come in this case from the triune God, and each of the three persons of the Godhead is named in turn.

The description of God the Father, which resembles the divine name made known to Moses in Exodus 3:14, shows the oddity of some of John's language. Its grammar has been smoothed out in the RSV; but what he actually wrote was the Greek equivalent of 'Grace and peace *from he* who is . . .'. Surely it should be 'from him'? Perhaps John was seeing God as one who is always 'he', the subject of every sentence, who governs every other part of speech and is himself governed by none.[1] We shall find in Revelation many declarations, much more explicit than this, of what is called in Hebrews 6:17 'the unchangeable character of his purpose'. At any rate the disjointed grammar is only on the surface, and may be due to the breathtaking sequence of his visions; for their deeper truth is perfectly consistent, and forms an interlocking grammar of the spirit.

It is in fact the Spirit, who is before the throne, at the heart of the Godhead, and thus knows the deep truth of God (1 Cor. 2:10 f.), who is mentioned next. John's vision is going to take him into the heavenly sanctuary, of which the Jewish Tabernacle was a copy and shadow (Heb. 8:5); and perhaps the unusual order of the Trinity here (Father, Spirit, Son) corresponds to the plan of the earthly sanctuary, where the ark in the Holy of Holies represents the throne of God, the seven-branched lampstand in the Holy Place before it represents the Spirit,[2] and in the courtyard before that stands the altar, with its priest and its sacrifice both representing, of course, the redeeming work of Christ.

If the description of the Father contains one of the first of John's solecisms, that of the Spirit contains one of the first of his mysteries. *Seven* spirits—do they mean the one Spirit in his

---

[1] 'Even a paraphrase of the name of the unchanging God must be preserved from declension!' (Kiddle, p. 7).

[2] Compare 1:4 with 4:5, 5:6, and Zc. 4:1-5, 10b: lamps = eyes = spirits. The symbolism of the lamps in 1:12, 20 is not so very different; here it is the Spirit, there the earthly dwelling-place of the Spirit (1 Cor. 3:16), which is being depicted.

essential nature, as the seven churches stand for the one church as she really is? Or do they mean the Spirit equally present in each of the churches (see 5:6)? Or do they mean the sevenfold gifts of the Spirit (*cf.* Is. 11:2)? We cannot know for sure. But we are duly warned that for some of the locked doors of Revelation, keys may be hard to find.

God the Son has the fullest description. Its Old Testament roots are in Psalm 89:27, 37, and it portrays him in his threefold office of Prophet, Priest, and King. Here the Trinity is earthed, and theology (verse 5a) turns into praise (verses 5b, 6). Jesus Christ is the Prophet who came into the world to bear witness to the gospel of salvation (for although the word for 'witness' is *martys*, 'a martyr', the basic thought is not the death he dies so much as the testimony he bears); and that loving condescension is for *us*. He is the Priest who has offered himself and died, and then risen from the dead, to obtain new life also for the rest of God's children. To be 'washed' in his blood (AV) is a perfectly acceptable biblical metaphor, found for example in 7:14; but the RSV's reading, *'freed* . . . by his blood', is not only better attested, but calls up the associations of the exodus—the death of the passover lamb, and the rescue of Israel from Egypt. At Calvary a more far-reaching rescue has been effected; and that deliverance is for *us*. He is now exalted as King of kings, and as Israel was brought out of slavery to be God's kingdom of priests (5:9, 10; Ex. 19:6), so a share in his kingdom is available to *us*. And one day he will return, as he himself has said; for it was not John, but Jesus, who first brought together the two prophetic pictures of clouds and mourning tribes in connection with his second coming (Dn. 7:13; Zc. 12:10; Mt. 24:30). Those who pierced him will at last recognize him, and bewail the lost opportunity of salvation. But his own people will be expecting him, knowing that he is 'the Alpha and the Omega',[1] both Beginning and End of all things. And thus his work will be completed.

This is the Almighty God who is sending grace and peace to us his servants in the long letter which follows. Grace and peace, be it noted—not perplexity and a puzzle; and we must read it in

---

[1] The first and last letters of the Greek alphabet, equivalent to 'A to Z'.

the expectant spirit that looks for his blessing. The letter is to be cast in the form of a drama; and after the Title and Greeting which together form its Prologue, the curtain rises, and the drama begins.

$I{:}9{-}3{:}22$

SCENE 1:
THE CHURCH IN THE WORLD:
seven Letters dictated

THE REPEAT OF PATTERNS

THE opening Scene of the drama is a stupendous vision of the living Christ, who dictates to John a series of individual Letters addressed to the seven churches for whom the entire book is being written. What is said we shall consider shortly. First we notice how it is said.

In a brief preview we have already glimpsed a repetition of Old Testament patterns, where the teaching of Balaam and Jezebel is recurring in the church life of these New Testament Christians. Now, as the whole Scene unfolds before us, we see how rich it is in such repetitions. Pattern echoes pattern throughout its length, as in an intricate poem. It positively rhymes.

Some of these echoes can be perceived without any background knowledge at all. Every Letter starts with a description of Christ which repeats part of the total description of him at the beginning of the Scene. Every Letter corresponds in shape to every other, beginning with the names of the addressees and the sender, continuing with statements about the former and messages to them, and ending with a command and a promise. Indeed, it is hard not to see in the basic structure of most of the Letters (though John does not draw attention to this) a seven-beat rhythm which echoes the broader rhythm of the Scene as a whole. In the first Letter, for example, it runs thus: (1) To the Ephesians (2) speaks the Holder of the seven stars: (3) I know certain good things about you, (4) but a bad thing too, (5) so repent. (6) Hear what the Spirit says; (7) the victor shall eat of the tree of life.

For readers familiar with other parts of the Bible, deeper echoes sound. The promises to those who conquer will be repeated in later Scenes of Revelation: the tree of life (2:7) in chapter 22, the escape from the second death (2:11) in chapter 20, and so on. The portrayal of Christ has already appeared in earlier scriptures; the glory itself is the same that shone on the mount of transfiguration (Mk. 9:2, 3)—if the writer of Revelation was the apostle John, he himself had already seen on a hilltop in Palestine what he now saw on a hilltop in Patmos. What goes with that glory (the sound of trumpet-voices and many waters, the dazzling whiteness and the glowing bronze) was also the accompaniment of divine appearances in the Old Testament (Ex. 19:16; Ezk. 43:2; Dn. 7:9; Ezk. 1:7). The Son of man's title and the general description of him are there too (Dn. 7:13; 10:5 f.).

Nor is it simply words and phrases that are repeated. The warnings to Christ's churches here correspond at several points with the warnings to his disciples in Matthew 24 (e.g. 2:4 and Mt. 24:12; and see pp. 85 ff.). The solemn declaration 'I will give to each of you as your works deserve' (2:23) is both 'Christ's invariable rule' and that of his apostles also.[1]

Once you begin looking for this sort of thing elsewhere, it is remarkable how much of it you will find. Repetition is one means by which the psalmists 'rhyme' their poetry; what is echoed from line to line is not the sound but the sense—'The earth is the Lord's and the fulness thereof, the world and those who dwell therein; for he has founded it upon the seas, and established it upon the rivers' (Ps. 24:1, 2). It gives force to the words of the prophets: 'For three transgressions of Damascus, and for four ... for three transgressions of Gaza, and for four ... for three transgressions of Tyre, and for four, I will not revoke the punishment' (Am. 1:3, 6, 9). It is to be found on the grandest scale in the 'types' or patterns of biblical history, the great vertical pillars which show at every level something of the plan of the whole building, and to which our attention is most clearly drawn in the Letter to the Hebrews. It is equally to be found in some of the smallest bricks that go to make up the building— tiny phrases, most of them hidden behind the plaster of an English translation, though at least one remains visible.

This is a fragment of a verse in the AV of Luke's Gospel, which

[1] Swete, p. 25; and see Rom. 2:6; Jas. 2:14-26.

yields the clue to why Scripture is so full of repeated patterns. One purpose of repetition, as we have seen, is to show how relevant the Bible is. If what happened in the time of Balaam could happen again in the time of John, we are warned that it is equally likely to happen today. But repetition has another purpose. The RSV of Luke 22:15 reads, 'I have earnestly desired'; what Luke wrote in Greek was, as the AV translates, 'with desire have I desired'. Genesis 31:30 has the same sort of phrase: in the RSV, 'you longed greatly'; in Hebrew, 'you longed with longing'. Repetition of this kind has in fact been taken over into New Testament Greek from Old Testament Hebrew, where it is the regular way of expressing emphasis. To say a thing twice is to intensify it. To repeat means to underline.

And this is what God is doing constantly. He has basically just one message for men, the good news of salvation. But in his concern to get it across, he knows that one statement of it will not be enough. 'Once God has spoken', says the psalmist, but 'twice have I heard' (Ps. 62:11). Thus Pharaoh is given two different dreams which convey the same message, to impress him with its validity (Gn. 41:32). The disciples are shown two separate miracles which convey the same truth, to teach them a particular lesson (Mt. 16:5-12). The purpose of hitting the same nail several times is obvious: to drive it home.

God is plainly teaching by this method throughout the rest of Scripture. And with good reason. The mind of man is incurably centrifugal, for ever flying off at a tangent. He must be brought back to the great central truths—made, literally, to concentrate. Those truths God outlines for him again and again, sometimes by a pencil sketch, sometimes by a more detailed pen drawing, sometimes by brushfuls of paint. The likelihood therefore is that he is doing the same in Revelation; and unless we have good reason to believe the opposite, we may expect the truth conveyed in this book to be intensive rather than extensive. In other words, what we are shown here is more likely to be a working over in colour of a picture we already know in outline, than to be an extra piece of canvas tacked on to the original picture.[1]

[1] See pp. 171, 180.

I. SCENE I OPENS:
THE CHURCH CENTRED ON CHRIST (1:9-20)

I John, your brother, who share with you in Jesus the tribulation and the kingdom and the patient endurance, was on the island called Patmos on account of the word of God and the testimony of Jesus. [10]*I was in the Spirit on the Lord's day, and I heard behind me a loud voice like a trumpet* [11]*saying, 'Write what you see in a book and send it to the seven churches, to Ephesus and to Smyrna and to Pergamum and to Thyatira and to Sardis and to Philadelphia and to Laodicea.'*

[12]*Then I turned to see the voice that was speaking to me.*

And on turning I saw seven golden lampstands, [13]*and in the midst of the lampstands one like a son of man, clothed with a long robe and with a golden girdle round his breast;* [14]*his head and his hair were white as white wool, white as snow; his eyes were like a flame of fire,* [15]*his feet were like burnished bronze, refined as in a furnace, and his voice was like the sound of many waters;* [16]*in his right hand he held seven stars, from his mouth issued a sharp two-edged sword, and his face was like the sun shining in full strength.*

[17]*When I saw him, I fell at his feet as though dead. But he laid his right hand upon me, saying, 'Fear not, I am the first and the last,* [18]*and the living one; I died, and behold I am alive for evermore, and I have the keys of Death and Hades.* [19]*Now write what you see, what is and what is to take place hereafter.* [20]*As for the mystery of the seven stars which you saw in my right hand, and the seven golden lampstands, the seven stars are the angels of the seven churches and the seven lampstands are the seven churches.'*

Up to the day when he heard the trumpet-voice, John's banishment must have seemed much more the sharing of Jesus's tribulation than the sharing of his kingdom. The mountains and mines of Patmos were surroundings calculated to depress, not to encourage. But though John was physically 'in Patmos' (*en Patmō*), on this particular Lord's day he was also 'in the Spirit' (*en Pneumati*), and as for Jacob long before, the stony wilderness of exile proved for him the very gate of heaven. The voice spoke: the saint turned: the Mediterranean island scene faded behind him, and before him opened the vision of another kind of reality altogether.

It was the circle of seven lamps which first caught his eye. The lamps mean the churches, as we are told immediately. Even without verse 20 we might deduce this meaning from such passages as Philippians 2:15, 16. Those who shine like lights in the world, says Paul, are those who hold the word of life. So Christ, who is *the* light of the world (Jn. 8:12), gives his disciples the same title (Mt. 5:14).

The meaning of the other cluster of lights, the stars, is less easy. Suggestions that the 'angels' are leaders of the churches, or messengers from them, or their 'spirit' in the modern sense of character or ethos, raise a number of difficulties. It seems simplest to take the word at face value. Scripture does seem to show (and not only in apocalyptic writings) that both individuals (Mt. 18:10; Acts 12:15) and nations (Dn. 10:13; 12:1) can each have an 'angel', a spiritual counterpart on the heavenly level; presumably the same may be true of churches. At any rate the angel and his church members are closely identified; Christ's message is addressed to him or to them indiscriminately; and both star and lamp, in different ways, give light to the world.

But the lesser lights of earth and sky pale before the splendour of the sun. This opening scene is dominated by 'the glory of our great God and Saviour Jesus Christ' (Tit. 2:13)—we know from verse 18 that it can be none other—and the sight is literally breathtaking (verse 17). John certainly sees him as God; he gives him the attributes of deity by using the same kind of language that Ezekiel and Daniel use to describe God, and recalls Christ's own claim in John 14:9, 'He who has seen me has seen the Father.' From this point onwards, the centrality of Christ is the ruling theme of Revelation. All things depend on their relation to him.

This may explain one curious feature here. The seven lampstands cannot help but recall the one that stood in Moses' Tabernacle. Moses, who like John was given a vision of spiritual reality, was told to construct a replica of what he had seen, and the seven lamps which (among other things) he duly made were united in a single lampstand. John's lampstands, however, are separate. Perhaps we are meant to see in them the church as she appears in the world, congregations located here and there, which can be isolated and indeed destroyed (2:5). But on the heavenly level, the church is united and indestructible, for she is centred on Christ. The lampstands are scattered across the earth; but the stars are held together in the hand of Christ.

So it must be for all who are his people. The tribulation and kingship and endurance which Jesus knows, John knows also, and if we are truly his companions we shall share the same experience. *En Patmō* we suffer; but *en Pneumati* we reign. The practical result at which Revelation aims is to make us see the first in the light of the second. Even the progression from Scene 1, set entirely in this world, to Scene 8, set entirely in the next, serves the same purpose. This world the Christian knows because he lives in it; but as to what it means, where it is going, why it treats him so capriciously, how can he know these things? Only let it be related to *that* world, and he begins to understand. He comes to see a plan in history, and to grasp what is really happening, where he fits in, and how it will all end. He perceives the grand design on the right side of the tapestry which explains the tangle of crossed threads and loose ends on the side he is more familiar with. So he learns to link in his mind the church as he sees it, lamps that gleam here and there across the dark world, ever seemingly threatened by extinction, and the church as Christ shows it, a cluster of inextinguishable stars in the hand of their creator. He is able to face the tribulation, because of what he knows of the kingdom: to confront the storm, because his foundations are deep in the rock. 'The tribulation and the kingdom' produce 'the patient endurance'. That is the object of the book of Revelation.

2. THE FIRST LETTER: TO EPHESUS (2:1–7)

'To the angel of the church in Ephesus write: "The words of him who holds the seven stars in his right hand, who walks among the seven golden lampstands.

2 *" "I know your works, your toil and your patient endurance, and how you cannot bear evil men but have tested those who call themselves apostles but are not, and found them to be false; 3I know you are enduring patiently and bearing up for my name's sake, and you have not grown weary.*

4 *" "But I have this against you, that you have abandoned the love you had at first.*

⁵ ᶜ *"Remember then from what you have fallen, repent and do the works you did at first. If not, I will come to you and remove your lampstand from its place, unless you repent.* ⁶ *Yet this you have, you hate the works of the Nicolaitans, which I also hate.*

⁷ ᶜ *"He who has an ear, let him hear what the Spirit says to the churches. To him who conquers I will grant to eat of the tree of life, which is in the paradise of God."* ʼ

If the traditions about John are correct, his pulse would have quickened as he heard that the first of the seven Letters was destined for the church at Ephesus, for there, it is widely believed, he himself was for many years bishop. As might be expected, the character of the church came to reflect the character of its leader. The two sides of the John of the New Testament—an apostle of love, yet a 'son of thunder'—are seen again, interestingly enough, in two stories that have been handed down concerning his later years at Ephesus: on the one hand his refusal to stay under the same roof as the heretic Cerinthus, and on the other hand his reduction of all his message to a sermon of one sentence, which in extreme old age he used to repeat at every church meeting: 'Little children, love one another.' We can tell from Acts and Ephesians that the early church there was likewise characterized by both love and zeal. As the city of Ephesus claimed to be the 'metropolis', or mother city, of the whole of Asia, so its church could claim by her evangelistic and pastoral concern to be the mother church of that province, and Paul could write of her 'love toward all the saints' (Eph. 1:15).

By the time John writes, some years have passed. How is the church now? Her zeal is undiminished. Her works, toil, and patient endurance are all commended, and especially the value she places on sound doctrine. Though she gladly endures suffering, she will certainly not endure false teaching, whether from evil men in general or from pseudo-apostles and Nicolaitans in particular.[1] According to the letter written to the Ephesians not long after this by Ignatius, bishop of Antioch, the report that has reached him is of a church so well taught in the gospel that no unorthodox sect can gain a hearing among her members, a church which has taken seriously the warnings of Paul at the

[1] We shall consider the latter when they reappear in 2:15.

time of his last contact with her leaders.[1] Nor does the message
from Christ in any way belittle their concern for purity and
soundness; would that all the Lord's people were keen-sighted
enough to know when and how to say with the Psalmist (Ps.
139:21), 'Do I not hate them that hate thee, O Lord?'

But in her keenness for the truth, the church at Ephesus has
lost her love, 'the one quality without which all others are worth-
less'.[2] It is noteworthy that only in the first and last of the seven
Letters is a church threatened with actual destruction, and in each
case the reason is the unnerving, purely negative one, that *it
lacks fervent devotion*. 'You have abandoned the love you had at
first', says Christ. Do not misunderstand me; 'you hate the
works of the Nicolaitans, which I also hate'; I commend your
zeal. But where is your *love*? For on that your very survival as a
church depends.

Such a failure is only too possible. It has to be confessed by all
Christians who have cast themselves in the role of Mr Valiant-
for-Truth, and forgotten that they are also expected to be Mr
Great-heart. To them Christ shows himself as equally zealous
for the right. He too shows strength and vigilance—but it is the
church he holds and patrols (verse 1). He too has a sharp eye for
wrong—but it is in the church that he detects it. He too will not
endure evil—but the evil he threatens to destroy is the church
herself, if she will not repent.

And the first lamp was indeed removed. Church and city
together have vanished; all that remains is the place-name
Ayasaluk—and that, ironically, commemorates not Ephesus
but John.[3] There is still the promise of life in paradise for the
individual who remembers from what he has fallen, and returns
to his first works and his first love. But let the loveless church
beware. 'If I have prophetic powers, and understand all mysteries
and all knowledge, and if I have all faith, so as to remove mountains, but have not love, I am nothing' (1 Cor. 13:2).

[1] Acts 20:28–31; Eph. 5:3–17; Ignatius, *To the Ephesians* 6, 9.
[2] Caird, p. 31. 'It is not clear whether this is love for Christ ... or
for one another ... or for mankind at large. It may well be that a
general attitude is meant which included all three' (Morris, p. 60).
[3] Ayasaluk comes from *hagios theologos* (saint-theologian), the name
of the fifth-century church built there and dedicated to John.

3. THE SECOND LETTER: TO SMYRNA (2:8–11)

'And to the angel of the church in Smyrna write: "The words of the first and the last, who died and came to life.

9' "I know your tribulation and your poverty (but you are rich) and the slander of those who say that they are Jews and are not, but are a synagogue of Satan.

10' "Do not fear what you are about to suffer. Behold, the devil is about to throw some of you into prison, that you may be tested, and for ten days you will have tribulation. Be faithful unto death, and I will give you the crown of life.

11' "He who has an ear, let him hear what the Spirit says to the churches. He who conquers shall not be hurt by the second death." '

One does not need background knowledge of Smyrna to understand the message to the church there, but still it is illuminating to learn that the beauty of this city, which rivalled Ephesus, was the beauty of a resurrection. Seven hundred years before, old Smyrna had been destroyed, and had lain in ruins for three centuries. The city of John's time was one which had risen from the dead. In sharp contrast to the fields which once were Ephesus, Smyrna thrives even today as Izmir, second largest city in Asiatic Turkey. And resurrection was to be the experience of its church also.

The immediate prospect was one of suffering and even death. This was a certainty—a fact which has lessons for those of us who live in comparative ease. Would we be taken aback to find persecution knocking at our door tomorrow? Many a church has had to learn to live with that prospect, and so ought we. For the great tribulation that John sees bringing this age to an end he also sees in miniature, recurring constantly in the experience of God's people. And it is a test. It is the devil's action, but God's intention.

The persecution at Smyrna was made especially poignant by the fact that the great enemy was the local community of Jews. These were God's people racially, but not really (Rom. 2:28), and were in fact blaspheming God as they persecuted his church under the guise of doing him service (Jn. 16:2). Perhaps it was economic pressure from these Jews that brought the church to poverty, and slanderous accusations by them (for 'Satan' means 'slanderer') that led to imprisonment and death.

But let the Christians take heart. For the Christ who unveils this dismaying prospect is one who has himself been through a Smyrna-experience. Like their city, their Lord also 'died and came to life', and guarantees a resurrection for them too. The enemy is strong. Behind these Jews stands Satan; it is he, not Abraham, who is their spiritual father (Jn. 8:33, 44). But behind Satan stands God, and God is in final control. If one great lesson is that suffering is certain, the other is that it is limited. For the Smyrnaeans, it would be for 'ten days' some time in their near future: there would in the goodness of God come an eleventh day, and all would be over. God's control does not mean that Satan is prevented from inflicting pain and hurt. Nowhere does the New Testament promise freedom from suffering in this life; indeed, without the cross there will be no crown. But what God does guarantee is that though the church may suffer even the death of the body, she will not suffer the death of the soul.[1] So Paul, having himself learnt these two lessons, demonstrates a true Christian sense of proportion in the face of tribulation: 'I consider that the sufferings of this present time are not worth comparing with the glory that is to be revealed to us' (Rom. 8:18).

The message therefore is that Smyrna must be not *fearful*, but *faithful*—to look not at the suffering, but beyond it to the all-controlling God.

4. THE THIRD LETTER: TO PERGAMUM (2:12–17)

'*And to the angel of the church in Pergamum write: "The words of him who has the sharp two-edged sword.*

13' "*I know where you dwell, where Satan's throne is; you hold fast my name and you did not deny my faith even in the days of Antipas my witness, my faithful one, who was killed among you, where Satan dwells.*

14' "*But I have a few things against you: you have some there who hold the teaching of Balaam, who taught Balak to put a stumbling block before the sons of Israel, that they might eat food sacrificed to idols and practise immorality.* 15 *So you also have some who hold the teaching of the Nicolaitans.*

[1] See pp. 82ff., 195.

16' "*Repent then. If not, I will come to you soon and war against them with the sword of my mouth.*

17' "*He who has an ear, let him hear what the Spirit says to the churches. To him who conquers I will give some of the hidden manna, and I will give him a white stone, with a new name written on the stone which no one knows except him who receives it.*" '

If Ephesus was the New York of Asia, Pergamum was its Washington, for there the Roman imperial power had its seat of government. There also was built the earliest temple for the state-sponsored worship of the Emperor. Whether or not this was what Christ meant by 'the throne of Satan', it emphasizes the kind of difficulties the Pergamene Christians had to face. For them Satan is not merely, as at Smyrna, a slanderer working through a group of ill-disposed Jews. He appears as 'the ruler of this world', to take a phrase from John's Gospel (Jn. 14:30); and what John's first Letter would call 'the world' (1 Jn. 2:15 ff.) is in fact the great enemy of the church at Pergamum.

It includes the power of other institutions besides the machinery of state. The enormous Pergamene library (the town gave its name to 'parchment'), the famous healing ministry of the priests of Aesculapius, and crowning the city's acropolis the Greco-Asiatic altar of Zeus the Saviour—all this paraphernalia of an 'alternative society', catering for mind, body, and spirit, is added to the overt demands of the Roman state. (In the same way we shall find in Scene 4 the beast from the earth joined by the beast from the sea to offer men a viable life-structure outside the kingdom of God. But that story must wait its turn: anticipating John's further revelations is a fruitful way of misunderstanding them.)

In brief, Satan is working here through the pressures of non-Christian society. He persecutes; the suffering which will come to Smyrna has already come to Pergamum, and one at least has died a martyr's death (verse 13b). He seduces; the Nicolaitans we met at Ephesus are here also, and though we know practically nothing about them, their teaching is apparently of the same kind as that of Balaam, who had led God's people into sin long before (Nu. 31:16; 25:1-3). Both the sins mentioned in verse 14 may be taken literally. Both appeared in the time of Balaam, both reappeared in the New Testament church (1 Cor. 5 and 8), and the pathway to them is the kind of temptation which is typical of worldliness in any age: 'Where is the harm in it? Everyone else does it; why shouldn't you?'

Seduction, or persecution—a choice of evils which the world offers the church. For a soft-centred permissive society can be curiously hard on those who refuse to go along with it. 'They are surprised that you do not now join them in the same wild profligacy, and they abuse you' (1 Pet. 4:4). The gay streets of Vanity Fair can still lead to prison and a stake: either you buy or you burn. This is not, indeed, the ten days' reign of terror which Smyrna was to expect. Antipas was apparently the only member of the church at Pergamum who had actually been martyred. But how does Christ's commendation read? 'You did not deny my faith *even* in the days of Antipas'; implying that it was always a temptation, though especially of course at that time.

For some the temptation is too strong, and they give way. Compromise creeps in; the distinction between the church and the world is blurred; there is too much tolerance, too little discipline. 'The fault of Pergamum is the opposite of the fault of Ephesus: and how narrow is the safe path between the sin of tolerance and the sin of intolerance!'[1]

Nevertheless in the end it is Christ they have to reckon with. The power of the sword rests not with the rulers of Rome nor with the ruler of this world, but with him (verse 12). It is the sword of judgment in two senses, discerning the truth (Heb. 4:12) and punishing the evil (Rom. 13:4), and he will use it even against those in the church who will not repent (verse 16).

But there remains a promise to those who do repent and overcome. It is not easy to understand, and many suggestions have been made, especially about the meaning of the white stone (verse 17). Since the context speaks of feasts of idol-meat and the feast of manna which God spread for Israel in the desert, perhaps the reference is to an ancient use of square stones as tickets of admission to some public entertainment. So the promise of eternal life which ends each of the first two Letters is repeated here in terms appropriate to the Christian who will not compromise with worldly pleasures and idol-meat banquets. Christ gives that

[1] Caird, p. 41.

man a personal invitation to the true pleasures of the banquet of heaven, which are, in fact, himself: for 'all the promises of God find their Yes in him', and he is the true manna, the heavenly bread (2 Cor. 1:20; Jn. 6:31-35).

5. THE FOURTH LETTER: TO THYATIRA (2:18-29)

'*And to the angel of the church in Thyatira write: "The words of the Son of God, who has eyes like a flame of fire, and whose feet are like burnished bronze.*

19' "I know your works, your love and faith and service and patient endurance, and that your latter works exceed the first.

20' "But I have this against you, that you tolerate the woman Jezebel, who calls herself a prophetess and is teaching and beguiling my servants to practise immorality and to eat food sacrificed to idols. 21 I gave her time to repent, but she refuses to repent of her immorality.

22' "Behold, I will throw her on a sickbed, and those who commit adultery with her I will throw into great tribulation, unless they repent of her doings; 23 and I will strike her children dead. And all the churches shall know that I am he who searches mind and heart, and I will give to each of you as your works deserve. 24 But to the rest of you in Thyatira, who do not hold this teaching, who have not learned what some call the deep things of Satan, to you I say, I do not lay upon you any other burden; 25 only hold fast what you have, until I come.

26' "He who conquers and who keeps my works until the end, I will give him power over the nations, 27 and he shall rule them with a rod of iron, as when earthen pots are broken in pieces, even as I myself have received power from my Father; 28 and I will give him the morning star. 29 He who has an ear, let him hear what the Spirit says to the churches." '

The sins in the church at Thyatira, like those at Pergamum, are immorality and compromise with idol worship. Here, as there, we may take them literally, though they also constitute the spiritual adultery of which God's people have often been guilty. The biblical metaphor is that the true God is Israel's husband; the false gods are her lovers (Je. 3; Ezk. 16; Ho. 2, *etc.*). Jezebel, like Balaam, was in the Old Testament story an outsider who seduced God's bride into this kind of unfaithfulness (1 Ki. 16:31; 2 Ki. 9:22).

There are however differences between the two situations. Against beleaguered Christians like those at Pergamum, Satan uses the pressures of the world to 'squeeze' them 'into its own mould' (Rom. 12:2, JBP); but where the church is noted for its growth and vigour (verse 19), he knows that he can do most damage not by pressure without but by poison within. So in Thyatira a particular woman takes on both the evil character of Jezebel and the prophetic role of Balaam, and begins to teach, as if from God, new 'deep things' which some members of this strong and lively church are only too willing to explore.[1]

Bishop Butler was unjust to accuse John Wesley of 'pretending to extraordinary revelations and gifts of the Holy Ghost'. But many have so pretended, and their revelations, when divorced from what Scripture has already revealed, can be 'a very horrid thing' indeed. Their sinister voice is often heard in the midst of surging spiritual enthusiasms. As the Reformation gathers momentum, John of Leyden proclaims himself Messiah at Münster. As the idealism of the Children of God makes a bid for the loyalty of modern youth, Christian parents are dismayed to find their offspring being encouraged to abandon their home ties. 'No other gods before me', 'Honour your father and mother'—mere dull traditionalism compared with the exciting voices of the new prophets.

The fact that such voices are to be expected in a lively church is no excuse for her allowing them to go unchecked. Rather the reverse. The more favoured she is, the more severely she will be judged. Christ of the piercing eyes and the trampling feet comes to her like the sun shining in full strength (1:16), infinitely more terrible than the pagan sun-god Apollo, whose temple at Thyatira was famous. His glory searches her mind and heart,

---

[1] Interpreters differ over the phrase in verse 24, 'what some call the deep things of Satan'. It has been discovered that for a small town Thyatira had a remarkable number of trade guilds, and many of the Christians there would have been involved in membership of them, with the attendant problems of conscience, as in verse 20b. Some therefore hold that 'Jezebel' recognized these idol feasts as Satanic temptations, but taught that Christians should be strong enough in spirit to be able to explore 'the deep things of Satan'. It is equally possible, however, that 'Jezebel' taught what she simply called 'deep things', and that it is Christ who brands them as Satanic. The latter view, since it does not rely on external evidence, is followed here.

and 'there is nothing hid from its heat' (verse 23; Ps. 19:6). Those who will not repent he threatens with suffering and death, certainly in a spiritual sense and possibly also (with these punishments as with the sins of verses 20, 21) in a physical sense. To those who will repent, he promises that with this one major hindrance removed, they will become the splendid missionary church they have it in them to be. Verse 27 is a Greek adaptation of the Hebrew of Psalm 2:9; the first half of the verse is ambiguous in both languages, but the curious wording which results here does express the double effect of the preaching of the gospel. For the 'authority over the nations' which is given to Christ in Psalm 2, and to the church here, is authority to proclaim the rule or kingdom of God. He who rejects that rule will perish; but he who accepts it will live (2 Cor. 2:15, 16; Jn. 20:23; Lk. 24:47). What is more, to the church which is a faithful gospel-lamp in the dark night of this world Christ also promises himself as the morning star (22:16), the assurance of the coming dawn, when lamplight will be swallowed up in the light of eternal day.

6. THE FIFTH LETTER: TO SARDIS (3:1–6)

'And to the angel of the church in Sardis write: "The words of him who has the seven spirits of God and the seven stars.

' "I know your works; you have the name of being alive, and you are dead.

²' "Awake, and strengthen what remains and is on the point of death, for I have not found your works perfect in the sight of my God. ³Remember then what you received and heard; keep that, and repent. If you will not awake, I will come like a thief, and you will not know at what hour I will come upon you. ⁴Yet you have still a few names in Sardis, people who have not soiled their garments; and they shall walk with me in white, for they are worthy.

⁵' "He who conquers shall be clad thus in white garments, and I will not blot his name out of the book of life; I will confess his name before my Father and before his angels. ⁶He who has an ear, let him hear what the Spirit says to the churches." '

In spite of their faults, in all the churches so far addressed Christ has recognized much good. What will he find to commend in

Sardis? Nothing. The only 'good' she has is a good reputation, for which there is in fact no basis. Christ's verdict on her is devastatingly brief: in name she is alive, in fact she is dead.

Let us make no mistake about Sardis. She is not what the world would call a dead church. Perhaps even by her sister churches she is considered 'live'. Indeed, since Christ tells her to 'wake up', and warns her that his coming to judge her will be quite unexpected, it seems that she herself is not aware of her real spiritual state. All regard her as a flourishing, active, successful church—all except Christ. Her works do not in fact measure up to the standard he expects; not one of them has really been 'completed' (verse 2, NEB). If he threatens not to confess her before God, the reason is that in spite of all her activities she is not in fact confessing him (verse 5; Mt. 10:32).

Failure to complete? Failure to confess? None would be more surprised at the accusations than she herself. But 'When we remember what "complete" fulfilment of the Christian life meant to the Christians of Smyrna . . . we shall better understand what John demanded of the church at Sardis': secure, complacent, like the city she lived in, untroubled by persecution or heresy, she 'set herself the task of avoiding hardship, by pursuing a policy based on convenience and circumspection, rather than whole-hearted zeal'.[1]

It is not quite accurate to say that her reputation is the only good thing she has. There are a few things about her which are not yet dead, though they are dying (verse 2). There are a few people in her whose righteousness is still unstained (verse 4). Above all, there are memories of her first response to the gospel, 'how she received and heard' (verse 3, RV). The word is 'how', not 'what'—if only she can recapture that 'how', the spirit of penitence and commitment of those early days! Otherwise Christ threatens to come in a surprise visitation of judgment, like a thief in the night. What he describes in this way could be his return at the end of the age, as in Matthew 24:36–44, but is likelier to be some more immediate punishment. John 'expected the final coming of Christ to be anticipated in more limited but no less decisive visitations'.[2] The experience of the church of

[1] Kiddle, p. 45.
[2] Caird, p. 49.

Sardis will be like that of the citadel of Sardis, never taken by assault and thought to be impregnable, but more than once captured by stealth.

Even the promise of verse 5 carries a warning. There is no mention here of the kingdom and the power and the glory which in the other Letters are explicitly the reward of victorious Christians. All that Christ promises to the victors of Sardis is non-deletion from the book of life, and the white robe of his righteousness—simply, that is, their acceptance before God; as if to underline that the church as a whole is likely to forfeit even that.

If Christ alone can see and expose the plight of Sardis, certainly he alone can deal with it. And this he is ready to do. He is the one 'who has the seven spirits of God and the seven stars'; and when he brings together the stars, who are the angelic representatives of the churches, and the sevenfold Spirit, two things can happen. The seven spirits are the eyes of God, from whom nothing is hidden (5:6): hence the message of severity we have just heard. But they are also the life-giving power of God; and in Sardis, as in all the seven cities, Christ has in his hands both the needy church and the life-giving Spirit. He can bring the two together, not only to diagnose but also to revive the dead. And we may be sure that if Sardis remembers and heeds and repents, he will do so.

7. THE SIXTH LETTER: TO PHILADELPHIA (3:7-13)

'*And to the angel of the church in Philadelphia write: "The words of the holy one, the true one, who has the key of David, who opens and no one shall shut, who shuts and no one opens.*

8' "*I know your works. Behold, I have set before you an open door, which no one is able to shut; I know that you have but little power, and yet you have kept my word and have not denied my name.*

9' "*Behold, I will make those of the synagogue of Satan who say that they are Jews and are not, but lie—behold, I will make them come and bow down before your feet, and learn that I have loved you.*

10' "*Because you have kept my word of patient endurance, I will keep you from the hour of trial which is coming on the whole world, to try those who dwell upon the earth.* 11*I am coming soon; hold fast what you have, so that no one may seize your crown.*

¹²' "*He who conquers, I will make him a pillar in the temple of my God; never shall he go out of it, and I will write on him the name of my God, and the name of the city of my God, the new Jerusalem which comes down from my God out of heaven, and my own new name.* ¹³He who has an ear, let him hear what the Spirit says to the churches." '

Apart from Smyrna, Philadelphia is the only church with which Christ has no fault to find. Whatever sternness there may be in his tone is due not to the finding of faults, but to the facing of facts. For a testing-time approaches—not, surely, the last great tribulation, as though John were mistakenly expecting that to be imminent, nor yet some local persecution, which could hardly be a 'trial . . . coming on the whole world'; but the perennial ordeal, of which all particular trials and especially the last one are embodiments. And the church has no great strength to meet it. Christ does not minimize the difficulties.

But he does encourage the church. It faces both opposition and (possibly) opportunity, and his intention is to overcome the one and to confirm the other.

Philadelphia is again like Smyrna in that it has to face the opposition of the 'synagogue of Satan' (2:9). We can catch the flavour of the Greek word for 'lie' by thinking of these people as '*pseudo*-Jews'. They claim, falsely, to be the holy people of God. In contrast, Christ speaks as the true Holy One (verses 9, 7). He refers to the ancient prophecies of how God's people will one day be vindicated and the rest of mankind will bow before them. The fulfilment of these prophecies, he tells the church, will be the reverse of what the Philadelphian Jews expect: *they* will have to 'bow down before *your* feet', and acknowledge 'that I have loved *you*'. Let the Christians take heart, for it is on them that the Lord has set his favour.

Frequently in Revelation John joins the other apostolic writers in teaching that the privileges and promises given to Old Testament Israel have been inherited by the Christian church.[1] The doctrine is here, for example, in the Letter to Philadelphia and its biblical background. Enquiry as to the meaning of the 'key of David' takes us to the book of Isaiah; we shall find allusions from every part of it here in Revelation 3. The 'key'

[1] See pp. 79ff.

appears in Isaiah 22:22, together with the promise that its custodian Eliakim, steward of the household, shall have the same authority that Christ has here to open or shut. To open or shut what? The entrance to the house of David. And for what purpose? The gates are opened, says Isaiah, 'that the righteous nation which keeps faith may enter in' (26:2). Then, just as Eliakim himself is fastened 'like a peg in a sure place, and ... a throne of honour to his father's house' (22:23), so in consequence the weak, the despised, and the converted outsider will be given 'in my house and within my walls a monument and a name' (56:5). The nations shall come in too, in humble submission (60:11); 'all who despised you shall bow down at your feet' (60:14; cf. 49:22, 23). The whole group of ideas thus concerns entry to the house of David, the kingdom, city, and temple of God.[1] What happens to it we may follow step by step. The Lord condemns Jewish legalism ('Woe to you, scribes and Pharisees ... you shut the kingdom of heaven against men; for you neither enter yourselves, nor allow those who would enter to go in', Mt. 23:13) and transfers the doorkeeper's authority to the apostolic church ('I will give you the keys of the kingdom of heaven', Mt. 16:19). So Peter and his associates have the privilege of first admitting not only Jews, but also Samaritans and Gentiles, to permanent membership of the kingdom (Acts 2, 8, 10). In this way the entire concept—key, door, city, temple, and pillar—becomes a Christian one, and the basis for the reversal mentioned above. The Jews will 'learn that I have loved *you*'.

This undeserved favour is at the root of it all. In a sense, Christ keeps (or preserves) his people because they keep (or observe) his word (verse 10), and the encouragements for Philadelphia, as for Smyrna, are intended for all who are loyal to him. But the chain of cause and effect goes further back: they obey his word only because he has first set his love on them. It also goes further on: the final result of his loving care for them will be that this church of 'little power' will be established as an immovable pillar in the temple of the heavenly Jerusalem (verse 12). She will be thrice sealed, as belonging to God, belonging to God's

[1] This would relate the 'open door' of 3:8 to that of 4:1, which admits John to the realm and presence of God; there it is a matter of revelation, and here one of salvation.

city, and belonging to God's Son. His tender promise to those
who are painfully aware of weakness and insecurity is that they
shall finally *belong*.

Until they reach that destination he calls them to endurance;
and also, no doubt, to service. Elsewhere in the New Testament
the 'open door' is a picture of opportunity (1 Cor. 16:9; 2 Cor.
2:12); and though, as we have seen, it here means primarily
their own assured entry into the New Jerusalem, it is also the
way by which others are to be brought in—even (if the picture
in Isaiah is totally reversed) Jews converted from the synagogue
of Satan. So they are doubly encouraged, for Christ who nulli-
fies the opposition also magnifies the opportunity. The door has
been opened by him, and none can shut it. Let them again take
heart, and use the strength they do have in the service he sets
before them.

8. THE SEVENTH LETTER: TO LAODICEA (3:14-22)

'*And to the angel of the church in Laodicea write: "The words of the
Amen, the faithful and true witness, the beginning of God's creation.*

15' *"I know your works: you are neither cold nor hot. Would that you
were cold or hot!*

16' *"So, because you are lukewarm, and neither cold nor hot, I will
spew you out of my mouth.* 17 *For you say, I am rich, I have prospered,
and I need nothing; not knowing that you are wretched, pitiable, poor,
blind, and naked.* 18 *Therefore I counsel you to buy from me gold refined
by fire, that you may be rich, and white garments to clothe you and to keep
the shame of your nakedness from being seen, and salve to anoint your
eyes, that you may see.* 19 *Those whom I love, I reprove and chasten; so be
zealous and repent.* 20 *Behold, I stand at the door and knock; if any one
hears my voice and opens the door, I will come in to him and eat with him,
and he with me.*

21' *"He who conquers, I will grant him to sit with me on my throne,
as I myself conquered and sat down with my Father on his throne.* 22 *He
who has an ear, let him hear what the Spirit says to the churches."* '

Archaeology has filled in much interesting background to this
Letter. Laodicea was a banking centre and a textile town, famous
also for the manufacture of a certain kind of eye ointment (see

verse 18); lime-laden water flowed, tepid and sickly, from nearby springs (see verse 16). So Christ's words to the church there were uncomfortably apt. But even without such background knowledge, we could not mistake his judgment on her. 'If only you were cold or hot!'—what more terrible condemnation could there be of a church's condition, than that the Lord would prefer even a cold Christianity to the sort he actually finds in her?

Elsewhere in Asia we have seen that the state of a church has often corresponded to the state of its city. At Laodicea, however, the two are contrasted. The church is the image of the city reversed in a black negative. Financiers, physicians, clothing manufacturers are among its notable citizens; but 'poor, blind, and naked' is the verdict on its church. 'It has failed to find in Christ the source of all true wealth, splendour, and vision.'[1]

The lukewarmness of Laodicea is the worst condition to which a church can sink. It is worse even than Sardis, where a glimmer of life remained. The only good thing in Laodicea is the church's thoroughly good opinion of herself—and that is false. She claims to have everything, and has nothing; and did we not remind ourselves that in 1:16, yes, there *are* seven stars held in the hand of Christ, we might well doubt whether she is a true church at all. Can we therefore be shocked by Christ's outspoken opinion? We may find it hard to accept what in effect he says in verse 16: 'You make me sick.' But it is the Amen, the faithful and true Witness, who speaks these words, and they are of a piece with those other frightening scriptures which speak of the Lord's loathing (Ps. 95:10) and his derision (Ps. 2:4).

Yet even Laodicea has a chance. The fact that he rebukes her shows that he still loves her (verse 19); and the threat of total rejection if she will not repent is balanced by the promise of total reinstatement if she will. For the sake of this disastrous church, he presents himself in verse 14 as the beginning, or (less misleadingly) the origin, of God's creation, the one who is able to go right down into the chaotic abyss of Laodicea's failure and make her anew, as he once made the world.

But *if she will*: that is the nub of the matter. Divine sovereignty is by no means undercut by this. Christ alone can provide the riches and the robes and the ointment; his is the persuasive voice

[1] Caird, p. 57.

which counsels Laodicea to accept his offer; he comes, he stands, he knocks, he calls. His sovereignty is implicit in his being the 'origin of creation', and that truth she had been taught long since, when Paul's Letter to Colosse had come to her also (Col. 1:15-18; 4:16). But the question for her is whether *she* will open the door and let him in again. For 'the only cure for lukewarmness is the re-admission of the excluded Christ.'[1]

Should the church even yet be deaf to his appeal, he addresses himself to its members one by one, for 'when Christ says *if any man* . . . he is appealing to the individual. Even if the church as a whole does not heed the warning the individual may.'[2] And to any in the Laodicean church who give evidence of this hoped-for repentance, he promises in verses 20 and 21 perhaps the most majestic reward of all, a seat at the divine banquet and a place on the throne of heaven.

[1] G. Campbell Morgan, quoted by Walvoord, p. 97.
[2] Morris, p. 84.

4:1-8:1

SCENE 2:
SUFFERING FOR THE CHURCH:
seven Seals opened

THE MEANING OF NUMBERS

WE saw in Scene 1 how the Bible, like a good teacher, repeats its lessons again and again in different ways in order to impress them on us. If repeating a thing underlines its importance, then the more frequent the repetition, the more important the lesson must be.

Following this line of thought into Scene 2, however, brings us into difficulties. We begin to realize how very repetitious the book is in one particular respect. Even more than story patterns or picture patterns, it seems to repeat number patterns. We may have wondered why in Scene 1 churches, lamps, stars, and spirits all appeared in groups of seven. We now find not only twenty-four elders, and four living creatures with six wings each, but another group of seven lamps and a scroll with seven seals, and as we read on we shall find a great assortment of other numbers both simple and complex. In ordinary life we distinguish between statistical numbers, which answer the question 'How many?' (*e.g.* 1,200 people at a meeting), and symbolic numbers, which stand for something other than mere counting (*e.g.* 1200 hours, meaning midday). The numbers of Revelation are hardly likely to be meant for statistics, as though we might be spiritually benefited by the mere fact of knowing how many elders and creatures and wings there are. This is not the case with the Old Testament, where the divine plan of redemption is being prepared for by a dramatized run-through in the actual historical experience of Israel, so that we expect to find there numbers which are plain statistics as part of the concrete evidence of historicity. But now in the fullness of time God's plan has been completed, and Revelation, with a wealth of picture language, is summing up its spiritual meaning and universal effects. In such a book, numbers are much more likely to be symbols than statistics. And these symbolic number patterns clearly have great importance, or the drama would not include such a lot of them.

The trouble is, what do they mean? '*Four* angels ... at the *four* corners of the earth, holding back the *four* winds' (7:1)— we feel like ignorant foreigners hunting through our phrase books to find out the meaning of words like this which John, a native in these parts, repeats so insistently. He seems to think we really ought to understand what he is getting at.

There have been commentators who have gone too far, and treated the book as though it were basically a mathematical puzzle. This cannot be right. It promises to yield its secrets to any humble Christian reader; the equipment he needs is not mathematical ingenuity, any more than it is specialized historical knowledge, but simply the Word and the Witness. So we must be careful not to go beyond what God really has told us about the meaning of numbers. Consider, for example, the calculation by which some would 'prove' that the 144,000 of 7:4 represent the whole church of Christ. According to Scripture, they would say, 3 is God's number; 4 stands for creation, or the world; $3 \times 4 = 12$, which means the church, through which God is at work in the world; $12^2 = 144$, the whole church; 10 means completeness; $10^3 = 1000$, three-dimensional completeness; $12^2 \times 10^3 = 144,000$, the whole church in all its completeness.

Asserting these things, however, is not the same as explaining them. When we are told 'This means that', we are still entitled to ask why. The Bible may authorize some of the steps in the argument above. But where does it tell us that 3×4 means one thing, while $3 + 4$ means something else? And why should 12 be squared and 10 cubed, and not *vice versa*? And which biblical tens are indisputably symbols of wholeness? The plagues of Egypt, the laws of the Old Testament, the secessionist tribes of Israel, and the lepers in the Gospel might all indicate, if anything, the opposite!

All we can honestly say is that if the 144,000 seem *from the context* to represent the whole church, it is an interpretation supported by the links there seem to be between some of its factors (3, 4, and 10) and certain basic biblical ideas.

With caution, therefore, we approach three of the numbers which feature in Scene 2, to see whether Scripture attaches to them meanings of which we ought to be aware in seeking to learn the lessons the author wants to teach us.

a. Twenty-four (4:4)

Practically the only places where the number twenty-four occurs in the Bible are the half-dozen mentions, here in Revelation, of the elders who surround the throne of God.[1] The number twelve, however, is frequent, and cannot help but recall the 'twelve tribes of the sons of Israel' and the 'twelve apostles of the Lamb'. These two groups are brought together in 21:12-14. There we see the city of God, its gates labelled with the names of the former and its walls with the names of the latter. The two twelves are linked as those on whom the people of God in Old Testament and New Testament days respectively is founded.

Since in any event they are given the title of 'elder', which is generally accorded to church leaders, we can scarcely doubt that the twenty-four represent the whole church of God, both before and since the time of Christ.

This interpretation has been objected to on the grounds that the church will not be seated, white-robed and crowned, in the presence of God in heaven until after judgment day; and since that day is not described till much later in the book, and at this stage the church is not yet triumphant, but still militant here in earth, the elders must stand for angels or some other kind of heavenly being. The objection is worth mentioning, not because it has any substance, but because it highlights a common mis-understanding of Revelation's time structure. The subject will be dealt with on pages 85-89. For the moment we merely note that the order in which events are shown to John may not be—in some cases cannot be—the order in which they happen his-torically. In any case, the elders do not necessarily represent the church triumphant. We learn from Ephesians 2:6 that 'in the heavenly places' (*i.e.* on the level of spiritual reality) we our-

---

[1] The twenty-four divisions of the priesthood (1 Ch. 24) support the suggestion to be made here, being representative of the people of God in the worship of the Temple.

selves, the church still militant here on earth, are already seated with Christ. John himself has hinted as much in 1:5, 6.

b. Seven (4:5)

In contrast to twenty-four, the number seven occurs frequently throughout the Bible. Traditionally it has been taken to mean completeness, just as 'to sail the seven seas' means to travel all the oceans of the world. A number of biblical examples can be adduced to support this idea. But a careful consideration of the Bible's sevens in general brings to light a more intriguing possibility.

Though found everywhere, they cluster especially thickly in the chapters which describe Old Testament religion—days and years, altars and sacrificial animals, sprinklings of water and oil and blood, again and again in groups of seven. We are not told why. It is simply that the activities concerned with this basic function of the life of man, his relationship to his Maker, seem to go in sevens. The use of the same number then spreads from his religious to his social relationships: it is the root of the chief Hebrew word for swearing an oath, and thus mutual trust between man and man is also based on the sacred seven. Further, it confronts us on the first page of Genesis, God's six days of work and a seventh day of rest when the world was made; and we have already begun to notice how here in Revelation, as the surface noise of history is cleaned off the record, the music of eternity is reverberating with the same seven-beat rhythm.

Again we are not told why it should be so. It simply is so. Creation, religion, society, all seem to go in sevens. It is not only that children on the beach look to see if every seventh wave is bigger than the rest; scientists in the laboratory, and politicians in totalitarian states, puzzle over why the human constitution should have a mysterious response to seven-cycle vibrations, and should rebel against a work/rest pattern whose 'week' has more than seven days. May it be that seven represents not the *entirety* of a thing, but the *essence* of it? Under the swirl of notes, the steady tread of a basic rhythm—'This is the way things are'. Though the seven churches of Asia do indeed stand for the church in general, it is because they represent not so much the *whole* church, as the *real* church. And if the seven Letters show the church as it really is, the seven Seals show the world as it really is; and so with the seven Trumpets and the seven Bowls— God's warnings as they really are, then his judgments as they really are.

If this is so, there is no question of John's artificially constructing a book full of sevens. As the classical dramatists of England habitually wrote in five-beat blank verse, and those of France in six-beat rhyming couplets, so these seven-beat rhythms seem to be the natural cadences of the voice of God. Even in those scenes of Revelation which are not explicitly subdivided, we may well discover that the meaning is brought out most clearly by a division into seven.

c. Four (4:6; 7:1)

Twenty-fours are rare enough in the Bible, and sevens common enough, to give a fairly clear idea of what their symbolic meaning might be. Fours are a different matter. There are a good many of them; but the difficulty is to know first which are symbols and which are statistics, and then what we are to understand by those which are symbols.

Take, for example, the four-horned goat in the vision of Daniel 8:8. 'Horns' mean kings, the successors of Alexander the Great; but does 'four' mean anything other than that there were in fact four of them? Or take Peter's vision in Acts 10:11, of a sheet let down by the corners and full of unclean animals. The sheet represents the Gentile world; but does it have four corners because four is symbolic of the world, as some have suggested, or simply because most sheets do? Fours like these do not help a great deal in interpreting the places where the number turns up in Revelation. We shall have to seek a meaning elsewhere.

The most important fours of the book all make their first appearance in this scene. If they are symbolic of anything, it could perhaps be the created world. Starting no doubt from the universally acknowledged compass points, north, south, east, and west, the Bible speaks (as we do) of the four corners of the earth, and the four winds of heaven. Naturally the angels who stand at earth's corners and restrain the winds are also four in number (7:1).

Are we supposed to see similar meaning in the four living creatures of 4:6?[1] In this case we may find greater help in their name than in their number. 'Living creatures' like these were seen by the prophet Ezekiel in his first extraordinary vision (Ezk. 1), and though the six wings apiece recall the seraphs of Isaiah's vision (Is. 6), most of the description tallies with that of the beings whom Ezekiel saw, and whom he elsewhere calls cherubs (Ezk. 10:20). The cherubs of the Bible are very far from being chubby infants with wings and dimples. They are awesome creatures, visible indications of the presence of God. So when we are told (Ps. 8:10) that the Lord travels both on a cherub and on the wings of the wind, we may begin to see a link between the four living creatures of 4:6 and the four winds of 7:1. We might call these cherub-creatures 'nature', so long as we remember what nature really is—an immense construction throbbing with the ceaseless activity of God. At any rate they could well represent what Paul calls God's 'eternal power and deity . . . clearly perceived in the things that have been made' (Rom. 1:20). Perhaps their faces (4:7; Ezk. 1:10) represent his majesty, his strength, his wisdom, and his loftiness, and their numberless eyes his ceaseless watchfulness over every part of his creation. It is appropriate then that there should be four of them, corresponding to the points of the compass and the corners of the earth, and standing for God's world, as the twenty-four elders stand for God's church.

1. SCENE 2 OPENS:
CREATION CENTRED ON CHRIST (4:1—5:14)

After this I looked, and lo, in heaven an open door! And the first voice, which I had heard speaking to me like a trumpet, said, 'Come up hither, and I will show you what must take place after this.'

4:2 At once I was in the Spirit, and lo, a throne stood in heaven, with one seated on the throne! 3 And he who sat there appeared like jasper

---

[1] The old translation 'beasts' (4:6, AV) caused needless confusion between these and the really 'beastly' creatures of later Scenes (13:1, *etc.*). In fact John uses two quite different Greek words.

and carnelian, and round the throne was a rainbow that looked like an emerald. ⁴*Round the throne were twenty-four thrones, and seated on the thrones were twenty-four elders, clad in white garments, with golden crowns upon their heads.* ⁵*From the throne issue flashes of lightning, and voices and peals of thunder, and before the throne burn seven torches of fire, which are the seven spirits of God;* ⁶*and before the throne there is as it were a sea of glass, like crystal. And round the throne, on each side of the throne, are four living creatures, full of eyes in front and behind:* ⁷*the first living creature like a lion, the second living creature like an ox, the third living creature with the face of a man, and the fourth living creature like a flying eagle.*

4:8 *And the four living creatures, each of them with six wings, are full of eyes all round and within, and day and night they never cease to sing, 'Holy, holy, holy, is the Lord God Almighty, who was and is and is to come!'* ⁹*And whenever the living creatures give glory and honour and thanks to him who is seated on the throne, who lives for ever and ever,* ¹⁰*the twenty-four elders fall down before him who is seated on the throne and worship him who lives for ever and ever; they cast their crowns before the throne, singing,* ¹¹*'Worthy art thou, our Lord and God, to receive glory and honour and power, for thou didst create all things, and by thy will they existed and were created.'*

5:1 *And I saw in the right hand of him who was seated on the throne a scroll written within and on the back, sealed with seven seals;* ²*and I saw a strong angel proclaiming with a loud voice, 'Who is worthy to open the scroll and break its seals?'* ³*And no one in heaven or on earth or under the earth was able to open the scroll or to look into it,* ⁴*and I wept much that no one was found worthy to open the scroll or to look into it.* ⁵*Then one of the elders said to me, 'Weep not; lo, the Lion of the tribe of Judah, the Root of David, has conquered, so that he can open the scroll and its seven seals.'* ⁶*And between the throne and the four living creatures and among the elders, I saw a Lamb standing, as though it had been slain, with seven horns and with seven eyes, which are the seven spirits of God sent out into all the earth;* ⁷*and he went and took the scroll from the right hand of him who was seated on the throne.*

5:8 *And when he had taken the scroll, the four living creatures and the twenty-four elders fell down before the Lamb, each holding a harp, and with golden bowls full of incense, which are the prayers of the saints;* ⁹*and they sang a new song, saying, 'Worthy art thou to take the scroll and to open its seals, for thou wast slain and by thy blood didst ransom men for*

God from every tribe and tongue and people and nation, [10] *and hast made them a kingdom and priests to our God, and they shall reign on earth.'*

5:11 *Then I looked, and I heard around the throne and the living creatures and the elders the voice of many angels, numbering myriads of myriads and thousands of thousands,* [12] *saying with a loud voice, 'Worthy is the Lamb who was slain, to receive power and wealth and wisdom and might and honour and glory and blessing!'*

5:13 *And I heard every creature in heaven and on earth and under the earth and in the sea, and all therein, saying, 'To him who sits upon the throne and to the Lamb be blessing and honour and glory and might for ever and ever!'* [14] *And the four living creatures said, 'Amen!' and the elders fell down and worshipped.*

The second Scene concerns a sealed scroll (5:1). But not till chapter 6 shall we come to the breaking open of the Seals. First the Scene must be set, and John needs two full chapters to do it.

Before we try to visualize what he saw, we should note two statements in the opening verse (4:1) whose meaning is not as obvious as it might seem.

What, first, is the 'heaven' into which John looks? The Bible uses this word for (1) the region where the birds fly, and (2) the region where the stars shine. But John's ascent in 4:1 is not the kind that could be made either in a balloon or in a spaceship; he is taken up, as Paul had once been, to the 'third heaven' (2 Cor. 12:2), the region where God is. Even then the word could have at least three further meanings. Does it here mean (3) a place of perfection which exists even now, alongside our own imperfect world; or (4) the perfect order of things which will exist after this world is done away; or (5) the 'heavenly places' of Ephesians (already referred to in the introduction to this Scene), which denote, not a place without evil, but the sphere of spiritual reality, where the masks are off and both good and evil are seen for what they really are? Since the vision includes the present creation, and a church which is still living on earth and needing to pray in order to contact God (5:8, 10, 13), the likeliest meaning seems to be the last of the five.

This sheds light on the other ambiguous phrase of 4:1, 'what must take place after this'. Of course it denotes a future. But is it John's own immediate future? Or the whole subsequent history of the church? Or *our* future, reckoning that these are prophecies practically none of which have yet been fulfilled?

Caird's illuminating suggestion helps towards a proper understanding of these chapters. By the voice of 4:1 John 'is summoned to the control-room at Supreme Headquarters ... a room lined with maps, in which someone has placed clusters of little flags ... It is war-time, and the flags represent units of a military command. The movement of flags may mean one of two things: either that changes have taken place on the battlefield, with which the map must be made to agree, or that an order is being issued for troop movements, and the flags are being moved to the new positions the units are expected to occupy ... The strange and complex symbols of John's vision are, like the flags in this parable, the pictorial counterpart of earthly realities; and these symbols too may be either determinative' (what is to happen) 'or descriptive' (what has happened).[1]

In itself, the phrase 'what must take place after this' does not necessarily mean anything but 'events from now on', from John's vision onwards, or even from that moment in the vision onwards. And if, in Caird's analogy, the flags in the map of Revelation show how things have come about as well as how they are going to develop (which is demonstrably the case), then the visions which begin here are a heavenly map of the total war, and not just a schedule of proposed operations.

Now what did John actually see?

Chapter 4 focuses first on the throne where sits the eternal God. Perhaps 'focus' is the wrong word, so hard is it to see clearly what is at the heart of that dazzling splendour. Still, though the sun may be hard to descry, the world it illuminates has clear enough outlines. Before the throne stand seven lamps and a crystal 'sea'; the four 'living creatures' encircle it, and around them are the thrones of the twenty-four elders.

Of course, John saw more than this. The Presence on the throne, the living creatures, and the surrounding rainbow could not fail to bring to his mind's eye all the associated marvels of the vision Ezekiel had had (Ezk. 1); the rainbow shone also from a far remoter past, the days of the Flood (Gn. 9:12 ff.). Thunder and lightning recalled the revelation of God at mount Sinai

[1] Caird, pp. 60, 61.

(Ex. 19:16 ff.). There were a 'sea' (a great bronze basin for ritual washing) and a seven-branched lampstand in the Temple at Jerusalem (Ex. 25:31 ff.; 2 Ch. 4:2–6). Then as well as all these extra dimensions to the vision, John must have seen their inner meanings: the majesty, mercy, glory, purity, and power of God. The picture is in fact a merging of many Old Testament images of divine truth, and presents God the Creator as worthy of universal praise (4:11). All that exists is under his sovereign sway; that is why the divine throne is the central and primary feature in the vision (4:2).

Chapter 5 amplifies the vision by bringing the drama of the New Testament into the tableau of the Old. To the central place now comes Jesus Christ, God the Son, to take and to open the sealed scroll. He bears the emblems of his lion-like greatness, the seven horns and eyes which show him to be 'the power of God and the wisdom of God' (1 Cor. 1:24), and the marks of his lamb-like humiliation, 'Those wounds yet visible above, In beauty glorified',[1] which make him equally worthy of praise. Around him are not only the circles of the elders and living creatures, but an outer circle of multitudes of angels; and beyond them, the entire creation is offering its praise to God.

We take it that the elders and the living creatures represent God's people and God's world.[2] The world of nature, which was cursed when man was cursed (Gn. 3:17), is also to be redeemed when man is redeemed (Rom. 8:19–21). So nature joins the church in praising God, and for both he is not only Creator (4:11) but also Redeemer (5:9, 10). Their song is even more glorious than that of the angels, who though they praise the slain Lamb, yet 'know not Christ as Saviour, but worship him as King'.

What is the scroll with seven Seals? Numbers of suggestions have been made; perhaps the most sensible one is to let him open it, and then we shall see! But whatever may turn out to be the meaning of the scroll itself, there is the immediate question in chapter 5 as to what is meant by the Lamb's opening of it. Is he simply revealing its contents, or (since the thought that it might remain closed is so grievous, verse 4) is he doing something more than that? Many commentators note that it is his redeeming

[1] M. Bridges and G. Thring.
[2] See pp. 61, 64.

death which qualifies Christ to break the Seals (verse 9), and infer, thinking of the cross primarily as a great achievement, that the events to be described in chapter 6 are also in some sense 'achieved' by Christ, and not merely revealed by him. The language of chapter 5 might best be accounted for, however, if his action were seen to be an unveiling of events *within the divine order*: they are being *explained* by him. We do not need Christ to tell us that the world is full of troubles. But we do need his explanation of history if its troubles are not to be meaningless.

We may link this thought with an incident in Christ's earthly life, when at the outset of his ministry (as here at the beginning of his Revelation) he 'went to synagogue' one sabbath day. There before the assembled elders 'he stood up to read the lesson and was handed the scroll of the prophet Isaiah' (Lk. 4:16, 17, NEB). His reading concerned the fulfilment in his own person of God's plan for humanity, as foretold in the Old Testament. Only in Christ crucified is to be found the answer to the riddle of life; no angel 'in heaven', no man 'on earth', no teacher from the past, now 'under the earth', can explain it—only Judah's Lion, David's Root, the Jew from Nazareth who is also the Lamb of God.

The whole Scene, then, if it is not too prosaic to look at it diagrammatically, is a series of concentric circles. From every point on every circle a radius of praise is drawn inwards to the centre: and at the centre, by his Father's throne, is Christ. So he was among the lampstands in Scene 1. So he will be throughout the drama. The reason why such importance is attached to the setting of the Scene will become clear as its action unfolds, and to that action, the opening of the seven-sealed scroll, we now turn.

2. THE FIRST SEAL: CONQUEST (6:1, 2)

Now I saw when the Lamb opened one of the seven seals, and I heard one of the four living creatures say, as with a voice of thunder, 'Come!' 2 And I saw, and behold, a white horse, and its rider had a bow; and a crown was given to him, and he went out conquering and to conquer.

The visions which follow the breaking open of the first four Seals are linked, as a series within a series, by a number of common features. These we shall deal with later, considering for the moment what is distinctive about each vision.

Many commentaries point on from verse 2 to another Scene much later in the drama, and from there back to a certain passage in the Gospels. In 19:11, as here, a crowned conqueror appears riding a white horse, and there he is actually named as King of kings, Lord of lords, and The Word of God, that is, Jesus Christ. So it is suggested that the horseman of 6:2 also is Jesus Christ.[1] If we then ask what Christ is doing here, in such gruesome company as that of the second, third, and fourth riders, we are referred back to Mark 13:10 and its parallels, which tell us to expect in the course of this age not only the spread of evil but also the spread of the conquering gospel.

We may or may not feel that this is sufficient evidence to identify the first horseman. To this question we shall return. The important thing which John has to record, at all events, is that some kind of conquest follows the opening of the first seal.

3. THE SECOND SEAL: STRIFE (6:3, 4)

When he opened the second seal, I heard the second living creature say, 'Come!' 4 And out came another horse, bright red; its rider was permitted to take peace from the earth, so that men should slay one another; and he was given a great sword.

If the first horseman is Christ and the conquering gospel, does the second stand for the warfare of the world, as a contrasting evil; or for divisions between men that are caused when the gospel is accepted by some and rejected by others (Mt. 10:34-36); or for persecution of the church by the world? If on the other hand the first horseman is not Christ, is he instead a personification of the glory of war, while the second personifies its horrors?

[1] He wears a different kind of crown and carries a different kind of weapon, but that is comparatively unimportant if the identification seems right on other grounds. Neither is it a serious objection to say that if Christ is the Lamb opening the seals, he cannot be one of the riders as well. Different functions of a single reality may need to be described by more than one symbol at once; we have already seen, for example, the right hand of Christ simultaneously holding the seven stars and resting on John's head (1:16, 17).

Biblical evidence has been brought forward for all these views, some of it from verse 4 itself. A more accurate rendering might change 'slay' into 'butcher', for example, and might explain that 'sword' could well mean a sacrificial knife. What the rider is actually said to do, however, is simply to take away peace. Trying once more to see through John's eyes, we may content ourselves for the present by saying that the vision is in essence simply one of strife and conflict.

4. THE THIRD SEAL: SCARCITY (6:5, 6)

When he opened the third seal, I heard the third living creature say, 'Come!' And I saw, and behold, a black horse, and its rider had a balance in his hand; [6]*and I heard what seemed to be a voice in the midst of the four living creatures saying, 'A quart of wheat for a denarius, and three quarts of barley for a denarius; but do not harm oil and wine!'*

With its references to weights and measures, wages and prices, the third vision describes an economic situation; not strictly famine, but certainly scarcity. The RSV's quarts and denarii do not mean a great deal to us; JB conveys the sense better: 'A ration of corn for a day's wages, and three rations of barley for a day's wages'. Good food (wheat or corn) is available—at the price of a man's entire wages! He will have to be content with poorer fare (barley) if he is to feed his family as well as himself, but even that does not take into account the cost of clothing and housing. The supply of oil and wine, however, is unaffected. Whether these commodities represent the luxuries, the caviare and champagne, which even in the hardest times continue inexplicably to furnish the tables of the rich, or whether they are staple items which are protected when other foodstuffs become scarce, so that the third rider stands for partial hardship rather than total famine, the situation described is at least one of great economic difficulty and inequality.

5. THE FOURTH SEAL: DEATH (6:7, 8)

When he opened the fourth seal, I heard the voice of the fourth living creature say, 'Come!' [8]*And I saw, and behold, a pale horse, and its rider's name was Death, and Hades followed him; and they were given power over a fourth of the earth, to kill with sword and with famine and with pestilence and by wild beasts of the earth.*

The meaning of the fourth rider and his fell companion is explicit. Men killed one another in the conflicts of Seal 2; but there we saw strife, the cause, while here we see death, the result.

The wiping out of a quarter of the human race sounds like a disaster of the first magnitude, until one realizes that nothing has been said to indicate that this is a single catastrophic event. After all, every man dies sooner or later, and what is probably meant here is that a sizeable proportion of those deaths are the unnecessary ones caused by war and famine and kindred evils.

6. THE FIFTH SEAL: THE SUFFERING OF GOD'S WITNESSES (6:9-11)

When he opened the fifth seal, I saw under the altar the souls of those who had been slain for the word of God and for the witness they had borne; [10] they cried out with a loud voice, 'O Sovereign Lord, holy and true, how long before thou wilt judge and avenge our blood on those who dwell upon the earth?' [11] Then they were each given a white robe and told to rest a little longer, until the number of their fellow servants and their brethren should be complete, who were to be killed as they themselves had been.

Three phrases call for comment at this stage concerning the events of Seal 5.

'Under the altar' the blood of sacrifices was poured out (Lv. 4:7). The martyrs who have given their lives (for 'the life . . . is in the blood', Lv. 17:11) may represent all who suffer in any way for Christ's sake, and all such devotion is a sacrifice acceptable to God.

'Those who dwell upon the earth', or rather (as in JB) 'the inhabitants of the earth', is a technical term in Revelation. It means not humanity in general, but those who are 'at home in the present world order'[1] as opposed to those who hold to the Word and Witness of God. John, being in 'the heavenlies', sees

[1] Caird, p. 88.

everything in black and white. 'He who is not with me is against me' (Mt. 12:30); there is no middle ground, and all men are either citizens of heaven (Phil. 3:20) or inhabitants of earth.

'Avenge our blood', cry the souls of God's witnesses, and in the light of the above, their cry becomes not only excusable but right. For the inhabitants of earth are those who are irredeemably committed to the cause of evil, and the martyrs are expressing not personal vindictiveness but an objective desire that justice be done.

7. THE SIXTH SEAL: THE FINAL CATACLYSM (6:12–17)

When he opened the sixth seal, I looked, and behold, there was a great earthquake; and the sun became black as sackcloth, the full moon became like blood, 13 and the stars of the sky fell to the earth as the fig tree sheds its winter fruit when shaken by a gale; 14 the sky vanished like a scroll that is rolled up, and every mountain and island was removed from its place. 15 Then the kings of the earth and the great men and the generals and the rich and the strong, and every one, slave and free, hid in the caves and among the rocks of the mountains, 16 calling to the mountains and rocks, 'Fall on us and hide us from the face of him who is seated on the throne, and from the wrath of the Lamb; 17 for the great day of their wrath has come, and who can stand before it?'

At last we have a sure reference point. Commentaries sometimes state dogmatically that 'Of course X means Y', when a little thought will show that there is no 'of course' about it. But here the meaning is unmistakable. Strings of biblical references to the events of this paragraph are gathered together in Christ's own magisterial discourse (Mark 13 and its parallels), where the description is that of the *parousia*, his return to this earth and the unveiling of the face of God. Verse 17 actually identifies it as 'the great day of their wrath'.

The question of whether the earthquake, the darkened sun, and so on, are to be taken literally or metaphorically, misses the point. That day will spell the end of the entire universe as we know it (Heb. 12:26), the end of the planets and galaxies as well as the end of the human institutions they may symbolize.

Now we return to the first four seals, and consider not their distinctive features but the ones they share.

Their common pattern may begin to make us rethink our
identification of the first horseman as Jesus Christ. That identification is largely based on the vision of 19:11. But is not the
meaning of Seal 1 more likely to be of a piece with that of Seals
2, 3, and 4, which are so closely related to it, than with another
vision which is not only thirteen chapters away, but thirteen
chapters *ahead*—that is, which John himself will not see for some
time yet? If he has not yet seen a white rider representing Christ,
is it not more natural to assume that he saw all four riders in
chapter 6 as evil powers?

Evil though they may be, it is God who allows them to ride
forth; each is 'given' authority (*cf.* Jb. 1:12; 2:6). It may be said
that Christ's authority also was given him by the Father (Mt.
28:18); but the gift to him was very much more than mere permission, whereas the repeated 'given' of 6:1–8 indicates that the
first rider's authority is of the same sort as that of the other
three. Again, therefore, it seems he represents something evil,
and not the conquering gospel of Christ.

A third bond between the visions—this time between all six,
not simply the first four—is the correspondence between them
and the Gospel passage already referred to, Mark 13 (= Mt. 24;
Lk. 21). This is particularly noticeable if we compare Matthew's
version, the fullest of the three, with the chapter before us. We
should not be surprised that these passages correspond, since the
same person is dealing with the same subject in each case. There,
Jesus speaks; here, the Lamb opens his book. In both places he is
revealing something about the future (4:1; Mt. 24:3). Since he is
'the faithful witness' (1:5), the truth to which he witnesses must
be consistent, and so indeed it proves to be. The two passages
are most clearly linked at the events of Seal 6 (6:12–17 = Mt.
24:29–30), but there is no difficulty in connecting those of Seals
2, 3, and 4 also with the earlier part of the Gospel passage. In fact
we do not have to strain the text in any way to postulate that
Christ is not only expounding the same subject, but expounding
it in the same order, in both places. The two chapters engage
at point after point like the two sides of a zip. According to this
parallel, it is the earthly warfare of Matthew 24:6, not the con-

quering gospel, which is represented by the rider of Seal 1; the troubles of Matthew 24:7, 8 are those of Seals 2, 3, and 4; the suffering church (Mt. 24:9-12), which nevertheless bears indestructible witness to its sovereign Lord (Mt. 24:13, 14), is described under Seal 5. We skip Matthew 24:15-28, which refers to the fall of Jerusalem, because by the time the prophecies of Revelation 6 were written this event was already past; and so we come on to verses 29, 30, which correspond, as we have noted, to Seal 6.[1]

In the light of Matthew 24, then, we begin to see the over-all meaning of this scene of the drama. What does the future hold? Conquest and strife, scarcity and death; 'but the end is not yet . . . all this is but the beginning of the birth-pangs' (Mt. 24:6, 8). In view of the frequent misunderstanding which takes the 'wars and rumours of wars' passage to be a prediction of the end, it is worth stressing that that is precisely what Christ says it is not. The terrifying events of the first four Seals, which those who have to live through them might imagine to be signs of Christ's return and of the close of the age (Mt. 24:3), are in fact the commonplaces of history. The four horsemen have been riding out over the earth from that day to this, and will continue to do so.

This may also explain the cry of the four living creatures as these Seals are broken open. On other interpretations, they appear to be little more than a convenient foursome of characters who happen to be available to usher in the riders. But why? And why do they call 'Come!'? They are not calling John: he has already been called to the vantage-point from which he is surveying the whole scene (4:1).[2] They are not calling the riders: remembering that they probably represent nature, God's world, we can hardly believe that they would be inviting the ruin of that world. In any case, three of the horses do not 'come' at all, but are simply

[1] On the basis of the traditional view, according to which the son of Zebedee, the writer of the fourth Gospel, and the writer of Revelation are one and the same person, Matthew 24 and Revelation 6 would be in effect the same discourse. What John had heard 'in the flesh' on the Mount of Olives, but for various reasons omitted from his Gospel, he now saw 'in the spirit', repeated in dramatic form, to be included here in Revelation. See pp. 85 ff. for further comparison between the two passages.

[2] They do simply say 'Come!' (RSV); AV's 'Come *and see*' is incorrect.

revealed to view. Whom then do the living creatures call? There is someone whose coming is both promised and desired. Hear the cry of 22:20: ' "Surely I am coming soon." Amen. Come, Lord Jesus!' Hear the echo of 1:6, 7: 'Amen. Behold, he is coming!' The same Greek word used there, in the first and last chapters of Revelation, is the cry of the living creatures here,[1] and is followed by the corresponding cry of 'How long?' from the souls under the altar. Both God's people and God's creation yearn for the coming of Christ to deliver them from suffering (Rom. 8:19-22).

As the Lamb unseals the book of history the immediate impression we get is of a suffering world. If he is in control, though, surely within that world his church is protected from these woes? Did not Ezekiel, threatening the same 'four sore acts of judgment' as in verse 8, promise nevertheless that the faithful would be delivered (Ezk. 14:21, 22)? The answer of Seal 5 (= Mt. 24:9-12) is No: the church is not exempt. Assaults from without and within will test to the limit those who are prepared to stake everything, even life, on the Word and Witness of God. But how long will this go on? Will there never be a respite for his suffering people? Again the answer is No, not in this world: only with the end of the world, and the completion of the total number who are to witness and suffer for Christ, will there come the day of vengeance on their persecutors (verse 11). In other words, rampant evil will be abroad, bringing suffering to the world in general and to the church in particular, through the entire period from the time of John's vision to the time of Jesus's return (Seal 6 = Mt. 24:14b, 29, 30). Seals 1 to 5 portray different aspects of the whole of history; Seal 6 describes the day which will end it.

Now we can see why the scene for these dramatic events was set in such detail. In chapter 6 John is shown the succession of woes which will sweep to and fro across the world throughout the course of history, and which often cause men to wonder whether the forces of evil are not altogether out of control. Even the church is not safe from them; so even Christians may be tempted to think that, as despairing Englishmen said in the anarchy of the reign of King Stephen, 'God and his angels sleep.'

[1] A different word is used in 17:1 and 21:9.

The setting in chapters 4 and 5, therefore, is intended to impress on John's mind, and through him on ours also, where the true power lies. Not only in the church's internal affairs (Scene 1) but in the world as a whole, Christ stands at the centre. It is he who is finally in control. God *is* still on the throne.

To reassure Christians of this, chapter 7 takes the general truth of chapters 4 and 5 and makes crystal-clear its particular lesson for them: that though they may, indeed will, have to go through temporal suffering, their eternal safety is never in question.

8. YET THE CHURCH IS INDESTRUCTIBLE (7:1-17)

After this I saw four angels standing at the four corners of the earth, holding back the four winds of the earth, that no wind might blow on earth or sea or against any tree. [2] *Then I saw another angel ascend from the rising of the sun, with the seal of the living God, and he called with a loud voice to the four angels who had been given power to harm earth and sea,* [3] *saying, 'Do not harm the earth or the sea or the trees, till we have sealed the servants of our God upon their foreheads.'*

[4] *And I heard the number of the sealed, a hundred and forty-four thousand sealed, out of every tribe of the sons of Israel,* [5] *twelve thousand sealed out of the tribe of Judah, twelve thousand of the tribe of Reuben, twelve thousand of the tribe of Gad,* [6] *twelve thousand of the tribe of Asher, twelve thousand of the tribe of Naphtali, twelve thousand of the tribe of Manasseh,* [7] *twelve thousand of the tribe of Simeon, twelve thousand of the tribe of Levi, twelve thousand of the tribe of Issachar,* [8] *twelve thousand of the tribe of Zebulun, twelve thousand of the tribe of Joseph, twelve thousand sealed out of the tribe of Benjamin.*

[9] *After this I looked, and behold, a great multitude which no man could number, from every nation, from all tribes and peoples and tongues, standing before the throne and before the Lamb, clothed in white robes, with palm branches in their hands,* [10] *and crying out with a loud voice, 'Salvation belongs to our God who sits upon the throne, and to the Lamb!'*

[11] *And all the angels stood round the throne and round the elders and the four living creatures, and they fell on their faces before the throne and worshipped God,* [12] *saying, 'Amen! Blessing and glory and wisdom and thanksgiving and honour and power and might be to our God for ever and ever! Amen!*

¹³ *Then one of the elders addressed me, saying, 'Who are these, clothed in white robes, and whence have they come?'* ¹⁴ *I said to him, 'Sir, you know.' And he said to me, 'These are they who have come out of the great tribulation; they have washed their robes and made them white in the blood of the Lamb.* ¹⁵ *Therefore are they before the throne of God, and serve him day and night within his temple; and he who sits upon the throne will shelter them with his presence.* ¹⁶ *They shall hunger no more, neither thirst any more; the sun shall not strike them, nor any scorching heat.* ¹⁷ *For the Lamb in the midst of the throne will be their shepherd, and he will guide them to springs of living water; and God will wipe away every tear from their eyes.'*

a. The sealing: when? (verses 1–3)

'After this', after the events of chapter 6, come the events of chapter 7. Or do they? It is dangerous to assume that the order in which John writes is the order in which the things he describes will happen; and here we have a notable example of that danger. For chapter 6 describes what is surely a 'harming of the earth'; yet 'after this' we come to a vision in which the earth has not yet been harmed (7:3). Chapter 7 may follow chapter 6 in John's visions, but it does not seem to follow it in the order of actual events. It will not do to try and find subtle distinctions between the chapters, and say that, in some mysterious sequence of events, first it is humanity which will suffer (chapter 6), then the church will be sealed, and only then will come the 'harming' of the inanimate creation, earth and sea and trees. For Seal 6, which ends chapter 6, is one of the most readily identifiable items in this Scene, and covers the events accompanying the return of Christ; with it, the history of the world comes to an end; after it, there can be no further harming of the earth—there will be no earth left to harm.

So we are forced back to the plain text of 7:1. John does not say 'After six unsealings of the book comes the sealing of the servants of God, and after that the harming of the earth.' He says 'After the six unsealings *I saw . . .*'. We have seen John's shifts of focus often enough already to imagine the focus changing once more. What the six seals have revealed is in fact a fearful and comprehensive harming of the earth, symbolized by the dread horsemen. In chapter 7 the depth of focus increases, our plane of vision is, so to speak, nearer to God, and where we saw four horsemen, with a veiled reference to a divine permission allowing them to ride forth, we now perceive four winds, which have power to harm the earth, but are controlled by four angels of God. It is a new view of the same thing, and the corresponding visions in the prophecy of Zechariah support this identification by linking four horse-drawn chariots with the four winds of God (Zc. 6:1-5, RV). But the further truth which here comes into focus is this: God's control over the horsemen/ winds ensures that his church is sealed and secure *before they ride forth.*

The Old Testament parallel to this is in Ezekiel 9, where 'a man clothed in linen' is told to 'put a mark upon the foreheads' of God's faithful people, before the six 'executioners of the city' smite it with his wrath (verses 1-4). The New Testament explanation of it is given by Paul in Ephesians 1:13 f. We were sealed with the promised Holy Spirit when we first put our faith in Christ. From that moment forward, our ultimate safety was guaranteed. So when the searing winds begin to blow, the servant of God is found to have been sealed already against their power. The horsemen ride out on their career of destruction; but the church has been made indestructible.

b. The sealing: who? (verses 4-12)

There has been much dispute over these verses. Who are the 144,000 of verse 4, who are the innumerable crowd of verse 9, and what is the relation between them? But it is less of a puzzle than might first appear. Verse 3 has told us who are sealed: it is God's servants. We have no reason to limit this in any way. The servants of God, all of them, Old Testament and New, all his believing people, are sealed.[1] If we are his servants, the message is for us as much as for any (1:1), and we too are sealed.

But if this is so, how can the sealed be described in verse 4 as 144,000 Israelites? Many theories, as wild as they are unnecessary, have been built on this description. The plain fact is that if we are God's servants, we have been sealed. If we are then told

[1] Rom. 4:11; Eph. 1:13 f.

that we number 144,000, when we know very well that there are millions of us, the figure is presumably another of the symbolic figures of Revelation, and indeed it looks too stylized to be anything else—the suspiciously tidy sort of number that is much more likely to be a symbol than a statistic. If we next find ourselves described as 144,000 *Israelites*, when most of us are Gentiles, this is in line with the regular New Testament teaching which applies to the Christian church the titles and privileges of Israel, and which we have already noted in 3:9.[1] If our numbers are specified even more closely, and oddly, in that each of the twelve tribes, whether large or small, contributes just 12,000; and if the tribes are listed in an order found nowhere else in the Bible; and if one of them (Dan) is omitted altogether, and the lack made up by including one of Joseph's sons as well as Joseph himself; then the description of us is very stylized indeed. But it is the kind of description we should expect if this is a 'diagram' of the church. Like every diagram, it sacrifices one kind of accuracy to clarify another; as when a map projection will sacrifice true distance in order to depict true area, or *vice versa*.

Then what about the innumerable crowd of verse 9? What is the relation between them and the 144,000? They are one and the same. For whatever else the white-robed multitude may be, they are certainly servants of God; and if they are servants, they are sealed (verse 3); and if they are sealed, they are the 144,000 (verse 4). But how can this be—how can a limited number, all Israelites, be the same as a numberless multitude drawn from

[1] Morris's survey of the biblical evidence for this, in his comment on 7:4, is worth quoting in full. 'The church can be referred to as "the twelve tribes" (Jas. i. 1; cf. Mt. xix. 28, Lk. xxii. 30), and this is probably the thought when a letter is sent to "the Dispersion" (1 Pet. i. 1, mg.). The Christian appears to be the true Jew (Rom. ii. 29) and the church "the Israel of God" (Gal. vi. 16). Descriptions of the old Israel are piled up and applied to the church (1 Pet. ii. 9 f.; cf. Eph. i. 11, 14). It is the church which is God's "peculiar people" (Tit. ii. 14), and Christ's own who are "Abraham's seed" (Gal. iii. 29) and "the circumcision" (Phil. iii. 3). Many hold that "Israel after the flesh" (1 Cor. x. 18) implies an "Israel after the Spirit".' Here in Revelation, John in the same way 'speaks of those "which say they are Jews, and are not, but are the synagogue of Satan" (ii. 9; cf. iii. 9). He regards the new Jerusalem as the spiritual home of Christians (xxi. 2, etc.), and it has on its gates the names of the twelve tribes (xxi. 12)' (Morris, p. 114).

every nation? Yet again, we put ourselves in John's place. What he *heard* was a voice from heaven, declaring the results of God's census of his people. More than once in Old Testament times, and again, significantly, at the coming of Christ (Lk. 2:1–7), they were caused to 'stand up and be counted'; and here is God's own count of them. The total may be a symbolic number, but it is still a *number*. If God can count the very hairs of our head (Mt. 10:30), a counting of the heads themselves is unlikely to be beyond him! 'The Lord knows those who are his' (2 Tim. 2:19), and what John heard was God's declaration of their total, given symbolically as '144,000'. What he *saw*, on the other hand, was that this definite total, known to God, is from the human point of view a numberless multitude. Similarly, from God's standpoint they are all 'Israel', his people; from our standpoint, they come from every nation under heaven.

Now for the third time the group of actors dominating the stage changes. We saw the angels, elders, and living creatures of chapters 4 and 5 give way to the horsemen of chapter 6; they in turn gave way to the four wind-angels of 7:1–10; and now, in 7:11, 12, we are back with the *dramatis personae* with whom the Scene began. God's people, whose final redemption is now guaranteed by their being sealed, are here represented not by the saints beneath the altar (6:9 ff.) or the innumerable '144,000' (7:4, 9), but once more by the twenty-four elders who first appeared in 4:4. God's world, which could not be hurt until its own final redemption had been assured by that same sealing (for its redemption depends on theirs),[1] is represented by the four living creatures, who first appeared in 4:6. And now the myriads of angelic spectators, first seen in 5:11, come into view again also. 'The great congregation His triumph shall sing, Ascribing salvation To Jesus our King'[2]—that was the song of the redeemed in verse 10; here in a yet vaster panorama we see all creation, bringing to God all its worship, for all that he does, through all the ages.

'Therefore with Angels and Archangels, and with all the company of heaven, we laud and magnify thy glorious Name,

[1] See pp. 73 f.
[2] C. Wesley.

evermore praising thee and saying: Holy, holy, holy, Lord
God of hosts, heaven and earth are full of thy glory; Glory
be to thee, O Lord most High. Amen.'[1]

c. The sealing: why? (verses 13–17)

The representative elder asks for, and gives, a definition of the
white-robed throng, in terms of what brings them where they
are. 'These are those who have come through the great oppression: they have washed their robes . . . That is why they
now have their place before the throne' (verses 14, 15, JBP).

Some have thought that the white robes therefore indicate
only those who have died, or at least suffered physical persecution, for their faith. Others hold that the 'oppression', or
'tribulation' (RSV), is a particular event still in the future, and thus
narrow down even more the number of those who will go through
it.[2] On both these views, of course, the phrase 'These are those
who have come through the great oppression' contradicts the
view put forward above, that the numberless throng is in fact all
the servants of God.

So far from complicating the issue, however, this phrase
clarifies it. Why do these stand before God's throne? What
qualifies them to be there? The twin facts that they *have washed*
their robes in the blood of the Lamb, and *do emerge* from suffering.
He who is numbered among that multitude is the man who has
been cleansed from his old life of sin (a past event) and been given
an irrepressible new life which no tribulation can quench (a
present experience).[3]

For the vision of verses 13 to 17 'refers, not only to the glory
of the blessed ones in heaven, but to the life of the Christian soul
in the world here and now. And who that, in this present
pilgrimage, has been granted some glimpse of the "unsearchable
riches of Christ" will affirm that the language of the seer is

---

[1] Holy Communion, the Book of Common Prayer.
[2] But we read too much into John's Greek wording if we say that
his use of the definite article must imply a particular event ('the
Tribulation') rather than a general concept (simply 'tribulation', which
is the lot of every Christian; *cf.* 1:9; Acts 14:22).
[3] The RV, almost alone among the versions, conveys the tenses
(aorist and present) correctly.

extravagant?'[1] Indeed the whole point of this Scene is that God's people are safe amid the troubles of *this* life: 'More happy, *but not more secure*, The glorified spirits in heaven.'[2] It is here and now, in this life, that they serve in God's temple—not in the *hieron*, the outer court, but in the *naos*, the innermost sanctuary. It is in this life that he spreads his tabernacle, his tent, over them (verse 15, RV). Tabernacle and temple, in the Old Testament God's own dwelling-places, are now the dwelling-place of his people, and the promises of the ninety-first Psalm are theirs:

'He who dwells in the shelter of the Most High,
who abides in the shadow of the Almighty,
. . . will not fear the terror of the night,
    nor the arrow that flies by day,
nor the pestilence that stalks in darkness,
    nor the destruction that wastes at noonday' (Ps. 91:1, 5, 6).

Of course neither Psalm 91 nor Revelation 7 means that Christians are insulated against trouble. Seals 1 to 4, which showed us the world suffering, were followed by Seal 5, which reminded us that the church must suffer too, and there will be no escape from suffering till the world ends with Seal 6. But the Christian has an inner security which is not affected by external trials. 'It is impossible that any ill should happen to the man who is beloved of the Lord,' wrote Spurgeon. 'Ill to him is no ill, but only good in a mysterious form. Losses enrich him, sickness is his medicine, reproach is his honour, death is his gain.'[3] Rupert Brooke, a poet of a very different kind from the Psalmist, nevertheless echoed his meaning perfectly:

'Safe shall be my going,
Secretly armed against all death's endeavour;
Safe where all safety's lost; safe where men fall;
And if these poor limbs die, safest of all.'

[1] Maycock, p. 89.
[2] A. M. Toplady.
[3] C. H. Spurgeon, *Treasury of David*, on Ps. 91:9, 10.

8. THE SEVENTH SEAL: 'THE REST IS SILENCE' (8:1)

When the Lamb opened the seventh seal, there was silence in heaven for about half an hour.

Seal 6 covered the end of history; and though we have learnt to beware of treating the sequence of John's visions as the historical sequence of the events they portray, it is hard to imagine that Seal 7 would cover anything other than the events which follow the end of history. When Seal 7 is actually broken open, however, there is silence—a silence which confirms our interpretation of Scene 2. For in this scene Christ is revealing to John what will be the experience of the church in the world; so concerning what will happen after the end of the world, he naturally at this point has nothing to say. There *is* a seventh Seal; that is, there is another world to come; but the revelations dealing with it are reserved for later Scenes. Meanwhile we are to learn that the church need never expect to be preserved from the common ills of mankind, as long as this world endures; but that God is still on the throne, Christ is still at the centre of all things, and his people are indestructible.

So begins a half-hour of silence. In terms of actual history and eternity, half an hour is nothing. But in terms of a drama depicting them, it is a lengthy interval, in which John can meditate on Scene 2 before Scene 3 begins.

8:2–11:18

SCENE 3:
WARNING FOR THE WORLD:
seven Trumpets sounded

THE SEQUENCE OF EVENTS

AFTER the Seals, the Trumpets. Or rather, after John has seen the Seals, he hears the Trumpets; which is not quite the same thing. Certainly seven trumpet-blowing angels are the next personages to appear in Revelation. But do they represent the next events to occur in history? This question, whether the order of Revelation is the order of history, has been touched on already,[1] but has to be dealt with thoroughly now if we are to understand the connection between Scenes 2 and 3.

The starting-point of our argument is the comparison between two descriptions of the parousia, Christ's return at the end of the world. One is in his own discourse on the Mount of Olives (Mt. 24:29 ff. is the most convenient version for our purpose),[2] and the other is here in Revelation (6:12–17, the sixth Seal). The Revelation sequence is the subject of our enquiry, and the Matthew sequence will be our control.

Beginning then from 6:12–17, the order *in the drama* is: (1) Seal 6; (2) a vision of the church's security for all time; (3) Seal 7, a half-hour silence; (4) the seven Trumpets. But what is the *chronological* order? We have seen that in real time (2) comes before (1); we cannot therefore take it for granted that (3) and (4) will necessarily follow in that order. Once we have allowed the principle of the 'flashback' in one case, we cannot deny that it might obtain in others. Where then in the sequence do the Trumpets belong?

[1] See p. 61.
[2] Not every commentator agrees that this passage refers to the parousia. Our own comments are based on the view that the total picture of Matthew 24:29–31 is too final and universal to represent anything else.

We seek help in Matthew 24 and 25. Beginning from the same point, the end of the world and Christ's appearing (24:29 ff.), we look to see not what Christ says next, but what he says *will happen* next. What follows in his discourse is a series of warnings (24:32—25:30). But what follows *in the sequence of events* is judgment and then eternity (25:31-46). That is Christ's master plan, and into that the Trumpets must fit somewhere.

a. Do they follow Christ's appearing?

There is no mention of them in Matthew, and no time gap between Matthew 24:30 (the appearing) and 25:31 (the judgment) into which they could fit. If such a complex Scene of the drama, occupying practically four chapters of Revelation, does indeed describe things which will happen between the appearing and the judgment, it seems odd that Christ should have given no indication of it in his master plan. But more than that. The appearing of Christ will bring with it a total cataclysm, in which, among other things, the light of the heavenly bodies will be put out.[1] If the sun, moon and stars are extinguished when Seal 6 is opened, how can the darkening of a mere third of their light (the fourth Trumpet, 8:12) take place later? We conclude then that the Trumpets, though following the Seals in John's vision, cannot follow them chronologically.

b. Do they accompany Christ's appearing?

That is, are they somehow incorporated in Seal 7 and attached to Seal 6? Matthew 24 gives no indication of that either. Furthermore, we again recall that there the return of Christ is accompanied by a total destruction of the world. The partial destruction heralded by the Trumpets is therefore as incongruous during the parousia as after it.

Arguments from silence are usually bad arguments. But not here. The fact that in the passage following Matthew 24:29[2] Christ omits to mention any event resembling the trumpet-events

[1] Rev. 6:12–17 = Mt. 24:29, 30 = 2 Pet. 3:10 = Heb. 12:26, 27.
[2] The great trumpet of Mt. 24:31 bears no relation to the Trumpets of Revelation, except perhaps Trumpet 7 (Rev. 11:15 ff.).

is of the greatest importance. For as has been said, Matthew 24 and 25 are Christ's master plan of the future. They are his answer to a double question from his disciples. First they had asked, in 24:3, 'When will this be?' (*i.e.* the destruction of Jerusalem, which he had mentioned in 24:2, and with which Revelation is not concerned, since it had already happened by the time John wrote); and secondly, 'What will be the sign of your coming—your parousia—and of the close of the age?' This is Christ's answer; and it is a full and detailed one. How full, we may judge from its very first words: 'Take heed that no one leads you astray.' Prophecy, the future, the end of the world—what more fruitful field for the growth of odd and misleading theories? The sheer number of the different interpretations of Revelation demonstrates that growth. For every interpretation which comes anywhere near the truth, there must be dozens which lead away from it. So, 'Take heed that no one leads you astray.' And for two long chapters Christ sets out his own magisterial teaching, explicitly designed to guard his disciples against being deceived in these matters.

We must therefore beware of any theory about the future which adds unwieldy extras to the perfectly proportioned outline given us here. We must view with suspicion any interpretation which tries, for example, to insert four chapters of Revelation between two words of Matthew 24. It will not do to say that Revelation is as authoritative as Matthew. That is beside the point. Interpreters who find in Revelation extensive prophecies which cannot be found in Matthew 24 and 25 are in fact casting aspersions on Christ's teaching in the latter place, and implying that it is defective, or at least badly proportioned, and inadequate to preserve his disciples from error.

Where then do the Trumpets fit in to the Mount of Olives discourse?

c. Do they precede Christ's appearing?

In that case they would coincide with events before Seal 6. A comparison between Trumpets and Seals seems to support this. Both their likeness and their unlikeness seem to point out a parallel between the two series.

They are alike in that both series depict trouble and suffering; in each, the first four sections are not a sequence of events so much as various aspects of the same situation; in each, the fifth section probes beyond external troubles to the inner characters of men; in each, the sixth and seventh seem to portray some final disaster and what follows it.

They are unlike in that whereas the fifth Seal shows Christians suffering (6:9), the fifth Trumpet shows the world of un-believers suffering (9:4); so indeed do all the Trumpets, as the following considerations make plain. The last three of them are denounced expressly against 'those who dwell on the earth' (8:13);[1] the plagues of Trumpets 1 to 6 clearly recall the plagues with which God smote unbelieving Egypt (8:7-9, 12; 9:3; and Ex. 7-10); the humans who people these trumpet-visions are either destroyed by the plagues, or unrepentant in spite of them (9:20 f.); the coming of the kingdom of Christ, with Trumpet 7 is a 'woe' (11:14), and only for impenitent unbelievers could it be so described. This difference between the two Scenes actually confirms their unity. They are the two sides of the same coin. Suffering will come to the world in general (the 'world' in the sense of God's creation, including the church): that is Scene 2. It will also come, with a special divine purpose, upon the 'world' (in the other sense, *viz.* ungodly human society): that is Scene 3.

In a word, the two scenes are parallel. The breaking open of the Seals shows what will happen throughout history, up to the return of Christ, with particular reference to what the church will have to suffer. The Trumpets, starting again from the same point, and also declaring what will happen throughout history up to and including the return of Christ, proclaims a warning to the unbelieving world. Note in passing that the Olivet dis-course confirms this by *following* the description of the parousia in Matthew 24:29-31 with a long section of warnings to those living in the age *before* the parousia.

As we look back, we can see how this method of writing follows the principle of the 'repeat of patterns', which we noted in con-nection with Scene 1. Realizing how integral this principle is to the

[1] The inhabitants of the earth—the phrase is the same as that in 6:10. See p. 72.

book, and indeed to the whole Bible, we should not be surprised
to find it extended into a parallelism between entire Scenes.
Looking forward, we shall find the same ground covered again
and again in this way. As each Scene ends, having traced history
through to its end and beyond, the drama returns to the same
beginning and retraces the same course through the next Scene.

This has a bearing on the way Revelation is approached by
two influential schools of thought, known as the 'historicist'
and the 'futurist'. Historicists hold that the book is a detailed
account of events covering the whole period from the first
coming of Christ to the second: from John's point of view,
almost entirely prediction, or 'history written beforehand'.
Futurists also believe the book to be mostly predictive, but
because they expect a more literal fulfilment of its prophecies,
they hold that even today the greater part of it has not yet come
true. The tendency of both types of interpretation is to string
the Scenes of the book end to end—to assume, for example, that
since in the drama Trumpets follow Seals, the events they depict
will also occur in that order.

We have seen that this is not necessarily so. Our own reading
proceeds on a different assumption, namely that the various
sections of Revelation cannot be taken *a priori* to be either consecutive or repetitive. One has to decide on other grounds
whether this thing is meant to follow that, or whether it is
instead a matter of doubling back and restatement. Such de-
cisions can generally be reached from internal evidence within
the book, and parallels in other parts of Scripture, such as the
Mount of Olives discourse; so these should provide sufficient
framework for all the sections to be fitted together in a reason-
ably simple order.

I. SCENE 3 OPENS: GOD HEARS HIS PEOPLE'S CRY
(8:2–6)

*Then I saw the seven angels who stand before God, and seven trumpets
were given to them.*

*³And another angel came and stood at the altar with a golden censer;
and he was given much incense to mingle with the prayers of all the saints
upon the golden altar before the throne; ⁴and the smoke of the incense*

rose with the prayers of the saints from the hand of the angel before God. [5] Then the angel took the censer and filled it with fire from the altar and threw it on the earth; and there were peals of thunder, loud noises, flashes of lightning, and an earthquake.

[6] Now the seven angels who had the seven trumpets made ready to blow them.

'At the round earth's imagined corners blow Your trumpets, angels,' cries John Donne, no doubt with this Scene in mind, and linking it, in the lines that follow, with the last trumpet which shall wake the dead.[1] But the Bible itself warns us not to identify these trumpets too readily. The sounding of trumpets might signalize a day of remembrance (Lv. 23:24), or a triumph (Jos. 6:4), or a coronation (1 Ki. 1:34), or a warning (Je. 4:5 f.). The great trumpet we heard in chapter 1, so far from waking the dead, all but slew the living (1:10, 17). There is nothing yet in chapter 8 to indicate which, if any, of these meanings should be attached to the trumpets of this scene, and we shall be wise to suspend judgment.

There is much less doubt about the altar and the incense of verses 3 to 5. They form one of the links between the last scene and this one. When Seal 5 was opened we saw an altar with the blood of the saints running down from it. Here we see an altar with the prayers of the saints rising up from it. In the furnishing of the Temple, the altar of sacrifice and the altar of incense were separate; as so often, the single truth of heaven needs many different representations to display all its facets. But there is only one altar in 'the heavenlies', and in it both the earthly altars are merged. We saw it already under Seal 5 as the focus of two kinds of offering: that of the saints' lives, and that of their prayers. It is out of the latter—the altar regarded as an incense altar, from which rises a fragrant smoke representing the prayers of God's people[2]—that the whole of Scene 3 grows. The connection is a sobering one, but three considerations establish it practically beyond doubt. First, Trumpets 5 to 7 (and by implication 1 to 4

[1] Mt. 24:31; 1 Cor. 15:52; 1 Thes. 4:16.
[2] The Greek of verse 3 does not make clear how the incense and the prayers are related, but 5:8 has already shown that the one is (no doubt in both places alike) a symbol of the other.

also) call down woes on the 'inhabitants of the earth'[1]; and it was for justice to be done on these same 'inhabitants of the earth' that the saints were praying when Seal 5 was opened. Second, the plagues of Trumpets 1 to 5, recalling the plagues of Egypt, also recall the solemn preface to those plagues in Exodus 3:7 f.: 'The Lord said, "I have seen the affliction of my people who are in Egypt, and *have heard their cry* . . . and I have come down to deliver them." ' Third, the censer from which the fire is poured out on earth is the same censer from which the prayer was sent up to heaven.

Now this may seem somewhat remote from normal Christian experience. In Scene 2 the church is assured that she will suffer, though her final safety will never be in question. But she is not accepting the suffering meekly. She is calling for vengeance on those who cause it. And lest we should imagine that this is a merely human prayer, which in the stress of the moment has lost sight of the divine command to pray for (not against) one's persecutors, we are then shown in Scene 3 that God hears and answers it in a horribly comprehensive way.

Two unanswered questions go with us, then, into Scene 3. Do the Trumpets mean triumph, doom, life, death, or what? And does the censer really mean that God's people are to pray for trouble to strike the world?

2. THE FIRST TRUMPET: THE EARTH STRICKEN (8:7)

The first angel blew his trumpet, and there followed hail and fire, mixed with blood, which fell on the earth; and a third of the earth was burnt up, and a third of the trees were burnt up, and all green grass was burnt up.

The riders of Scene 2 were unimaginable, so we accepted that they must be symbolic. Hail that burns, however, is only too easy to visualize in the atomic age, and one may be tempted to see in it not a symbol but an actuality. Certain assumptions have been made on the basis of this: that for nineteen centuries no such hail was known; that when it eventually did come, it would therefore be a portent of the end of history; that it has appeared for the first time in our own day; and that consequently we are near the

[1] See p. 72.

end of history. This reasoning will not in fact stand up to scrutiny. Men have often believed that some momentous event of their own day was what this or that prophecy mentioned as a sign of the end. The barbarian invasions of the fifth century, the coming of the fateful year 1000, the turmoils of the Reformation, the Lisbon earthquake of 1745, each caused some Bible students to say 'Now at last we are seeing a literal fulfilment of prophecy; now at last judgment day is near.' But neither conclusion was true—not, at any rate, in the sense they meant.

For these reasons we should resist the temptation to interpret the hail as something like atomic fallout. And for two other reasons also. (1) If it is true that Scene 3 describes plagues sent to the wicked 'inhabitants of the earth' in answer to the prayers of God's people, it seems rather odd that the first of them should not have come till the mid-twentieth century, and that sixty generations of the wicked should have gone unscathed even by that plague (let alone the rest, which, if literal, have not happened even yet). (2) If it is true that Scene 3 is parallel to Scene 2, the first five Trumpets are likely to resemble the first five Seals in revealing not datable events, but aspects of the world situation which may be true at any time.

On this view, the hail, fire, and blood symbolize any kind of destruction which at any time damages the earth on which man lives.

3. THE SECOND TRUMPET: THE SEA STRICKEN (8:8, 9)

The second angel blew his trumpet, and something like a great mountain, burning with fire, was thrown into the sea; ⁹and a third of the sea became blood, a third of the living creatures in the sea died, and a third of the ships were destroyed.

The effect of Trumpet 2 recalls the first of the plagues of Egypt (Ex. 7:20 ff.), as the effects of Trumpet 1 recalled the seventh plague (Ex. 9:24 ff.). The fouling of the seas and the consequent destruction of marine life might be another aspect of environmental damage, like the damage to the land which followed Trumpet 1. The particular mention of the loss of shipping, though, may mean that while the first plague was directed against

man's environment, the second was directed against his commerce; for in New Testament times 'the sea' meant the Mediterranean, and the Mediterranean was a 'Roman lake', criss-
crossed by the trade routes of the Empire.

The means by which these dire effects are brought about is
dramatic in the extreme. But it is not unimaginable. The overthrow of Atlantis is to us a legend; the readers of Revelation
lived 2,000 years closer to the colossal disaster which gave rise to
that legend.[1] There may well have been extant in their day reports
of it as history, not fable, which would have given them some
conception of how a huge burning mountain might collapse into
the sea. Moreover, they had in their own time known the AD 79
eruption of Vesuvius; and it is not perhaps too fanciful to suggest
that that disaster must have struck many of John's readers as a
remarkable example of the teaching of this scene. For in AD 70
Jews all over the world, Jewish Christians included, had heard
with stunned disbelief how Roman armies had sacked God's holy
city. The smoke that went up from Jerusalem symbolized the
prayer of the people of God:

'They set thy sanctuary on fire;
    to the ground they desecrated the dwelling place of thy
    name . . .
How long, O God, is the foe to scoff?
Is the enemy to revile thy name for ever?' (Ps. 74:7, 10).

The smoke that went up from Pompeii and Herculaneum nine
years later, nine years which had done little to dim the memory of
Jerusalem's fall, must have seemed to many the answer to that
prayer.

4. THE THIRD TRUMPET: THE RIVERS STRICKEN (8:10, 11)

*The third angel blew his trumpet, and a great star fell from heaven,
blazing like a torch, and it fell on a third of the rivers and on the fountains of water. [11] The name of the star is Wormwood. A third of the
waters became wormwood, and many men died of the water, because it was
made bitter.*

[1] Perhaps an eruption of the volcanic Aegean island of Thera, in
about the sixteenth century BC. See J. V. Luce, *The End of Atlantis*
(Thames & Hudson, 1969).

We find this hard to visualize. But if the first century knew something like the burning mountain of Trumpet 2, and our own century knows something like the burning hail of Trumpet 1, something may well happen to men of a generation still future which they will ruefully compare to the burning star of Trumpet 3. Science fiction even in its early days dreamed of such possibilities, and 'The Star' of H. G. Wells's short story came near to accomplishing not a partial but a total destruction of the world.

But expectation of a literal fulfilment of any of these visions misses the point of them. What they tell us is that by agencies so far beyond human control that their divine origin should be obvious, terrible things happen to the world in which man lives. In this case God smites the fresh waters, presumably (since he specifies the drinking of them, and the consequent poisoning of those who drink) a symbol of the natural resources which ought to sustain human life.

5. THE FOURTH TRUMPET: THE SKY STRICKEN (8:12)

The fourth angel blew his trumpet, and a third of the sun was struck, and a third of the moon, and a third of the stars, so that a third of their light was darkened; a third of the day was kept from shining, and likewise a third of the night.

Still harder to imagine than the falling star is this one-third darkness during both day and night. Even recognizing that it is probably not the sun, moon, and stars themselves which would be affected, but rather our view of their light, what are we to visualize? Eclipses, or cloud-cover, or sandstorms? Or a radical change in the earth's movement which would extend permanent night over a third of its surface, though it would still not account for the darkening of moon and stars? From all such fruitless speculation, may the analogy of Scripture deliver us. For Scripture is not concerned with the mechanics of miracle. The supernatural events of the Bible are concerned not with 'How?'; but with 'Who?' and 'Why?' Trumpet 4 again points us back to the book of Exodus,[1] where the importance of the

[1] Ex. 10:21 ff. Trumpet 3 does not have an exact parallel among the plagues of Egypt; but see Ex. 7:24; 15:23 ff.

plagues which struck Egypt was precisely that men could not understand how they happened, and had to admit that God was at work (Ex. 8:7, 18 f.).

What then is God doing here? We draw together our conclusions about the first part of Scene 3. Fearful damage is done to the land and its vegetation, the sea and its ships, the waters which men drink, and the light by which they see—their environment, commerce, resources, and vision. But the damage is partial ('one third'), not total; which seems to show that the Trumpets are sounding not doom, but warning. The majority of mankind is allowed to survive, being shown God's wrath against sin, and given the chance to repent. Paradoxically, therefore, the miseries of Scene 3 are really kindnesses. The Seals showed the suffering church pleading for justice to be done. But the Trumpets show the wicked world being offered mercy. The offer is not accepted, and the world will not in fact repent (9:20 f.); but let it never be said that God has not done all in his power, even to the devastation of his own once perfect earth, in order to bring men to their senses.

6. LET THE WORLD OF MEN BEWARE THE REMAINING TRUMPETS! (8:13)

Then I looked, and I heard an eagle crying with a loud voice, as it flew in midheaven, 'Woe, woe, woe to those who dwell on the earth, at the blasts of the other trumpets which the three angels are about to blow!'

While the attention of readers is being drawn to the links between this Scene and the exodus, the eagle may recall to them that the frustrating of Egyptian wickedness was finally achieved by God rescuing his people 'on eagles' wings' (Ex. 19:4). On the other hand, the Bible does not distinguish between eagles and vultures (see Mt. 24:28) and this bird, warning of doom, may be a vulture circling over the dying body of mankind. Certainly the woes it proclaims for the inhabitants of the earth are of the same kind, and are precipitated by the same wickedness, as those proclaimed by Christ for the towns of Galilee. 'Woe to you, Chorazin! woe to you, Bethsaida! for if the mighty works done in you had been done in Tyre and Sidon, they would have repented long ago . . . And you, Capernaum, will you be exalted to heaven? You shall be brought down to Hades. For if the mighty works done in you had been done in Sodom, it would have remained until this day' (Mt. 11:21–24). The sin which brings doom is, as always, the wilful refusal to respond to what the humble eye sees to be the deeds of God.

Men suffer indirectly as the first four Trumpets affect their environment. Since they are still impenitent, the remaining Trumpets will now affect them directly. God is using, to expose the true character of the wicked, the same method which in the case of Job was used to expose the true character of the righteous (Jb. 1:8–12; 2:3–7)

7. THE FIFTH TRUMPET: TORMENT (9:1–12)

And the fifth angel blew his trumpet, and I saw a star fallen from heaven to earth, and he was given the key of the shaft of the bottomless pit; [2] *he opened the shaft of the bottomless pit, and from the shaft rose smoke like the smoke of a great furnace, and the sun and the air were darkened with the smoke from the shaft.* [3] *Then from the smoke came locusts on the earth, and they were given power like the power of scorpions of the earth;* [4] *they were told not to harm the grass of the earth or any green growth or any tree, but only those of mankind who have not the seal of God upon their foreheads;* [5] *they were allowed to torture them for five months, but not to kill them, and their torture was like the torture of a scorpion, when it stings a man.* [6] *And in those days men will seek death and will not find it; they will long to die, and death will fly from them.* [7] *In appearance the locusts were like horses arrayed for battle; on their heads were what looked like crowns of gold; their faces were like human faces,* [8] *their hair like women's hair, and their teeth like lions' teeth;* [9] *they had scales like iron breastplates, and the noise of their wings was like the noise of many chariots with horses rushing into battle.* [10] *They have tails like scorpions, and stings, and their power of hurting men for five months lies in their tails.* [11] *They have as king over them the angel of the bottomless pit; his name in Hebrew is Abaddon, and in Greek he is called Apollyon.* [12] *The first woe has passed; behold, two woes are still to come.*

Only the most extreme literalists take the events of Trumpet 5 at their face value, expecting to see in real life what John saw in his vision. Imagine a great hole opened somewhere in the earth's surface, and smoke pouring from it, bringing from the interior of the earth an immense plague of locusts, such as never were on sea or land—armed like scorpions, shaped like horses, crowned like kings, with the faces of men, the hair of women, the teeth of lions, armour-plated, winged, and moving with deafening noise; attacking people instead of vegetation, and able, into the bargain, to discern between Christians and non-Christians. Scripture forbids us to expect such a prophecy to be fulfilled literally. That some prophecy does have literal fulfilment, few will deny. But we have to distinguish that which does from that which does not; and the criterion is not whether such a fulfilment is imaginable by our minds,[1] but whether the analogy of Scripture leads us to take the prophecy in question symbolically or straight. We have had ample indication already that Trumpets 1 to 5 at least, like Seals 1 to 5, prophesy in symbols, and what they declare has in fact come true again and again throughout the centuries.

The object of introducing supernatural events into history is, as we noted in connection with Trumpet 4, that men should ask not 'How?', but 'Who?' and 'Why?' The important thing about the locusts is not how such creatures could exist, but what they mean. This was equally the point of the literal locust-plagues in the parallel Old Testament passages, Exodus 10:12–20 (yet another of the plagues of Egypt) and Joel 1 and 2. So these demonic hordes have spiritual significance. They emerge from the pit, the place of death; the pit is opened by someone who is a 'fallen star'—no doubt Satan (Lk. 10:18; *cf.* Is. 14:12); Satan is 'given' divine authority to do this. Their appearance is practically indescribable, but their effect is plain, being one of sheer terror; they torment men for nearly half a year, so that the breathing-spaces are scarcely longer than the periods of suffering; their sting is such that even death would be preferable.

Our interpretation means that whenever unbelievers suffer in this way, all the many-shaped ills which torment them, and which

[1] Some interpreters seem to reason in this way. Walvoord says about verse 6, '*literal* death is meant'; about verse 5, '*Probably . . . literally . . .* a period of five months'; about verses 7 ff., '*not* natural locusts, but a *visual representation* of . . . hordes of demons' (pp. 160 f. Our italics). Literalism reigns as far as the point where the mind begins to boggle, and beyond that symbolism is allowed to take over.

even kindly death will not come to relieve—chronic hardships, diseases, enmities, insecurities—these ills are the locusts of Trumpet 5, marshalled and led by the angel of the abyss, again perhaps Satan himself. Such is the warning of Trumpet 5, and the first of the woes directed against unbelieving men themselves, as distinct from their environment.

8. THE SIXTH TRUMPET: DESTRUCTION (9:13–21)

Then the sixth angel blew his trumpet, and I heard a voice from the four horns of the golden altar before God, 14 *saying to the sixth angel who had the trumpet, 'Release the four angels who are bound at the great river Euphrates.'* 15 *So the four angels were released, who had been held ready for the hour, the day, the month, and the year, to kill a third of mankind.* 16 *The number of the troops of cavalry was twice ten thousand times ten thousand; I heard their number.*

17 *And this was how I saw the horses in my vision: the riders wore breastplates the colour of fire and of sapphire and of sulphur, and the heads of the horses were like lions' heads, and fire and smoke and sulphur issued from their mouths.* 18 *By these three plagues a third of mankind was killed, by the fire and smoke and sulphur issuing from their mouths.* 19 *For the power of the horses is in their mouths and in their tails; their tails are like serpents, with heads, and by means of them they wound.*

20 *The rest of mankind, who were not killed by these plagues, did not repent of the works of their hands nor give up worshipping demons and idols of gold and silver and bronze and stone and wood, which cannot either see or hear or walk;* 21 *nor did they repent of their murders or their sorceries or their immorality or their thefts.*

There is a seventh Trumpet yet to sound, but Trumpet 6 is the last warning for the inhabitants of the earth. When Trumpet 7 sounds it will be too late (11:15–18). The warning is death, not one's own death but the death of others (verses 15, 18). One third of mankind is destroyed, with the object (unsuccessful, as it turns out) of moving the rest to repentance.

The cavalry armies are, like the rest of this scene, not to be taken literally. No age in history has yet seen the devastating coincidence of, on the one hand, pagan idolatry as the dominant religion (verse 20), and on the other, 200 million fire-breathing, snake-tailed horses rampaging out of Mesopotamia. Nor is the passage to be treated as symbolism of the kind which merely encloses words in inverted commas, so that the 'horses' mouths' are flamethrowers, the 'horses' tails' bombers, and so on, and the 'Euphrates' from which all this military paraphernalia comes is Russia, or China, or whatever the current bogey may be. Strict literalism pushes the whole episode into a near-unbelievable future; this kind of quasi-symbolism locates it in our present century. Neither would have had any meaning for readers over the past two thousand years.

No: it must all be not merely symbolism, but true biblical symbolism. Verse 13: it is from the altar that the church's prayers go up, and God's fiery answer is sent down (8:3-5). Trumpet 6, like the rest, is sounding the warning of God's wrath against sin in reply to the prayers of his people that evil should not go un-punished and that justice should be done. Verse 14: through much of Bible history the threat of destruction had come chiefly from the region of the Euphrates and Tigris, ever since 'the Assyrian came down like a wolf on the fold' in the eighth cen-tury BC. Even Rome looked apprehensively over its shoulder at the barbarians on its eastern frontier, and was by no means the last empire to do so. God's last and most potent warning, then, is to be a 'Euphratean' one of destruction and death. Verses 15, 16: the angels who will bring the destruction are unleashed at God's command, at a zero hour of God's planning, and with forces of God's numbering. Every single death they bring about will happen exactly as and when God plans it.

The death-dealing horsemen of Trumpet 6 are not tanks and planes. Or not only tanks and planes. They are also cancers and road accidents and malnutrition and terrorist bombs and peace-ful demises in nursing homes. Yet 'the rest of mankind, who were not killed by these plagues', still do not repent of their idolatry, the centring of their lives on anything rather than God, or of the evils which inevitably flow from it. They hear of pollution, of inflation, of dwindling resources, of blind politicians, and will not admit that the first four Trumpets of God are sounding. In the end they themselves are affected by these troubles, and for one reason or another life becomes a torment: the locusts are out, Trumpet 5 is sounding, but they will not repent. Not even when the angels of the Euphrates rise to the summons of Trumpet 6, and the cavalry rides out to slay—by any kind of destruction, not necessarily war—a friend or a relative, a husband or a wife: not even in bereavement will they repent. 'God whispers to us in our pleasures, speaks in our conscience, but shouts in our pains.'[1] If we will not hear the tremendous voice of the pains of bereavement, there can be no hope for us.

9. THE MEANING OF THE LAST TRUMPET (10:1–7)

Then I saw another mighty angel coming down from heaven, wrapped in a cloud, with a rainbow over his head, and his face was like the sun, and his legs like pillars of fire. [2] He had a little scroll open in his hand. And he set his right foot on the sea, and his left foot on the land, [3] and called out with a loud voice, like a lion roaring; when he called out, the seven thunders sounded. [4] And when the seven thunders had sounded, I was about to write, but I heard a voice from heaven saying, 'Seal up what the seven thunders have said, and do not write it down.'

[5] And the angel whom I saw standing on sea and land lifted up his right hand to heaven [6] and swore by him who lives for ever and ever, who created heaven and what is in it, the earth and what is in it, and the sea and what is in it, that there should be no more delay, [7] but that in the days of the trumpet call to be sounded by the seventh angel, the mystery of God, as he announced to his servants the prophets, should be fulfilled.

The angel who is to introduce Trumpet 7 first brings the tantalizing message of the seven Thunders. One wonders why John should have been given this particular revelation and then told not to reveal it to his readers. It was a notable vision, and the angel is a noble figure, resembling the Christ of chapter 1, and removing once and for all any lingering idea that angels are effeminate creatures who play languidly on harps. Clearly John heard and understood what the Thunders said. But as with Paul's experience related in 2 Corinthians 12:4, it was not to be divulged further.

We may still hazard a guess as to the kind of thing the Thunders spoke. The nearest biblical parallel is probably Psalm 29, where thunder is called the 'voice of God', and is mentioned seven

[1] C. S. Lewis, *The Problem of Pain* (Bles, 1940), p. 81.

times. What it does is to declare his greatness and majesty, so that
'in his temple all cry, "Glory!"' (Ps. 29:9). Perhaps then the
revelations of himself which God gives to the inhabitants of the
earth are even more comprehensive than we can realize. Perhaps
it is not good for Christians to know how very numerous are his
warnings to the world, or they might desist from their own duty
of evangelizing.

However that may be, the next event in God's calendar will
be Trumpet 7, and that will be the end. The New Testament use
of the word 'mystery', as we shall see,[1] shows that the 'mystery
of God' is not 'truth concerning God Himself which has not been
fully revealed',[2] but simply the gospel, the good news of how
any man may be reconciled to God through Christ.[3] Indeed in
verse 7 the word 'announced' is actually *euēngelisen*, 'preached the
gospel'. With Trumpet 7 the gospel age will be completed.

It is tempting to read with AV and RV, 'There shall be time no
longer', that is, that time will come to an end and be replaced by
eternity. There comes to mind the character in one of Charles
Williams' novels who in the real world is on his way to an
appointment, and in his dream world is descending a rope which
in a few moments will take him past the point of no return, into
everlasting hell. 'He thought: "I shall be just in time." He was,
and only just; as close to its end as to the end of the rope.'[4]

The RSV is certainly correct, however, in translating 'that there
should be no more *delay*'. This declaration had a double purpose.
First, it clarifies one of the relationships between Revelation and
the greatest of the Old Testament apocalyptic books, Daniel.
Among the many likenesses which Daniel's visions bear to
John's is the mighty oath, sworn by a similar dazzling figure,
concerning 'the end of these wonders'. Daniel is told that three
and a half 'times' are to elapse before the end (Dn. 10:5 f.;
12:6 f.). For John, by contrast, there is to be no more delay.
Where the earlier revelation was written as a prospect of history,
with the end still remote, this one brings the end right before us,
as part of the immediate perspective of life.[5]

[1] See pp. 153 f.
[2] Walvoord, p. 172.
[3] 1 Cor. 2:1, RV; Eph. 3:4-6.
[4] Charles Williams, *Descent into Hell* (Faber, 1949), pp. 216 f.
[5] See pp. 32.

Secondly, its purpose is pastoral. It reminds us that there is a limit to the patience of God. Six trumpet blasts represent every possible chance for repentance which he can offer to man. Even then it is not his patience, but man's ability to respond, which is exhausted. The stage is reached at which there is no point in offering further opportunities, for man has hardened himself beyond the possibility of repenting. It is then that the angel swears that Trumpet 7 shall be no longer delayed.

10. YET THE WORLD IS UNREPENTANT (10:8—11:14)

Then the voice which I had heard from heaven spoke to me again, saying, 'Go, take the scroll which is open in the hand of the angel who is standing on the sea and on the land.' 9So I went to the angel and told him to give me the little scroll; and he said to me, 'Take it and eat; it will be bitter to your stomach, but sweet as honey in your mouth.' 10And I took the little scroll from the hand of the angel and ate it; it was sweet as honey in my mouth, but when I had eaten it my stomach was made bitter. 11And I was told, 'You must again prophesy about many peoples and nations and tongues and kings.'

11:1Then I was given a measuring rod like a staff, and I was told: 'Rise and measure the temple of God and the altar and those who worship there, 2but do not measure the court outside the temple; leave that out, for it is given over to the nations and they will trample over the holy city for forty-two months.

11:3And I will grant my two witnesses power to prophesy for one thousand two hundred and sixty days, clothed in sackcloth.' 4These are the two olive trees and the two lampstands which stand before the Lord of the earth. 5And if any one would harm them, fire pours from their mouth and consumes their foes; if any one would harm them, thus he is doomed to be killed. 6They have power to shut the sky, that no rain may fall during the days of their prophesying, and they have power over the waters to turn them into blood, and to smite the earth with every plague as often as they desire.

11:7And when they have finished their testimony, the beast that ascends from the bottomless pit will make war upon them and conquer them and kill them, 8and their dead bodies will lie in the street of the great city which is allegorically called Sodom and Egypt, where their Lord was crucified. 9For three days and a half men from the peoples and

*tribes and tongues and nations gaze at their dead bodies and refuse to let
them be placed in a tomb,* ¹⁰*and those who dwell on the earth will rejoice over them and make merry and exchange presents, because these two
prophets had been a torment to those who dwell on the earth.*

¹¹:¹¹*But after the three and a half days a breath of life from God
entered them, and they stood up on their feet, and great fear fell on those
who saw them.* ¹²*Then they heard a loud voice from heaven saying to them,
'Come up hither!' And in the sight of their foes they went up to heaven in
a cloud.* ¹³*And at that hour there was a great earthquake, and a tenth
of the city fell; seven thousand people were killed in the earthquake, and
the rest were terrified and gave glory to the God of heaven.*

¹¹:¹⁴*The second woe has passed; behold, the third woe is soon to come.*

a. The sweet/bitter scroll (10:8–11)

The angel resembles Christ, and his scroll probably contains
the words of Christ, since John is told that having digested its
contents he is then to prophesy. The prophet Ezekiel is given a
similar experience (Ezk. 2:8—3:3). And every Christian will
agree with their testimony that the first taste of the gospel is, to
them, one of great sweetness: saints of all ages have found it so
(Pss. 19:10; 119:103). But there is bitterness in it when they
proclaim it to the unbelieving world, for it speaks of estrange-
ment from God, and wrath and hell for those who will not repent.

Whatever the message may be in detail, verse 11 makes clear
that it has universal meaning. This consideration has a bearing on
the next two sections.

b. The sacred/profane city (11:1–2)

Scene 3 is mostly about the world, but it does have something
to say about the church, concerning which we find a section here
that corresponds to the one preceding Seal 7 in Scene 2. Here as
there we find the church's security guaranteed, despite all its
outward sufferings.

For the temple cannot be taken literally. 'When John wrote,
the temple at Jerusalem had been in ruin for a round score of
years . . . When they were told that the temple was to be "measured" for preservation', John's readers 'must inevitably have

perceived an allegorical sense.'[1] Such a sense lay readily to hand in the teaching of the apostolic church, which frequently applied to itself the terms and concepts of Judaism, thinking of itself, for example, as 'God's temple' (1 Cor. 3:16; and see p. 83). So far as this vision is concerned, the temple means the church, while the city stands for the world; in harmony with 10:11, John is not speaking of Jerusalem in any narrow geographical sense, but as a universal symbol.

Between Seals 6 and 7, then, we find those who are sealed serving God in his temple, in the *naos*, the inner sanctuary. Here too, between Trumpets 6 and 7, although the unbelievers occupy not only the holy city but even the outer courts of the temple itself, God's people are safe in the inner sanctuary, which is then 'measured' (just as its occupants were numbered in 7:4) to indicate that they are all known to God and therefore safe in his care.

c. The power of the word and the power of the world (11:3–14)

Interpreters have not been lacking who have expected a literal fulfilment of this section, as of the rest. At some unspecified date in the future will begin, presumably in Jerusalem, the three-and-a-half-year preaching career of these two remarkable people, God's witnesses. It will be followed by their martyrdom, and then (to the consternation of all) by their resurrection and rapture, and chaos in the city.

If, however, the temple and city of verses 1 and 2 are symbolic, and the message of 10:11 is universal, it seems a great deal more likely that this passage also carries a non-literal meaning, especially as the length of the witnesses' career ties in with the symbolism of the last section (verse 3 with verse 2), and their title of 'lampstand' with the symbolism of Scene 1 (verse 4 with 1:20).

Accordingly, the following suggestions are offered.

The witnesses, declaring God's truth to the inhabitants of the earth, are the church in the world, God's people among the heathen nations, those to whom the gospel is sweet among those

---

[1] Kiddle, pp. 178 f. The whole of Kiddle's introduction to chapter 11 (pp. 176–188) is most illuminating.

to whom it is bitter, the sanctuary which remains God's own when not only the city but even the outer temple is profaned. They wear sackcloth to show the solemnity of their message. Various conjectures have been made as to why there are two of them, but the remarkable things they do in verses 5 and 6 recall perhaps most forcibly the two who witnessed to the glory of Christ on the mount of transfiguration, Moses and Elijah.[1] These two symbolize the witness of the whole church, and perhaps also the certainty of that witness, since the biblical principle is that 'the testimony of two men is true' (Jn. 8:17; see Acts 1:8). They are furthermore unquenchable, like the lamps which the prophet Zechariah saw connected directly to the source of oil in the living olive trees (verse 4; Zc. 4:2 ff.). They are untouchable, as is the church of Christ as a whole, though its individual members may be hurt (verse 5). They are invincible, producing proofs of God's power corresponding to those produced by Moses and Elijah (verse 6)—proofs which no more succeeded in evoking general repentance then than they do now, in spite of their perennial qualities of both strangeness and sternness. Of the strangeness, we may say that in all ages drought, blood, and plague result, whether literally or metaphorically, when the praying and prophesying of God's witnesses are on the one hand inspired by the Spirit but on the other rejected by men. Of the sternness seen in much of the ministry of the first Moses and Elijah, we may say that Jewish prophecy looked forward to another Moses and Elijah whose ministry was designed to make men listen to God before the day of judgment should come; that those predictions were chiefly fulfilled in Jesus and John the Baptist; and that continued witness of the same kind in the mouth of Christians ever since is 'an indication of their utter determination to bring men to repentance at whatever cost, before it is too late'.[2]

The witnesses preach for 1,260 days, which on the basis of a stylized month of thirty days are the forty-two months during which the nations occupy God's city (verse 2). This period cannot be literal either; for the literal 'times of the Gentiles' (or 'nations') were to begin, according to Christ, when Jerusalem was sacked

[1] Mk. 9:4; 2 Ki. 1:10; 1 Ki. 17:1; Ex. 7:17—11:10.
[2] Caird, p. 136.

by the Romans in AD 70 (Lk. 21:20–24), and no literal sequence of events remotely like those of verses 3 to 13 started on that date. To say 'The times of the nations are forty-two months' will lead us into great and unnecessary difficulties. To say, on the other hand, ' "Forty-two months" means the times of the nations', puts quite a different complexion on the matter. The figure becomes a symbol like the red cross or the swastika, a shorthand way of indicating the period during which the 'nations', the unbelievers, seem to dominate the world, but the 'people', God's people, maintain their witness in it.

After the forty-two months (three and a half years) of witness, follows a brief period (three and a half days) of apparent defeat for the church. It may not be altogether fanciful to see in the church's experience a reflection of Christ's experience, in his three days of death following three years of ministry, since his place of suffering is explicitly identified with hers (verse 8). The city where their corpses lie exposed to public gaze is no more literal than the rest. It cannot at one and the same time be literally both Sodom and Egypt; and if those names are used metaphorically, why should not 'the city . . . where their Lord was crucified' be metaphorical also? No; whenever we hear the gospel preached in the world, we know we are still living in the 'three and a half years'; and wherever we may be when the church seems finally to perish, we shall know we have arrived at the Christ-killing Jerusalem which is also Sodom at her most corrupt, and Egypt at her most oppressive.

For Scripture does seem to envisage a time (this is the first clear indication of it in Revelation) when at the very end of history an unexampled onslaught will be mounted against the church, and she will to all appearances 'go under'. Paul speaks of it as 'the rebellion', the coming of 'the man of lawlessness' (2 Thes. 2:3), and Christ hints at it in Matthew 24:11 f., 24. We shall hear more of it, and of the Beast who initiates it (verse 7), in chapter 20. But it will be brief; and at the end of it the church will rise again to meet its Lord, and the world in confusion will at last give worship to its Maker, not the willing worship of love but the grudging worship of compulsion. For the warnings will have been in vain. There are none so blind as those who will not see. Scene 2 showed how the church will suffer, yet be indestructible; Scene 3 now shows how the world will be warned, yet be unrepentant.

11. THE SEVENTH TRUMPET: THE WORLD IS NO MORE (11:15-18)

Then the seventh angel blew his trumpet, and there were loud voices in heaven, saying, 'The kingdom of the world has become the kingdom of our Lord and of his Christ, and he shall reign for ever and ever.' [16] *And the twenty-four elders who sit on their thrones before God fell on their faces and worshipped God,* [17] *saying, 'We give thanks to thee, Lord God Almighty, who art and who wast, that thou hast taken thy great power and begun to reign.* [18] *The nations raged, but thy wrath came, and the time for the dead to be judged, for rewarding thy servants, the prophets and saints, and those who fear thy name, both small and great, and for destroying the destroyers of the earth.'*

With Trumpet 7 the parousia has arrived. Although Scripture mentions some aspects of the victory of Christ in connection with his first coming,[1] there is no doubt that the language here describes the total triumph of his second. This is the 'final and overwhelming display' of the majesty of God.[2]

In the context of Scene 3, we should not be surprised that this glorious event is described as a 'woe' (11:14). The entire Scene has been a warning to the unbelieving world, and if the world has still not repented after the first six Trumpets, then Trumpet 7 will bring woe indeed. It is the final woe, because from it there is no appeal. Trumpets 1 to 4 proved God's power over the earth the wicked inhabit; Trumpets 5 to 7 are the three woes which prove his power over them themselves—he has power to hurt them, to kill them, and finally (which should give them greatest cause to fear, Mt. 10:28) to damn them.

Let there be no false pity for the unrepentant. The fond hope that God might give them one more chance after death is

---

[1] *e.g.* Jn. 12:31; Col. 2:14 f.; and see below, on 20:1 ff. (pp. 187 ff.)

[2] Swete, p. 143. Caird, contrasting the divine title in verse 17 with the one in 1:4, observes that the seventh Trumpet undoubtedly announces the end, since 'there can be no future once futurity itself has been removed from the very name of God' (p. 146).

contrary both to Scripture and to reason. If this life is the time of testing, the opportunities of this life are as complete as any man could wish for, and we have seen to what lengths God will go to warn them. If they hear not Moses and the prophets, they will not be persuaded though one rise from the dead. If they hear not the first six Trumpets, neither will they repent when Trumpet 7 ushers in eternity. For by that time the bent of their heart is established beyond redemption. 'He that is unjust, let him be unjust still: he that is filthy, let him be filthy still' (22:11, AV).

These things come about in answer to the prayers of the church. God forbid that we should pray for the punishment of particular individuals, of whose standing before God we know little. For all we know, he who seems to us most evil may, like Paul, be intended for a dazzling trophy of grace (1 Tim. 1:15 f.), and he who seems set for heaven may be an emissary of hell (2 Cor. 11:13 f.). But as we ought to pray that where there is a real work of grace in the heart it should be fostered, so we ought to cry to God that where there is irredeemable wickedness it should not go unpunished: 'that the evil man must not be left perfectly satisfied with his own evil, that it must be made to appear to him what it rightly appears to others—evil . . . that, soon or late, the right should be asserted.'[1] We must pray for justice to be done. And it will be done: the maximum of justice, with the maximum of mercy: for in the plan of God righteousness and peace have kissed each other (Ps. 85:10). And when they finally see it done, the twenty-four elders, representing the church, fall on their faces and worship him.

How much do we really care that right should triumph and that evil be defeated? It is the sanctimonious fashion in our violent age to recoil from violence. But how much of our dislike of the violence of Scene 3 is really little more than a blindness to the blacks and whites of the situation, a lack of hatred for Satan and his works and a lack of concern for the glory of God?

> 'I want a true regard,
> A single, steady aim,
> Unmoved by threatening or reward,
> To thee and thy great name;

[1] C. S. Lewis, *The Problem of Pain* pp. 108, 110.

A jealous, just concern
For thine immortal praise,
A pure desire that all may learn
And glorify they grace.'[1]

[1] C. Wesley.

11:19–15:4

SCENE 4:
THE DRAMA OF HISTORY:
seven Visions of cosmic conflict

THE ANALYSIS OF THE DRAMA

'SO Scene 4 begins one verse before the end of chapter 11. And Scene 2 ended one verse after the beginning of chapter 8. How come that the chapter divisions of Revelation are being discarded in favour of these "Scenes"? What basis is there for this analysis of the book as a drama divided into Scenes?'

Fair questions. Let us dispose of the chapter divisions first. They are not part of the New Testament as it was originally, and Revelation is one of the books where they are a positive hindrance to the understanding of the text. They were 'inherited from Latin Bibles of the later middle ages', as the Preface of the RV New Testament points out; and while, as it goes on to say, 'the arrangement by chapters and verses undoubtedly affords facilities for reference', it can be in other respects a tyranny from which we must try to escape. The proper analysis of a book is according to its subject-matter. It should arise naturally, from a study of the text itself.

a. Starting-point

In looking for the natural divisions of Revelation, we should remember two important facts: that it is a letter, and that it is a vision. *'Write* what you *see'* (1:11).

First we follow the progress of the letter. Having arrived at one of the Asian churches, it was to be read aloud in the hearing of the church members, which is the meaning of 1:3a. What we should try to visualize is a congregation perhaps different in some respects from those to which we belong: much nearer to John's ways of thinking and speaking, some of them able to

hear in their mind's ear the very lilt of his voice; more used to
the apocalyptic style of writing; come more freshly, and therefore more avidly, to the study of the Scriptures which had made
them wise unto salvation; untrammelled by nineteen centuries
of discordant interpretation of John's letter. Given that sort of
congregation, and the tumultuous vividness of the letter itself,
and a good reader who could make it come alive to his hearers
(a special blessing is promised to him as well as them, 1:3)—
given these things, we are half way to understanding the structure of Revelation.

.The other fact to remember is that it is a vision. We may be
among those who find the recounting of other people's dreams
a breakfast-time bore; needless to say, the vision revealed by
Christ to his apostle could never come under that condemnation!
Should we not rather imagine the little congregation at Philadelphia, for example, gathered in someone's home on the Lord's
day, hanging on every word of the one who was reading? And
as he came to the end of each paragraph, would they not be
saying eagerly, 'And what happens next? What does John see
next?'

It is with this question in mind that we have tried to analyse
the book. 'What does he see next?' There have been numbers of
different analyses, the more slapdash often not consistent, and
the more careful often smelling of lamp-oil and library dust. We
do not intend even to begin to comment on these exegetical
acrobatics, but offer instead an attempt at a plain and positive
scheme of our own.[1] From artificial plans based on ingenious
formulae and number schemes, we turn back to the artless
demand of the first humble hearers: 'And what does he see next?'

b. Analysis

When we read Revelation in this way an interesting fact emerges.
On the stage of his vision innumerable actors come and go;
there is constant action. But every so often comes a point at
which not only the actors change, but the scene itself changes;

[1] Since it arises from the contents of the book itself, it is not 'our
own' in any exclusive sense! It commended itself also, for example, to
the German commentator Zahn in the 1880s, and no doubt has done
so to many others of the throng of commentators on Revelation.

as though a curtain has fallen, then risen again to disclose a completely new scene, or even as though John himself has moved in order to look at a different stage.

What did John see? Up to 1:12, the scenery of Patmos. At that point, having heard a great voice behind him, he 'turned to see the voice'; and there behind him rose scenery of a very different order, Scene 1 of the drama that was to be revealed to him. Nothing moves in Scene 1. It is a vision of tremendous, flaming stillness, as the glorious Christ dictates his seven Letters.

Then at the end of it, there is 'a door opened in heaven', and the voice commanding John to 'Come up hither' (4:1). Scene 2 begins. A new panorama opens before him, the radiant circles of heaven with the throne of the Lamb at their centre. There is much activity and much shifting of focus in this Scene. On one plane, all creation (with the church represented as twenty-four elders) worships the Lamb; on another, the horsemen ride out and smite both the world and the church (now seen as martyrs beneath the altar); on another, the church (now a numberless multitude) is sealed before the winds of suffering can blow. But with all these comings and goings on the stage, it is still the same Scene that John is watching from his vantage-point of 4:1, 2.

Looking on through the drama, we shall find three other occasions on which an opened door leads John to a new viewpoint, and thus reveals a stage set for a new Scene. The temple of God in heaven is opened (11:19); the temple of the tent of witness in heaven is opened (15:5); heaven itself is opened (19:11). So there are four places where 'openings' of this kind mark the beginning of new Scenes. When the analysis is completed, they will fit into it as Scenes 2, 4, 5, and 7.

Now we return to Scene 2. It started with a double indication: there was an opened door, and there was an inviting voice. The latter is heard a second time at 17:1-3: ' "Come" ... and he carried me away ... into a wilderness'; a third time at 21:9, 10: ' "Come" ... and ... he carried me away to a great, high mountain.' This again is a change of viewpoint, like the 'openings' just noted. Here then are the beginnings of two more Scenes, which will in the event be numbered 6 and 8.

Thus seven times over some such phrase occurs. The only

place where we might expect it but find it absent is at 8:2, where the seven Trumpets first appear. But since the Trumpets are generally agreed to be a self-contained section of the book, on a par with the Letters, the Seals, the Bowls, and so on, in our analysis of the book as a drama we can safely count the Trumpets as a separate Scene like the others.

It will be observed that on this basis eight Scenes result. Alas for the tidy-minded, who, noting the prevalence of sevens, would like Procrustes-wise to lop the body to fit the bed, and ensure somehow that there should be only seven Scenes! But unless we combine Trumpets and Seals, which the test does not seem to warrant, eight is what we have. And maybe we shall find good reasons for even that mysterious number.[1]

c. Further evidence

Two points here in 11:19 should be noted in connection with this analysis. They are not sufficient in themselves to establish it, but if on the grounds suggested above it seems reasonable, they serve at least to confirm it.

One is the mention of the ark of the covenant which is revealed in heaven. It is the traditional chapter divisions, one feels, which have misled some writers into taking 11:19 with the rest of chapter 11, and propounding ingenious ideas as to why the seven Trumpets should be climaxed by the revealing of the ark. Ingenious they are, for no natural explanation springs readily to mind; whereas a reading of the following Scene will show that 11:19, a puzzle if it is the climax to Scene 3, falls magically into place as the introduction to Scene 4. By the ark's appearance within it, the opening of the heavenly temple is thus confirmed as the opening of a new section.

The other point is the lightnings, voices, thunders, earthquake, and hail which accompany the appearance of the ark. A combination of some or all of these phenomena occurs four times in the book (in 4:5, in 8:5, here in 11:19, and in 16:18), and has sometimes been pressed into service as the scaffolding for a different analysis of it. Now in 16:18 the thunder and lightning are explicitly stated to be the contents of the seventh Bowl, that

[1] See pp. 201 ff.

is, an occurrence within one of the Scenes. But if our analysis is correct, in the other three cases they come just as the curtain rises on a new Scene. May we guess that John's experience was like that of the man who arrives to find the show already in progress, and for whom, until he gets to his place, settles down, and begins to pay attention, the events on the screen or stage are just so many unrelated sounds and colours and movements? Or perhaps, more justly, is the music of the thunder an overture as the curtain rises on Scenes 2, 3, and 4?

d. Conclusions

All these suggestions we may summarize in a brief outline of the drama, complementing the one given at the beginning of this book.

1:1	Introduction
1:12	John turns to see who is speaking to him: Scene 1
4:1	In heaven a door is opened and a voice says 'Come': John is taken to a vantage point from which he can see the whole heavenly sphere: thunder and lightning: Scene 2
8:2	The angels with the trumpets appear: thunder and lightning: Scene 3
11:19	In heaven the temple is opened; thunder and lightning: Scene 4
15:5	In heaven the temple of the tent of witness is opened: Scene 5
17:1	An angel says 'Come': John is taken into a wilderness: Scene 6
19:11	Heaven itself is opened: Scene 7
21:9	An angel says 'Come': John is taken to a mountain top: Scene 8
22:20	Epilogue

e. Analysis of the present Scene

The same method needs to be applied within the present Scene. There are no numbered divisions to guide us, as there were with the Letters, Seals, and Trumpets; instead we notice that certain phrases are repeated at various points in the Scene, and may provide a useful analysis. This is not an artificial method based on the mere recurrence of a formula. We are again simply asking, 'What does John see next?'

We have just over three chapters to consider, from the opening of the temple in 11:19, where Scene 4 begins, to the opening of the 'temple of the tent of witness' (not quite the same thing) in 15:5, where Scene 5 begins. Within this section we are looking for what John *saw*. The Greek verb is *idein*, and it appears in two forms: usually 'And I saw', but also 'And I looked, and lo', for 'lo' represents the imperative of the same verb ('And I looked, and see!'). There are other phrases which might seem to introduce new divisions, for example 'a great portent appeared' (12:1), 'and I heard' (12:10; 14:13). But if we set these aside and base our analysis strictly on the two phrases mentioned above, this is what we find.

13:1	'I saw a beast'
13:11	'I saw another beast'
14:1	'I looked, and see! the Lamb'
14:6	'I saw another angel'
14:14	'I looked, and see! a white cloud'
15:1	'I saw another portent'
15:2	'I saw . . . a sea of glass'

An interesting result when we count the sections![1] And, we must insist, not an artificial one; for again we visualize the reader and his hearers at the Asian church meeting, they agog to know 'What did John see next?', and he pausing with impressive emphasis to let John introduce each of his seven Visions: '*And I saw*'.

I. SCENE 4 OPENS: BEHIND THE VEIL, GOD'S COVENANT (11:19)

Then God's temple in heaven was opened, and the ark of his covenant was seen within his temple; and there were flashes of lightning, loud noises, peals of thunder, an earthquake, and heavy hail.

[1] 'I saw' in 13:3, AV and RV, is not in the Greek, and so is rightly omitted in RSV.

A number of apparently familiar words need a closer look if we are to understand Scene 4. 'Heaven' here is not a place of perfection, for it contains war and evil and the forces of Satan. It must therefore be the heaven of Scene 2 and of Ephesians 6:12, the sphere of spiritual reality. Consequently the 'temple' means the place where God really is: not a particular sacred spot which is as it were officially dedicated to him, but the entire creation: for on a spiritual level, there is no place where he is not—'the whole earth is full of his glory' (Is. 6:1-3; Pss. 29:9; 139:7-10).

Of the ark, no more need be said here than that it is the symbol of God's covenant, or agreement, to rescue his people from their enemies; and the lightnings, voices, thunders, earthquake, and hail are often used in Scripture as signs that he is present and active[1]—in residence, so to speak, in his temple, and not on a journey, as the Baal-god apparently was when his prophets failed to raise an answer from him on mount Carmel.[2] Up to now God has given us the assurances of his character and its effects, that he is 'a God merciful and gracious . . . but who will by no means clear the guilty' (Ex. 34:6, 7). In this Scene he will show us, in seven Visions of cosmic conflict, something of the actual scheme by which he saves his people and destroys his enemies.

Elgar asked a friend's opinion of his setting of 'Praise to the Holiest in the height', in *The Dream of Gerontius,* and was delighted with the reply: 'It makes me think of great doors opening and shutting.' To the accompaniment of the music of heaven the great doors of God's temple now open, and the fourth Scene begins.

2. THE CHARACTERS (12:1-6)

And a great portent appeared in heaven, a woman clothed with the sun, with the moon under her feet, and on her head a crown of twelve stars; [2]*she was with child and she cried out in her pangs of birth, in anguish for delivery.*

[1] *Cf.* Ex. 19:16-18; Ps. 18:7-14. It is much less likely that these are signs of the end of the world. Perhaps it is again the misleading position of verse 19 at the end of this chapter which has led many to assume that it is a climax, rather than a beginning.

[2] 1 Ki. 18:27.

3 And another portent appeared in heaven; behold a great red dragon, with seven heads and ten horns, and seven diadems upon his heads. 4 His tail swept down a third of the stars of heaven, and cast them to the earth. And the dragon stood before the woman who was about to bear a child, that he might devour her child when she brought it forth;

5 she brought forth a male child, one who is to rule all the nations with a rod of iron, but her child was caught up to God and to his throne,

6 and the woman fled into the wilderness, where she has a place prepared by God, in which to be nourished for one thousand two hundred and sixty days.

Who are these characters on the heavenly stage? It is with them that Scene 4 is mostly concerned. The woman and the dragon are 'portents', or 'signs' (RV), symbolic figures with meanings beyond the superficial ones. They represent not a literal woman and a literal dragon, but something more. The third character, the child, is not a 'sign' in this sense, because he actually represents a human person. All three can be readily identified.

The dragon will be explained beyond doubt in verse 9. He is the serpent, the devil (or slanderer), the 'Satan' (or adversary), the deceiver. His heads probably mean not intellect (in the ancient world one thought with one's heart) but authority; and his crowns, unlike the woman's in verse 1, are royal crowns. If seven stands for what is 'essential',[1] his seven crowned heads mean that he really does have princely authority (Lk. 4:6; Jn. 14:30), and the ten horns perhaps that he deploys it with very great strength.

He is undoubtedly related to the dragon, or serpent, who appears in the mythology of many ancient peoples, and who in a number of Old Testament passages expresses certain theological truths for the Hebrews also. This would be a matter merely of academic interest were it not for references such as Psalm 74:13, 14. The dragon there is not only given a name (Leviathan), and several heads, like John's dragon here; most important, he is used as a symbol of Israel's ancient enemy Egypt. This symbol is taken up again in Ezekiel 29 and 32, and in Revelation becomes a ruling thought. Our minds have already been guided this way by Scene 3, where the trumpet-plagues resembled the plagues of

[1] See pp. 62 f.

the exodus, and the city which oppressed God's people was called 'Egypt' (11:8). Light is thus shed on the meaning of the 'wilderness' of Scene 4 (verse 6). The dragon is Egypt; the woman (as we shall see) is Israel; her flight into the wilderness is an exodus into a place not of hardship and suffering, but of safety and divine protection, till at the end of her 1,260 days' journey—forty-two months, like the forty-two stages mapped out in Numbers 33—she arrives in the promised land.

The child is sufficiently identified by the fact that he is to rule all nations. Such a destiny was promised, it is true, to victorious Christians in 2:6 f., but they have it only by derivation from the one to whom it properly belongs. The original prophecy in Psalm 2:7-9 is declared by many New Testament references to speak of Jesus Christ. It is against him that the dragon's hatred is primarily directed.

Some commentators hold that this Psalm is the background not only of the child's rule, in verse 5b (= Ps. 2:9), but also of his birth, in verse 5a (= Ps. 2:7, when he officially becomes God's son, at his coronation). In this case, the phrases 'brought forth' and 'caught up' would refer not to Christ's birth and ascension, but to his resurrection and ascension, as Romans 1:4 makes plain. Since, however, he is seen here as the child of the woman Israel rather than as the Son of God, the 'bringing forth' is more likely to mean his human birth at Bethlehem. In either case verse 5 is curiously selective. On the latter interpretation, his ministry, death, and resurrection are all omitted from it. The important facts in this summary are the nativity and the ascension: the point at which the Son himself first came within the dragon's grasp, and the point at which he finally escaped it for ever.[1]

The woman's identity has already been touched on. She is not simply Mary, the actual mother of Jesus; nor Mary's ancestress Eve, whose offspring was to be the serpent's great enemy (Gn. 3:15); nor even all mothers in the chosen line between them. For regarded as a 'sign', she is adorned with the splendour of sun,

[1] Joachim Jeremias refers to 'the characteristic Semitic way of only dwelling on the beginning and end of a story without reference to what happens between', and quotes several examples from the Gospels and Acts (*The Parables of Jesus* (SCM, 1954), p. 90, n. 5; p. 152, n. 65).

moon, and twelve stars, which in a parallel Old Testament dream (Joseph's in Gn. 37:9-11) represent the whole family of Israel. What is more, she continues to exist even after Christ's ascension, and lives on for 'one thousand two hundred and sixty days', the whole period of church history from his first coming to his second.[1] She is in fact the church: the old Israel, 'the human stock from which Christ came' (Rom. 9:5, Knox), and the new Israel, whom he has now left in order to go back to his Father— though he has not left her comfortless, because like those previously noted symbols of God's church, Moses and Elijah, she finds in the desert of the world a place of safety and the provision of her needs.[2]

3. THE PLOT (12:7-16)

Now war arose in heaven, Michael and his angels fighting against the dragon; and the dragon and his angels fought, [8]*but they were defeated and there was no longer any place for them in heaven.* [9]*And the great dragon was thrown down, that ancient serpent, who is called the Devil and Satan, the deceiver of the whole world—he was thrown down to the earth, and his angels were thrown down with him.*

[10]*And I heard a loud voice in heaven, saying, 'Now the salvation and the power and the kingdom of our God and the authority of his Christ have come, for the accuser of our brethren has been thrown down, who accuses them day and night before our God.* [11]*And they have conquered him by the blood of the Lamb and by the word of their testimony, for they loved not their lives even unto death.* [12]*Rejoice then, O heaven and you that dwell therein! But woe to you, O earth and sea, for the devil has come down to you in great wrath, because he knows that his time is short!'*

[13]*And when the dragon saw that he had been thrown down to the earth, he pursued the woman who had borne the male child.* [14]*But the woman was given the two wings of the great eagle that she might fly from the serpent into the wilderness, to the place where she is to be nourished for a time, and times, and half a time.* [15]*The serpent poured water like a river out of his mouth after the woman, to sweep her away with the flood.* [16]*But*

---

[1] See pp. 105 f.
[2] Moses at Sinai, with manna (Ex. 15, 16); Elijah at Horeb, with cakes and water (1 Ki. 19).

*the earth came to the help of the woman, and the earth opened its mouth
and swallowed the river which the dragon had poured from his mouth.*

Bearing in mind that the end of the church's three and a
half years in the desert (verse 6) is practically the end of history,
and that apart from the three and a half days right at the very end
when her witness seems to be extinguished[1] the next great event
will be the parousia, we may be warned against assuming too
readily that verses 7 to 16 are a straightforward sequel to verses
1 to 6. If we do assume this, it means that between the end of the
three and a half years and the actual return of Christ, presumably
therefore within the three and a half days, a war is fought; the
dragon is defeated; the kingdom of God comes—but the dragon's
fury is unabated, and still bodes ill for the earth; the woman
flies again to the desert, on this occasion for three and a half
'times';[2] again she is protected there from the dragon's hatred.
All this within the three and a half days at the very end of history.
But by the time we reach verse 14 the events have become so
similar to those of verse 6 that we cannot help wondering whether
this passage is that one repeated. It is by now fairly clear that
such a method—returning again and again to the beginning,
repeating, underlining—is part of the very warp and woof of
Revelation. Let us see how it would work in this case.

First we remind ourselves of the characters of verses 1–6:
the child, Christ; the woman, Israel, from whom he is born, and
who continues as the Christian church after his ascension; the
dragon, who seeks to destroy the child, and when foiled vents
his anger on the church. Now we begin again at verse 7. Michael
the archangel, appearing here for the first time in Revelation, is
according to Daniel 10:21 the heavenly champion of Israel; and
the dragon is the 'primeval serpent', the old, original one. (May
we be preserved from the modern heresy which considers 'old'
to be a term of pity or abuse! The 'old' serpent is older than any
other created being in evil and cunning, ripest and maturest in
malice and wickedness and the ability to deceive.) The opposition of verse 7 is the opposition of verse 4b seen at a different

[1] See p. 106.
[2] 'A time, and times, and half a time' almost certainly means $1+2+\frac{1}{2}$
'times'. The Old Testament parallel is Dn. 12:7.

depth of focus. The conflict between the two archangels, the good and the evil, is the conflict between Eve and the serpent, and between her offspring and its offspring, through the whole history of Israel, until the day when *the* offspring should come (Gal. 3:16; 4:4). Then the child is born; and his triumphant progress from nativity to ascension, unscathed by the dragon (for even his death is his own free choice), spells the dragon's defeat. It is at the time of Christ's incarnation that the downfall of Satan, and the coming of the kingdom of God and of the authority of Christ, take place.[1] From that time on, the people of the new Israel have been able to claim victory over the dragon, because of the Lamb's death and their witness to their own experience of its power. For the Lamb has suffered the penalty of all the dragon's accusations, and there remains 'no condemnation for those who are in Christ Jesus' (Rom. 8:1). Even the death of the body no longer matters to them (verse 11). God has brought them on eagles' wings to himself (verse 14; Ex. 19:4), and they are safe with him in the desert; the flood with which the dragon hoped they might be destroyed—characteristic of the power of Egypt, as brought out in the Ezekiel prophecies mentioned earlier—has become dry land for their sake (verses 15, 16; Ex. 15:12).

It might seem that verses 1 to 6 are the plot, being more eventful than verses 7 to 16, which amplify the characters. We reverse these headings, however, because on reading through Scene 4 we shall find its seven Visions are oddly static. The conflict they describe is not so much a sequence of events, a 'story', as a battle which is always in progress. And this is of a piece with the rest of Revelation. The substance of the book is a portrayal of truths which all its readers will find valid in their own experience, in whatever century and whatever society they may live. In this sense, therefore, it is merely incidental that verses 1 to 6 should provide a 'story', with verses 1 to 4 describing all the centuries BC, verse 5

---

[1] Lk. 10:18; Jn. 12:31; Mt. 12:28; 28:18. The coming of the kingdom spoken of here in 12:10 means Christ's first coming, and is not the same as when that kingdom will actually replace the kingdoms of this world, at Christ's second coming. Rev. 11:15 refers to the second; 12:10 to the first.

the thirty-odd years of Christ's earthly life, and verse 6 all the centuries AD. These dates are simply part of the character-identification. The actual plot, or most of it, has no dates. It concerns a beast, and another beast, and the Lamb's followers, and a trio of angels, and all these are active in every age. Only in the three last Visions does John point on into the future, as he had done with the last Seals and the last Trumpets.

4. THE PRELUDE (12:17)

Then the dragon was angry with the woman, and went off to make war on the rest of her offspring, on those who keep the commandments of God and bear testimony to Jesus. And he stood on the sand of the sea.

If Israel can be pictured as a wife, why should she not also be a mother? But though each in turn is a comprehensible symbol of her, it is not possible (strange to say) to visualize her as being both at once. Regard her as a wife, and Christ is married to her; she is the people of God. Regard her as a mother, and Christ is born to her; she is the *community* of the people of God, an abstract collective noun, to which each of us also may belong, and thus be reckoned along with Christ as 'the rest of her offspring'. To use her alternative name, in one sense we *are* Jerusalem, the bride (21:9, 10); in another, we are *the children of Jerusalem*—'she is our mother' (Gal. 4:26, 27; *cf.* Is. 54:1; 66:8). Against us, the people of 'the Word and the Witness', the dragon mobilizes his forces. The resulting cosmic conflict is the subject of the seven Visions which follow.

5. THE FIRST VISION: THE BEAST FROM THE SEA (13:1-10)

And I saw a beast rising out of the sea, with ten horns and seven heads, with ten diadems upon its horns and a blasphemous name upon its heads. ²*And the beast that I saw was like a leopard, its feet were like a bear's, and its mouth was like a lion's mouth. And to it the dragon gave his power and his throne and great authority.*

³*One of its heads seemed to have a mortal wound, but its mortal wound was healed, and the whole earth followed the beast with wonder.* ⁴*Men worshipped the dragon, for he had given his authority to the beast, and they*

worshipped the beast, saying, 'Who is like the beast, and who can fight against it?'

⁵And the beast was given a mouth uttering haughty and blasphemous words, and it was allowed to exercise authority for forty-two months; ⁶it opened its mouth to utter blasphemies against God, blaspheming his name and his dwelling, that is, those who dwell in heaven. ⁷Also it was allowed to make war on the saints and to conquer them. And authority was given it over every tribe and people and tongue and nation, ⁸and all who dwell on earth will worship it, every one whose name has not been written before the foundation of the world in the book of life of the Lamb that was slain.

⁹If any one has an ear, let him hear: ¹⁰If any one is to be taken captive, to captivity he goes; if any one slays with the sword, with the sword must he be slain. Here is a call for the endurance and faith of the saints.

As the indescribable beasts emerge on the scene, one's eyes glisten or else one's mind boggles, according to whether one does or does not have preconceived ideas about the interpretation of these chapters. What, though, would all this have meant to John's readers? They, at any rate, did not start with the disadvantage of being unfamiliar with the apocalyptic style, and would not have found the talk of beasts and horns as peculiar as we do. Furthermore, assuming them also to be well taught in their Scriptures, we may be sure that their minds would have gone at once to the Old Testament's own great apocalyptic work, the book of Daniel. As the beast rose from the sea, they would no doubt have said to one another, first, 'It looks like the dragon we have just been hearing about'; but then, 'It also looks like one of the visions of Daniel' (verses 1, 2).

Now the dragon's seven heads and ten horns showed that power was of his very essence. Of all the attributes of God, his omnipotence is what Satan aspires most to have. And the beasts of Daniel 7 are actually explained as being four great kings, or empires: there also power is of the essence. In fact it is the very word we use to describe them—the 'great powers'. So when we are shown a beast whose power is not that of wealth or of influence, but that of government ('diadems' and a 'throne'), who combines all the powers of Daniel 7, and whose authority is worldwide (verse 7), we see in him the principle of power politics: in a word, the state. For John this meant, of course, the Roman Empire; but every succeeding generation of Christian people knows some equivalent of it. To use a phrase which the Authorized Version has fed into common English usage, the beast from the sea represents 'the powers that be' (Rom. 13:1, AV).

But are we not told by Paul that the state is ordained by God? How then can its authority come from the devil, and be indeed so devilish that it actually begins to look like him (verses 1, 2; 12:3)?

Paul, of course, is right. 'There is no authority except from God' (Rom. 13:1); it was God who created the institution of human government. The devil never created anything. He could only pervert what was already there. As prince of this world, he took what God had instituted for mankind's welfare and made it an instrument of oppression. It is God's will that there should be law and order. It is the devil's achievement that there should so often be bad law and tyrannical order. He puts blasphemies in the mouth of the state, so that it proclaims 'I am God' by demanding from its subjects a total, unconditional allegiance, such as those whose names are written in the Lamb's book of life will never give to any but Christ. They will uphold the principle of law and order at all costs, to whatever repressive ends it may be perverted: 'If any one is to be taken captive,' well then, 'to captivity he goes'; they will not take up the sword to overthrow it; this is 'the endurance and faith of the saints' (verse 10). But neither will they worship at its shrine, and be swayed by its talk of 'patriotism', and give it 'the clerical blessing it so much desires'.[1] They reserve the right to criticize, and to discern continually between the state functioning properly *under* divine authority, and the state acting illegitimately *as* divine authority.

And what of the death-wound and its healing (verse 3)? This too we know. Just as the beast's blasphemies meant in those days the claims of emperors to be divine, but also mean something equivalent in every age, so it is with his 'death and resurrection'. These would be linked at that time with the widespread belief that the emperor Nero might return after death (if not in

[1] Alan Kreider, in Brian Griffiths (ed.), *Is Revolution Change?* (Inter-Varsity Press, 1972), p. 54.

his own person, then in the person of one of his successors), but they are also the pattern of something which can be seen in the realm of politics at any time in history. The communist sees in one place the failure or defeat of his political creed, and then in another its resurrection; and he is confirmed in his belief that it is immortal, it is the truth—'Great is the truth, and it shall prevail.' At the same time his opponent on the political far right is seeing the same thing happen with fascism. It may be dead, but it won't lie down. Even the liberal democracies—perhaps they most of all—lead men to put their faith in the beast by the miracle of his resurrection. Every true liberal knows that John Brown's body lies a-mouldering in its grave, but his soul goes marching on. Fear not the apparent death-wound, for good sense and democracy and the human spirit can never finally be put down. So it comes about that the whole earth follows the beast with wonder (verse 3), each one having seen how the head he idolizes can die yet rise again. And all whose hope is not ultimately in the blood of the Lamb have no hope except in some human system, to which either expressly or by implication they give the blasphemous name of God; yes, even in the residually Christian West, where it is the value and goodness of the human spirit, rather than the One who created it, which are 'worshipped, Trusted, and adored'.

The church may expect to suffer when it takes leave to question all these assumptions, and to criticize the ideals of the society in which it lives. The prophets of Baal said all the right things, and ate at the table of a queen; Elijah said all the wrong things, and was driven to exile in the wilderness. But it was Elijah, and not the representatives of official religion, who stood for the true church.

And how long is this to continue? The beast is 'allowed to exercise authority for forty-two months', the same 'three and a half years' during which God's city and the outer courts of his temple are trodden underfoot by the nations, while the church nevertheless survives despite attacks on her members (verse 7), and continues to preach.[1] Throughout the history of the church, then, the beast from the sea will be active, and Christian people

---

[1] For three and a half years the woman in the desert survives (12:6, 14), and the two witnesses preach (11:3). See pp. 118 f., 105.

will always have the dragon-manipulated state to take into account in their daily conflict.

6. THE SECOND VISION: THE BEAST FROM THE EARTH (13:11–17)

*Then I saw another beast which rose out of the earth; it had two horns
like a lamb and it spoke like a dragon.* ¹²*It exercises all the authority of
the first beast in its presence, and makes the earth and its inhabitants
worship the first beast, whose mortal wound was healed.* ¹³*It works great
signs, even making fire come down from heaven to earth in the sight of
men;*

¹⁴*and by the signs which it is allowed to work in the presence of the
beast, it deceives those who dwell on earth, bidding them make an image
for the beast which was wounded by the sword and yet lived;* ¹⁵*and it was
allowed to give breath to the image of the beast so that the image of the
beast should even speak, and to cause those who would not worship the
image of the beast to be slain.* ¹⁶*Also it causes all, both small and great,
both rich and poor, both free and slave, to be marked on the right hand or
the forehead,* ¹⁷*so that no one can buy or sell unless he has the mark, that
is, the name of the beast or the number of its name.*

Verses 11 to 13 make clear what the beast from the earth is. Its
looks are lamb-like but its voice dragon-like; it stands before the
first beast—another reminiscence of Elijah, who stood before
God (1 Ki. 17:1) waiting on his bidding, ready to act at his
command and speak with his authority; it is concerned with
worship, the religious aspect of human life; and it works miracles,
like bringing fire from heaven (Elijah yet again, 1 Ki. 18). The
coupling of Christlike appearance and Satanic message, the
status of prophet, the concern with worship, and the appeal to
the magical, all add up to one thing: false religion. The relationships between man and man, and between man and God, are both
provided for in the divine plan. The beast from the sea is Satan's
perversion of society, the first; and the beast from the earth is his
perversion of Christianity, the second.

To what, in the subsequent centuries of history, would John
have pointed and said, 'Yes, that is the beast from the earth'?
It would be a religion which in some way would encourage

devotion to the state instead of to God, and would do so by
supernatural means (verses 12 to 14). Now these seem at first
sight to be the characteristics of two different, and indeed
opposite, kinds of religion. On our right, churches which work
hand-in-glove with the state, preaching establishment politics
and patriotic crusades. On our left, sects which prove themselves
by signs—not just Montanists and Shakers and Snake-handlers,
but Mormons with their remarkable morality, and Jehovah's
Witnesses with their amazing assiduity, which attract the un-
committed by making them wonder whether there might not be
something in it after all.

But where is the beast from the earth who combines these
characteristics? For the 'establishment' churches do not normally
work miracles, and the 'lunatic fringe' sects rarely hold any brief
for the state—some repudiate its authority altogether. Yet on
reflection we can see that any church which is not the true church
does in fact show both the telltale marks. It promotes the worship
of the beast from the sea, not necessarily by crying up national-
ism, but by encouraging men to seek salvation in any human
system rather than in the grace of God in Christ; and the Jehovah's
Witnesses, for all their independence of the formal system known
as 'the state', are fostering that false allegiance just as much as the
church of Constantine ever did. On the other hand, its means of
persuasion are as supernatural in established churches as in the
outlandish sects. Where in the latter it may be miraculous cures or
miraculous earnestness, in the former it is the magic of ritual
and emotion. In other words, whenever the beast speaks he
causes men to say, 'This religion is so impressive, that we are
prepared to commit ourselves for salvation to the system to
which it points us.'

Religion, indeed, is too narrow an identification of the second
beast. He is, in modern parlance, the *ideology*—whether religious,
philosophical, or political—which 'gives breath to' any human
social structure organized independently of God. He is 'the
message'. When 19:20 labels him the false prophet, and thus
points us back to the passage about false prophecy in Deuteronomy, we find a warning which, for all its religious language, can
be applied to any kind of ideology: 'If a prophet arises among
you, or a dreamer of dreams, and gives you a sign or a wonder,

and the sign or wonder which he tells you comes to pass, and if he says, "Let us go after other gods," which you have not known, "and let us serve them," you shall not listen to the words of that prophet' (Dt. 13:1–3).

But by such deceiving messages the 'image of the beast' (*i.e.* of the first beast, the 'system') is made to have a seeming life of its own, apart from which man, apparently, cannot survive (verse 15). And as the invisible seal of the Spirit confirms the divine ownership of God's servants (7:3), so the mystical mark of the beast confirms those who thus sell themselves to the 'system'.

The true Lamb also offers a sign to lead men to embrace salvation. That is why the false lamb's Satanic message is so deceiving. But the true sign is himself, Christ's own miraculous life embodied in his church today, and the true salvation to which it points is also himself, the living Christ. All other signs and systems are the voice of the beast.

7. THE NUMBER OF THE BEAST (13:18)

This calls for wisdom: let him who has understanding reckon the number of the beast, for it is a human number, its number is six hundred and sixty-six.

What does the number of the beast mean? Any amount of ink has been spilt over this fascinating, and misleading, question. The number is said to stand for Nero, or Caligula, or Domitian, or the Caesars in general, or the Roman Empire, or any one of several solutions, mostly based on the fact that in Greek and Hebrew as well as in Latin, numerals were indicated by letters of the alphabet, so that the letters of various names had numerical values which could be added together to obtain the total 666.[1] For example, *qsr nrôn* (a Hebrew spelling of 'Caesar Nero') adds up to this—100 + 60 + 200 and 50 + 200 + 6 + 50.

It is our contention that all such answers are wrong, because the question itself is wrong. The number does not stand for any

---

[1] More recent candidates have included Mohammed, Cromwell, and Napoleon, not to mention Martin Luther and an assortment of popes. The number has also been used to calculate possible dates when the beast might appear.

particular person or institution. The number simply stands for *the beast*.

The yards of commentary devoted to working out the meaning of the number are redolent of the aforementioned smell of lamp-oil. We have scented it already in 8:1, 2, two verses which even that most acute of translations, the Revised Version, misleadingly combines into a single paragraph. Our friend Lamp-oil sits at his study desk, mesmerized by the look of the printed page, and reads: 'When the Lamb opened the seventh seal, there was silence in heaven for about half an hour. Then I saw the seven angels who stand before God, and seven trumpets were given to them.' He proceeds to explain how the Trumpets follow immediately after the breaking of the seventh Seal, or are even included within it, and how perhaps it is during the silent half hour that the Trumpet-angels are assembling, and so on and so forth. Had he tried to see the thing as John saw it, or hear the account as the Christians in the seven churches heard it, the result would have been somewhat different. Six Seals were opened; then with the seventh came a half hour interval, during which John would assuredly have been meditating on what he had heard and seen up to then. It is not beyond probability that the same thing would have happened when his letter was being read aloud at the Asian church meeting: that as the reader described the opening of the seventh Seal, a silence would have fallen there also, with the congregation lost in the glories of chapter 7—and the Trumpets would have been postponed for the next Lord's-day reading. But Lamp-oil forges straight on (supported inexplicably by the RV), when a half hour of silent meditation between 8:1 and 8:2 would have been of far greater value both to him and to the readers of his commentary.

In a moment we shall try to approach 13:18 in the same way. Before doing so, we consider the phrase, 'It is a human number', or 'It is the number of a man' (RV). Paul uses a similar turn of phrase several times,[1] when he is illustrating some spiritual truth by an analogy drawn from human experience. We have already found John doing the same in connection with times and numbers. One example is the duration of the church age. Jesus had already said that the length of time between his first and

[1] Rom. 3:5; 6:19; 1 Cor 9:8; 15:32; Gal. 3:15.

second comings was a matter known only to God: 'Of that day
and hour no one knows, not even the angels of heaven, nor the
Son, but the Father only' (Mt. 24:36); 'It is not for you to know
times or seasons which the Father has fixed by his own authority'
(Acts 1:7). The actual number of years involved was divinely
known, but was not to be humanly known. Nevertheless to the
human readers of Revelation a number *is* given, as a kind of code:
3½ years = 42 months = 1,260 days = the length of the church
age. It may be that this was thought an appropriate 'human'
number because it corresponded to the length of Christ's
ministry. If it was reckoned that something over three years
elapsed between his baptism and his ascension, then 'three and a
bit years', or three and a half years, would be an excellent symbol
for the period between the church's 'baptism' at Pentecost and
her 'ascension' to meet the Lord when he returns.[1]

Another example is the number of God's people. The actual
number is a secret, 'divine' one: only 'the Lord knows those
who are his' (2 Tim. 2:19), and when John was shown the whole
church it was a literally innumerable throng (7:9). But for the
convenience of human readers a code number, 144,000, is given
(7:4).

A third example will be found in 21:17, where the walls of
the heavenly city are measured as 144 cubits (probably thickness,
not height). This can only be what it is stated to be, a 'human
measurement', for unlike the earthly duration and the total
membership of the church, the heavenly Jerusalem simply does
not have dimensions that can be computed in human terms;
so an earthly measurement is given to it to help us imagine
something which is strictly unimaginable.

It is perverse to treat the beast and his number in any way
differently. The church is symbolized by pictures (the elders,
the woman, the witnesses) and by a number (144,000). The
church age is symbolized by pictures (the woman preserved, the
witnesses preaching, the nations occupying Jerusalem) and by a
number (three and a half years). False religion is symbolized by a

---

[1] It is also the period which the New Testament assigns to the
drought which was the result of Elijah's praying and prophesying
(Lk. 4:25; Jas. 5:17), and its months correspond, as we have noted,
to the forty-two stages of Israel's desert journey under the leadership
of Moses (Num. 33).

picture (the beast from the earth) and by a number (666). The number 666 does not mean Nero or Caligula or Rome. It simply means the beast, false religion.

And this is precisely what John says. Lamp-oil reads 13:18 in a single glance—is it not a single verse?—and interprets the whole verse as the setting of a problem: 'This calls for wisdom: let him who has understanding reckon the number of the beast, for it is a human number, its number is six hundred and sixty-six.' (Even a comma before the last clause, where the Greek has a full stop!) He assumes that the whole verse is the puzzle, with 666 as its starting-point, and that what is required is for the meaning of 666 to be worked out. So he embarks on the solemn discussion of Nero and the rest. But John did not say, 'Work out *the meaning* of the number.' He said, 'Work out *the number.*' His question runs as far as the full stop which should follow the words 'human number'; the rest is his answer. Puzzle: what sort of number do we think might be used to symbolize false religion? Solution: 666.

Let us therefore paraphrase the verse, as it might have been read to those original hearers. 'Let him who has understanding work out a number for the beast—a "human" number, a code such as we have already had symbolizing the church and the church age. What might we suggest?' 'How about something which tries to look like truth, but isn't?' 'A number as close as may be to perfection, but not achieving it?' 'And if the symbol of basic truth is seven, how about six for false religion?' 'That would be very appropriate. Actually, perhaps because the beast in all its activities is persistently missing the mark, the number John writes here is not just 6, but 666.' It may not have been exactly like that. But such an approach seems more consistent with Revelation's general use of symbolism than do Lamp-oil's flights of fancy.

8. THE THIRD VISION: THE LAMB AND HIS FOLLOWERS (14:1-5)

Then I looked, and lo, on Mount Zion stood the Lamb, and with him a hundred and forty-four thousand who had his name and his Father's name written on their foreheads.

2And I heard a voice from heaven like the sound of many waters and like the sound of loud thunder; the voice I heard was like the sound of harpers playing on their harps, 3and they sing a new song before the throne and before the four living creatures and before the elders. No one could learn that song except the hundred and forty-four thousand who had been redeemed from the earth. 4It is these who have not defiled themselves with women, for they are chaste; it is these who follow the Lamb wherever he goes; these have been redeemed from mankind as first fruits for God and the Lamb, 5and in their mouth no lie was found, for they are spotless.

The setting of Vision 3 recalls us yet again to the second Psalm. 'The "rage" of the heathen, and their vain attempt to cast off the divine sovereignty, has been shown at length; it is time to remember "Yet have I set my king upon my holy hill of Zion." So here on Zion's hill he stands, and his people round him.'[1] The 144,000 are the church, all God's people.[2] In the context of the over-all view of Revelation which we are taking, there is nothing in this passage which might lead to any other conclusion. They are named with the names of Christ and of God; they are the redeemed, and know the song of the redeemed; virginity, truth, and purity mark them as God's saints. They are the followers, or disciples, of Christ, and the first fruits of his harvest. Those who follow the Lamb form the *civitas Dei*, the city (or state) of God, as opposed to those who worship the beast from the sea, and form Satan's perversion of the state.

Neither is there anything to indicate that the 144,000 are only the church triumphant, and that we are looking either into the world of the departed or into the future. The first two Visions describe this world and the present time, and unless we have reason to suppose otherwise, we should take it that the third Vision does the same. It is quite in accord with Scripture to speak of the entire church, living and dead, as being with God on a Mount Zion which though not an earthly location is nevertheless a present spiritual reality (Heb. 12:22; Eph. 2:6; Jn. 4:20-24).

The virginity of the 144,000 has caused needless questioning. It is likely as anything in Revelation to be symbolic, especially

[1] Farrer, p. 160.
[2] See pp. 79 ff.

since the Bible places no special value on celibacy, and uniformly commends the institution of marriage.[1] In a similar paradox, Christ endorses what the law says about care for one's parents, yet also tells us we must hate them if we are to follow him.[2] But we know what he means. Love for parents, which he himself commands, is to be so far surpassed by love for him that it will seem in comparison like hatred. In the same way, he lays down, as an essential part of marriage, total commitment to one's partner (Mt. 19:3-6); and then says here in verse 4 that to follow the Lamb means a commitment on the spiritual plane so total that in comparison with it no other ties exist.

9. THE FOURTH VISION: THE ANGELS OF GRACE, DOOM, AND WARNING (14:6-13)

Then I saw another angel flying in midheaven, with an eternal gospel to proclaim to those who dwell on earth, to every nation and tribe and tongue and people; [7]and he said with a loud voice, 'Fear God and give him glory, for the hour of his judgment has come; and worship him who made heaven and earth, the sea and the fountains of water.'

[8]Another angel, a second, followed, saying, 'Fallen, fallen is Babylon the great, she who made all nations drink the wine of her impure passion.'

[9]And another angel, a third, followed, saying with a loud voice, 'If any one worships the beast and its image, and receives a mark on his forehead or on his hand, [10]he also shall drink the wine of God's wrath, poured unmixed into the cup of his anger, and he shall be tormented with fire and brimstone in the presence of the holy angels and in the presence of the Lamb. [11]And the smoke of their torment goes up for ever and ever; and they have no rest, day or night, these worshippers of the beast and its image, and whoever receives the mark of its name.' [12]Here is a call for the endurance of the saints, those who keep the commandments of God and the faith of Jesus. [13]And I heard a voice from heaven saying, 'Write this: Blessed are the dead who die in the Lord henceforth.' 'Blessed indeed,' says the Spirit, 'that they may rest from their labours, for their deeds follow them!'

The opening Visions showed that part of the world which is governed by Satan, its social system in the first Vision and its

[1] *E.g.* Gn. 2:18-24; Eph. 5:22-33; Heb. 13:4.
[2] Mk. 7:9 ff.; Lk. 14:26.

religious voice in the second. The third, the converse of the first, showed the members of God's society, so we should expect the fourth (corresponding to the second) to show their message. And this is what we find. The word 'angel' means messenger, and the message is threefold.

The first angel speaks of grace. He has a gospel to proclaim: good news of how to be in a right relationship with God. It is the absolutely basic gospel, more basic even than that which Paul preached to the pagans of Lystra or Athens;[1] it is the gospel which was preached to Adam in Eden, before the relationship had ever been spoilt; it is the hypothetical gospel with which Christ challenged the lawyer in Luke 10:28—'Do this, and you will live.' The first part of the message is: 'Recognize God as Creator and Judge, the Beginning and End of your existence, and all will be well.'

But all is not well, and the second angel has to say why. The Babylon he mentions has an entire Scene to herself later on, and will be dealt with fully in her place. Suffice it to say for the present that Babylon is another picture of the beast from the sea, the world system which is in rebellion against God. This angel's message is that the spirit of Babylon has infected all nations, and rendered men incapable of responding to the first angel's gospel; but for all her power, she is doomed to destruction.

The third angel therefore brings the personal challenge. He who identifies with the Babylon-beast will share its fate, and also 'drink the wine of God's wrath' (verses 9–11): he who identifies with Christ will similarly share his destiny, and endure to everlasting life (verses 12, 13).

Such is God's counterblast to the falsehoods of the beast from the earth, a message of 'sin and righteousness and judgment' (Jn. 16:8). It is most reasonable to suppose, in the context, that this fourth Vision is like the first three in describing what is happening throughout Christian history; the two phrases which seem to hint at some future date for it can both be understood as present truth.[2]

[1] Acts 14, 17.
[2] The hour of judgment (verse 7) and the fall of Babylon (verse 8) are indeed still future, in a sense. Yet judgment is already here (Jn. 3:19; 12:31); and Babylon is as good as fallen already—cf. 'he *shall be* tormented . . . they *have* no rest' (verses 10, 11).

For all the 'three and a half years' these four powers will be locked in conflict. In his book *Who Moved the Stone?* Frank Morison has a chapter entitled 'A Psychological Parallelogram of Forces'. That is the pattern here. In one corner, there is the state, or better 'the system'—mankind organized socially and politically as the dragon wants it to be, with the power structures which in any given situation will best serve his ends. Next to it, on the same side, are the ideologies which are held to justify the system and give it quasi-religious expression and mystical sanctions. Then over against 'the nations', the world that lies in the dragon's power, is the 'holy', or distinct, nation (1 Pet. 2:9): the church, God's redeemed society. In the fourth corner, opposite to the ideologies which are the life force of the dragon's world, is the gospel of truth which animates the church of God. Every event in history can be seen as part of the conflict between these four, two on one side and two on the other; the opposing messages, and the opposing societies from which they emanate and which embody them.

10. THE FIFTH VISION: THE FINAL REAPING (14:14–20)

Then I looked, and lo, a white cloud, and seated on the cloud one like a son of man, with a golden crown on his head, and a sharp sickle in his hand.

15 And another angel came out of the temple, calling with a loud voice to him who sat upon the cloud, 'Put in your sickle, and reap, for the hour to reap has come, for the harvest of the earth is fully ripe.' 16 So he who sat upon the cloud swung his sickle on the earth, and the earth was reaped.

17 And another angel came out of the temple in heaven, and he too had a sharp sickle.

18 Then another angel came out from the altar, the angel who has power over fire, and he called with a loud voice to him who had the sharp sickle, 'Put in your sickle, and gather the clusters of the vine of the earth, for its grapes are ripe.' 19 So the angel swung his sickle on the earth and gathered the vintage of the earth, and threw it into the great wine press of the wrath of God; 20 and the wine press was trodden outside the city, and blood flowed from the wine press, as high as a horse's bridle, for one thousand six hundred stadia.

'The harvest is the close of the age', when the angels will be sent forth to gather in both wicked and righteous (Mt. 13:30, 39). In contrast with the procedure of Vision 1, where the four beasts of Daniel 7 were condensed into one, Vision 5 distributes the harvesting between four distinct personages: two to reap, and two to tell them when to reap. The grape harvest, which is destined for the wine press of God's wrath and produces a monstrous tide of blood, is the reaping of the wicked; the land will be a blood bath from end to end (perhaps 1,600 *stadia*, or furlongs, means the length of Canaan, the 200 miles 'from Dan to Beersheba'), though the city itself is kept unsullied, for within it there is no place for such defilement (Heb. 13:11, 12). According to the parallels in the Gospels, the other harvest, presumably of wheat, is the reaping of the righteous; for though, in the Old Testament harvest is usually a symbol of judgment on the wicked only Christ spoke of the gathering in of both weeds and grain, and of bad fish and good (Mt. 13:24 ff., 47 ff.). Each of the two reapers, even the one like 'a son of man' (whom we take to be Christ, though some commentators disagree), has to wait on the word of authority from God before the work begins, for 'of that day or that hour no one knows, not even the angels in heaven, nor the Son, but only the Father' (Mk. 13:32).

As in Daniel 7 'one like a son of man' came on the clouds of heaven to put an end to the dominion of the beasts, so here his appearing is the decisive factor in this cosmic conflict. For the whole three and a half years the tension will have continued between the two societies, the beast's followers and the Lamb's followers, and between their respective ideologies. It will be terminated only by the final reaping, when on the one hand (to use a figure from the Old Testament) the iniquity of the Amorites is complete, and on the other hand all Israel is ready to be saved (Gn. 15:16; Rom. 11:26).

II. THE SIXTH VISION: A PREVIEW OF SCENE 5 (15:1)

Then I saw another portent in heaven, great and wonderful, seven angels with seven plagues, which are the last, for with them the wrath of God is ended.

The plagues poured out from the seven Bowls will form the next major section of Revelation. The question therefore arises as to whether that section (Scene 5) begins here at 15:1, or whether John is still watching Scene 4, the 'drama of history'.

If the answer were that the new section begins here, it would involve several peculiarities: (1) that Scene 5 would begin without the usual note of a change of scenery or viewpoint;[1] (2) that when a change of viewpoint did occur, in 15:5, it would not in fact introduce a new Scene; (3) that Scene 4 would be left consisting of five Visions instead of seven; (4) that at the suggested opening of Scene 5 there would be a song of triumph (15:2–4) which looks much more like a climax than a curtain raiser; (5) that it would be hard to see why this song should be slotted in between John's first sight of the plague-angels in 15:1 and their actual emergence in 15:5.

If, on the other hand, the new section begins at 15:5, all these oddities vanish. The phrase 'I saw', in 15:1 and 15:2, introduces the sixth and seventh Visions of Scene 4; Vision 7 (the triumph-song of 15:2–4) does form the climax of Scene 4, and the phrase 'the temple of the tent of witness in heaven was opened' does introduce Scene 5. The reason why Vision 6 is a preview of the following Scene is something which will become clear later in our study.[2]

12. THE SEVENTH VISION: THE SONG OF VICTORY (15:2–4)

And I saw what appeared to be a sea of glass mingled with fire, and those who had conquered the beast and its image and the number of its name, standing beside the sea of glass with harps of God in their hands.

[3] And they sing the song of Moses, the servant of God, and the song of the Lamb, saying, 'Great and wonderful are thy deeds, O Lord God the Almighty! Just and true are thy ways, O King of the ages! [4] Who shall not fear and glorify thy name, O Lord? For thou alone art holy. All nations shall come and worship thee, for thy judgments have been revealed.'

Moses has two songs in the Old Testament, the first in another

[1] Though Scene 3 admittedly did the same (8:2).
[2] See pp. 139 ff.

great fifteenth chapter, that of Exodus, and the second in Deuteronomy 32. The latter is a song of triumph on the grandest scale; but the earlier, though narrower in its reference, has great depths of prophetic meaning in the present context. 'Sing to the Lord, for he has triumphed gloriously', it begins (Ex. 15:1). He has smitten Egypt and saved Israel. Through the centuries that signal deliverance is recalled by the annual death of the passover lamb; and in the fullness of time, following the death of a greater Lamb, the real Israel is rescued and the real Egypt destroyed. The song of Moses and the song of the Lamb are one and the same. It would be wrong to say that the exodus was the 'real' deliverance while the cross and resurrection were 'only the spiritual' one. It would be truer to say that the spiritual deliverance by Christ is the real one, while the exodus was 'only historical'. The latter was a representation of the former on the stage of history, rather as the player-king's 'crime' in *Hamlet* was a dramatic representation—dramatic in both senses—of what King Claudius had actually done.

It is quite possible, as was noted in the case of Vision 3 (the Lamb and his followers), to understand this sort of Vision as a picture of the present situation and not just a future hope. The triumph of Christ and his people dates from the time of his earthly life, death, and resurrection. Nevertheless it seems more natural, since we saw the drama of history in Visions 1 to 4 and the end of history in Vision 5, to take Vision 7 as a sight of what lies beyond history after Christ's return and the final defeat of the beast. This seems to be how Charles Wesley takes it in his hymn 'Head of thy church triumphant':

> 'The world, with sin and Satan,
>   In vain our march opposes,
> By thee we *shall* break through them all,
>   And sing the song of Moses.'

15:5–16:21

SCENE 5:
PUNISHMENT FOR THE WORLD:
seven Bowls poured out

THE UNITY OF THE DRAMA

IT has already been explained in connection with 15:1 why (in our analysis) Scene 5 does not begin there, but here at 15:5. The question remains why, if this is so, there should be a preview of the plague-angels of Scene 5 back in 15:1, before Scene 4 has come to an end. The reason is not obvious. Neither however is the circumstance unparalleled, and two similar instances of it will between them shed light on why this sort of thing should happen in John's visions.

a. Examples

Jerusalem and Babylon, God's holy city and its evil counterpart, each puts in a first appearance in this way.

The name of Babylon first occurs, quite unheralded, at 14:8, in the middle of Scene 4. One of the four great forces that are in conflict throughout this age is what we have called the ideology of the Christian faith, which is summarized in Vision 4 of Scene 4 as a message of grace, doom, and warning. The second part of the triple message is a declaration of the downfall of Babylon the great, 'who made all nations drink the wine of her impure passion'. If her doom is meant to signify the doom of something mentioned earlier in Scene 4, the likeliest candidate for Babylon's 'other self' would seem to be one or both of the beasts.

The second occurrence is at 16:19, at the end of Scene 5, where the final disasters and the end of history are being described. As the cities of the nations collapse, we are told that 'the great city' also breaks up: Babylon is remembered by God.

It is after these two earlier mentions that Babylon comes into her own. Scene 6 is devoted entirely to her, showing her downfall and a great deal more besides.

Towards the close of Scene 6, Jerusalem is introduced as Babylon's rival and successor (19:7). Again at the close of Scene 7, beyond the end of history, she appears coming down from God out of heaven (21:2). Both these are previews of Scene 8, which (as with Scene 6 and Babylon) is devoted entirely to her.

It is of a piece with this procedure, whatever may be its meaning or object, that the plague-angels, who likewise have an entire Scene to themselves, put in an earlier appearance, being seen nearly at the end of Scene 4, before their own Scene 5 begins.

b. Conclusions

These considerations confirm the view already expressed that the basic arrangement of Revelation is not a chronological one,[1] and that what creates the unity of the drama is not the continuity of its events. At the end of Scene 4, Babylon is said to have fallen; at the end of Scene 5 she is coming to the notice of the avenging God, and is breaking up; in Scene 6 she is, at the beginning at any rate, vividly alive. It is clearer than ever that the order of the scenes as John saw them is by no means the chronological order of the events they describe. Whatever else may bind the drama together, it is not a straightforward narrative sequence.

The Scenes are unified in a more subtle way than this, as will be realized when their relationships are followed through with regard to the three subjects just mentioned—the plague-angels, Babylon, and Jerusalem.

Scene 4 concerns the perennial spiritual conflict of history. Four visions describing the four contending forces need to be supplemented by a fifth which shows that in the end God is in control, and will not allow the struggle to continue indefinitely. He will act when the harvest is ripe. And his action will be to deal finally with his opponents; for he is not only a God who is 'merciful and gracious', but also one 'who will by no means clear the guilty' (Ex. 34:6, 7). He is to be reckoned with as a God who punishes evil. Hence the sixth Vision, of the angels of punishment. This is the theme which is taken up after Scene 4 has been played out, and which forms the chief subject of Scene 5.

[1] See pp. 85 ff.

The same thing happens with regard to Babylon. The society and philosophy represented by the two beasts are what will in due course be called Babylon. The fact that she is doomed from the start forms an essential part of the Christian message, which is itself one of the forces opposing her (Scene 4, Vision 4). When the vision of the plague-angels in the same Scene is expanded to make a whole Scene of its own, Babylon appears there also as being ripe for punishment (Scene 5, Bowl 7). Then, when she has been introduced in this way, it is judged appropriate that she in turn should have a Scene to herself.

Scene 6 describes every aspect of her career to ruin, and the last declaration about her concerns her successor, the holy city Jerusalem (Scene 6, Word 7). Scene 7 follows with a recapitulation of the underlying realities, the 'drama behind history', and from that point of view also Jerusalem appears at the climax of the drama (Scene 7, Vision 7). What Scene 8 describes is beyond time and history altogether. Babylon and the dragon have vanished like a dream; the night is over, and the morning is come. The seventh sections of all the first seven Scenes are blended in one dazzling panorama of eternity. 'For I dipt into the future, far as human eye could see . . .' But John, in the nature of the case, could see a good deal further than the English poet,[1] and what he saw was Jerusalem, the holy city, occupying the whole of Scene 8; with which in due course we shall close this book.

I. SCENE 5 OPENS: BEHIND THE VEIL, GOD'S INESCAPABLE WRATH (15:5—16:1)

After this I looked, and the temple of the tent of witness in heaven was opened, ⁶and out of the temple came the seven angels with the seven plagues, robed in pure bright linen, and their breasts girded with golden girdles. ⁷And one of the four living creatures gave the seven angels seven golden bowls full of the wrath of God who lives for ever and ever; ⁸and the temple was filled with smoke from the glory of God and from his power, and no one could enter the temple until the seven plagues of the seven angels were ended.

¹⁶:¹Then I heard a loud voice from the temple telling the seven angels, 'Go and pour out on the earth the seven bowls of the wrath of God.'

[1] Tennyson, *Locksley Hall*.

The temple that was opened at the start of Scene 4 is opened again now. But it is not quite the same. Not that there are two temples: but though the temple always means the place where God is, there are different senses in which he is to be 'located'. In one sense, he is everywhere. Scene 4 portrayed a cosmic struggle, and the scenery revealed when the curtain went up was that of his 'temple' in a very broad sense—his whole creation. In another, religious, sense there are particular circumstances in which he promises to meet with man. In the time of Moses this meant the Tabernacle: 'There I will meet with the people of Israel' (Ex. 29:43). It is a confrontation of this kind with which Scene 5 is concerned. So it is not just the temple, but the temple in this special sense, which opens in order for the seven plague-angels to emerge.

The Tabernacle was known from its earliest days as 'the tabernacle of the testimony' or 'the tabernacle of the congregation'—to use the less cumbersome Anglo-Saxon words, the tent of witness or the tent of meeting (Ex. 38:21; 33:7). The first name meant that it witnessed to the presence and character of God, notably his holiness. The tribe of Levi, specially called to this service, looked after it and camped around it: 'If any one else comes near, he shall be put to death . . . The Levites shall encamp around [it], that there may be no wrath upon the congregation of the people of Israel' (Nu. 1:51, 53). The second name meant that this was where God, though of course present everywhere, actually let his presence be seen. The pillar of cloud and fire rested on it from the day it was erected (Nu. 9:15). This was where God would meet with his people. But his character was the same—holiness: the cloud was not only on the tent, but in it: 'The glory of the Lord filled the tabernacle' (Ex. 40:34, 35). In that first glorious demonstration of God's presence actually among his people, even Moses, who had spoken with him face to face on mount Sinai, could not enter the tent.[1]

But in Scene 5 of Revelation the holiness of God is a terrible thing. Fear pervades the scene, not the awe and reverence felt by Moses, Solomon, and Isaiah when they saw God's glory fill his house, but naked terror. This atmosphere is evoked from the outset by the clothing the angels wear and the Bowls they are

[1] Ex. 40:34 f.; and *cf.* 1 Ki. 8:10 f.; Is. 6:1-5.

given. Far from being sombre, their appearance is dazzling, like that of their Lord in 1:13 ff. They radiate the 'unapproachable light' in which God dwells (1 Tim. 6:16), 'light like solid blocks intolerable of edge and weight'.[1] The opponents of Christ cannot endure an onslaught of such goodness and purity.

The angels' Bowls, moreover, are filled with the wrath of the God who *lives* for ever and ever, and 'it is a fearful thing to fall into the hands of the *living* God' (Heb. 10:31). It means that though our life may end with its bang or its whimper, his life continues unaffected. The bomb goes up, the smoke clears, the dust dies down—he is still there. Or alternatively, the busy world is hushed, the fever of life is over, and our work is done, and we look forward to peace at the last—but he is still there to be reckoned with. 'Do not fear those who kill the body, and after that have no more that they can do. But I will warn you whom to fear: fear him who, after he has killed, has power to cast into hell' (Lk. 12:4, 5). It is the classic horror story situation, where you flee from the thing you fear, take refuge behind your barricades, and find you have locked it inside with you. It is the Hound of Heaven, only a hound of judgment, not of mercy. 'Who among us can dwell with everlasting burnings?' (Is. 33:14).

Such are the punishments of the holy, living God: sevenfold, like those which Israel asked should fall on the heathen (Ps. 79:12) but with which she herself was threatened when disobedient (Lv. 26:18 ff.), because they represent full, or rather *real*, punishment. And as 'the stars in their courses fought against Sisera' (Jdg. 5:20, RV), so here nature is the agent of the wrath of God, and it is accordingly one of the four living creatures who provides the actual plagues which the angels will pour out. 'He will arm creation to punish his enemies', says the Jewish book of Wisdom (5:17, JB).

2. THE FIRST BOWL: THE EARTH STRICKEN (16:2)

So the first angel went and poured his bowl on the earth, and foul and evil sores came upon the men who bore the mark of the beast and worshipped its image.

[1] C. S. Lewis, *The Great Divorce*, pp. 117 f.

The Trumpets ushered in troubles which were partial, with the object of bringing to a better mind those who survived them. They were God's warnings. The plagues poured out of the Bowls are total, because the opportunity for repentance has gone. All who have not been sealed as followers of the Lamb are irretrievably marked as worshippers of the beast, and all of them, not just a third of them, are to suffer. These are no longer warnings but punishments.

The classic biblical instance of holiness bringing a plague on the unholy is that of 1 Samuel 5, when the captured ark of Israel caused an epidemic in each Philistine city to which it was taken. That chapter is light relief alongside this one. We can even chuckle over the Philistines' growing panic as the ark made its infectious progress from Ashdod to Gath and from Gath to Ekron, because we know the story has a happy ending: the plague-sores were to them a warning which in the event they heeded. Revelation 16 is an altogether grimmer picture. It recalls the plagues of Egypt rather than that of the Philistines in this respect, that the Egyptian Pharaoh hardened his heart and was duly destroyed. So with the beast's worshippers. They have refused the warnings and must now take the consequences.

3. THE SECOND BOWL: THE SEA STRICKEN (16:3)

The second angel poured his bowl into the sea, and it became like the blood of a dead man, and every living thing died that was in the sea.

Bowl 2 concerns the sea, as Trumpet 2 did, and looking ahead we realize that though the effects of the Bowls are different from those of the Trumpets, the two scenes are nevertheless going to run parallel. Earth, sea, rivers, and sky are stricken in turn; then comes torment, then destruction, and finally the world is no more.

What happens to the sea, in both Bowl 2 and Trumpet 2, recalls the first plague of Egypt. The result here is particularly unpleasant, and again in contrast with the Trumpets it is total, not partial. The sufferings poured out from the Bowls are also directed more immediately against life itself; they are not the indirect Trumpet-warnings of a failing economy or a worsening environment. The sins of men are coming home to roost.

4. THE THIRD BOWL: THE RIVERS STRICKEN (16:4-7)

The third angel poured his bowl into the rivers and the fountains of
water, and they became blood. ⁵And I heard the angel of water say,
'Just art thou in these thy judgments, thou who art and wast, O Holy
One. ⁶For men have shed the blood of saints and prophets, and thou hast
given them blood to drink. It is their due!' ⁷And I heard the altar cry,
'Yea, Lord God the Almighty, true and just are thy judgments!'

The text does not read as though the angel with the third Bowl
is the same as the angel of the waters. The latter is perhaps the
representative on the spiritual level of the earth's rivers and
fountains, as we have seen angels standing for the churches
(1:20), the angels of wind and fire (7:1; 14:18), and the archangel Michael as the representative of the nation of Israel.[1]
If so, it is remarkable that his reaction to the Bowls of God's
wrath is not one of pain. It is one of recognition of divine justice. We have already noted that the Bowls are first given to the
angels by one of the four living creatures, the representatives of
nature. It is as if nature, though knowing that it will suffer when
the plagues come, is willing to lay itself open to whatever its
Maker may wish to do in pursuance of his scheme of judgment.

The last appearance of the altar was in Scene 2, Seal 5, when
from it the suffering saints cried out for vindication. The first
part of God's answer to that prayer was to send the world not
punishment but warning, with the Trumpets of Scene 3. But
now his answer is completed, literally with a vengeance. So
voices representing both God's world and God's church speak
with approval of his righteousness and justice and the deserved
retribution meted out to his enemies.

5. THE FOURTH BOWL: THE SKY STRICKEN (16:8, 9)

The fourth angel poured his bowl on the sun, and it was allowed to scorch
men with fire; ⁹men were scorched by the fierce heat, and they cursed the
name of God who had power over these plagues, and they did not repent
and give him glory.

[1] See p. 120, and the discussion on 1:20 (p. 41). There are related
beliefs in Rabbinic Judaism, Zoroastrianism, and classical paganism.

Sinners who would not repent when the sun's light was darkened are now punished by having its heat intensified. That, they sensed but ignored; this they cannot help but feel. By this time God's presence is recognized, but only to be blasphemed, not submitted to.

We have noticed how similar the plan of Scene 5 is to that of Scene 3. The more such likenesses appear between one Scene and another, the clearer it becomes that their relationship is not that of sequence. If the line of interpretation followed so far has commended itself, it is quite impossible to fit the seven Bowls into it as a sequence of events which will occur, and in this order, some time after the events of Scene 4. The connection between the Scenes is not chronological but logical. Again and again trouble will sweep the world (the Seals): whenever suffering is caused, God warns that it cannot be caused with impunity (the Trumpets); whenever his warnings go unheeded, he will in the end punish the wrongdoers (the Bowls).

6. THE FIFTH BOWL: TORMENT (16:10, 11)

The fifth angel poured his bowl on the throne of the beast, and its kingdom was in darkness; men gnawed their tongues in anguish [11] and cursed the God of heaven for their pain and sores, and did not repent of their deeds.

In each Scene from the Seals onwards, the fifth section has brought an extra turn of the screw, a 'not only . . . but . . .'. Not only will the world suffer conquest and scarcity, strife and death, *but* even the church will not be exempt—that was Seal 5. To warn man of the perils of sin, God not only interferes with his environment, commerce, resources, and vision, *but* also sends ills like locusts to gnaw at his personal life—that was Trumpet 5. Four great spiritual forces are engaged in the cosmic struggle of history, *but* the hand of God holds the trump card—that was Vision 5. Nor is it otherwise in this scene. God will punish unrepentant men by land and sea, by water and fire, *but* he will do more than this. When Bowl 5 is poured out, the entire human system is thrown into disarray; darkness falls upon it, like the ninth plague of Egypt.

There are few visions in Revelation more awe-inspiring than that of the fifth Bowl. The throne of the beast is in some ways Satan's master stroke. He has invaded the whole structure of society, as first planned by God, and perverted it to his own ends. The 'world', the organization of human society without reference to God, is the result. It is the Satanic counterpart of God's society, the church. It is the kingdom of the beast as opposed to the kingdom of Christ, and one of the four great powers in the cosmic conflict of Scene 4. And upon this—this mighty edifice, the laborious triumph of the dragon's skill, the kingdom crowned with the throne and the throne occupied by the beast—upon this the fifth Bowl is poured out: and confusion follows.

God is grimly vindicated when godless society, which rose so proudly against him and his church, and claimed to provide a viable alternative, is shown to be unequal to the task. The book of Daniel, who witnessed to the true God in the midst of the heathen world systems of his day, is full of this message: that 'the Most High rules the kingdom of men, and gives it to whom he will' (Dn. 4:17, 25, 32). He sees the statue representing the great empires shattered in fragments 'like the chaff of the summer threshing floors' (2:35), the great tree which was Nebuchadnezzar of Babylon hewn down (4:14), Belshazzar's kingdom numbered and finished (5:26). He sees visions of beasts, like the beasts of Revelation, which are great and powerful—till their dominion is taken away (7:12).

Even so, those who bear the mark of the beast will not turn to God on this account. They will suffer, by no means in silence, and throw the blame on God. But those who are sealed as the Lamb's followers will know what is happening when the system begins to break down, when (to borrow the title of one of E. M. Forster's stories) 'The Machine Stops', and will pray 'Hallowed be *your* name; may *your* kingdom come; may *your* will be done, on earth as it is in heaven.'

7. THE SIXTH BOWL: DESTRUCTION (16:12-16)

The sixth angel poured his bowl on the great river Euphrates, and its water was dried up, to prepare the way for the kings from the east. [13] *And I saw, issuing from the mouth of the dragon and from the mouth of the beast and from the mouth of the false prophet, three foul spirits like frogs;* [14] *for they are demonic spirits, performing signs, who go abroad to the kings of the whole world, to assemble them for battle on the great day of God the Almighty.*

[15] (*'Lo, I am coming like a thief! Blessed is he who is awake, keeping his garments that he may not go naked and be seen exposed!'*)

[16] *And they assembled them at the place which is called in Hebrew Armageddon.*

There are problems in this section, and the answers given here may not commend themselves to all. Tentative though they are, however, they do seem to follow from what has been understood so far.

Verse 12: we know that the Euphrates is the region from which destruction comes (Scene 3, Trumpet 6). We presume that, like the cavalry of Trumpet 6, the kings of the east represent the forces of destruction, whatever those forces may turn out to be in actual experience. The drying of the waters to make way for men to pass over is a commonplace of biblical history and prophecy.[1]

Verse 13: we know that the dragon is the devil, and the beast is the world, or the godless state system (Scene 4). We presume that the false prophet is the second beast, the one from the earth, and shall find this presumption confirmed when we compare 13:14 with 19:20. The reason that inspirations coming from this evil trio are likened to frogs is no doubt the reason which John himself gives, that the frog was in biblical times an example of an unclean creature.

But questions remain. The kings of verse 14 seem to be literal kings, or at least governments; but if they are, can we take the same word in verse 12 to mean something more metaphorical? Should not 'the kings of the east' also be actual political powers, emerging from the continent of Asia? Again, if (on the analogy of previous scenes) we are to understand the Bowls as describing the punishments that God *always* sends when his warnings are persistently ignored, why is the punishment of Bowl 6 given a date at the end of time—the great day of God Almighty, when Christ returns as unexpectedly as a thief

[1] Ex. 14:21; Jos. 3:16; 4:23; 2 Ki. 2:8; Is. 11:15, 16.

(verses 14, 15)? Again, what is the meaning of Armageddon, the 'hill of Megiddo'? This hill, a few miles south-east of the modern city of Haifa, overlooks the crossing-place of some of the most important routes of the ancient world, and as the 'crossroads of the Middle East' witnessed many of the crucial battles of history. Writers of science fiction, the apocalyptic of the twentieth century, are very familiar with the concept, and their doyen H. G. Wells wrote a story actually entitled 'A Vision of Armageddon'; will it be, as in his fictional 'eschatology', the final World War? The following interpretation is offered tentatively as being most in line with the general meaning of the book.

The pouring out of Bowl 5 punished the unrepentant by the tribulations of a society thrown out of gear. Things are bad enough when the beast's kingdom works properly; when its machinery runs amok, they are infinitely worse. Bowl 6 is the next and last stage of the divine punishment, and in it the purposes of God and Satan in a macabre way converge. Having seen his perversion of human society confounded, Satan says, 'If I can no longer pervert, I will destroy'; and he and the beast and the false prophet inspire the kings of the earth, no longer able to maintain the inconstant balance they call 'peace', to a frenzy of mutual slaughter. Armaments multiply, armies march, and men die—not their kith and kin, but they themselves; for as Trumpet 6 was the last warning, bringing death *before* them, Bowl 6 is the last punishment, bringing death *to* them. But while Satan is saying, 'I will destroy', God is saying, 'So you shall'. Satan's purpose is to assert his power; God's is to prosecute his justice. The result is the same: Armageddon.

Armageddon, therefore, is the end. When 'the great day of God the Almighty' comes, the powers of this world will find themselves suddenly confronted by their rejected Lord, coming as unexpectedly as the quotation of his words comes into this chapter at verse 15. That battle will be the last: the torment of the fifth Bowl followed by the destruction of the sixth, as darkness in Egypt was followed by death, on the night of the first Passover.

But though it is to the last day that Bowl 6 chiefly refers, we ought not to forget that whenever destruction comes upon the impenitent sinner, that is for him the 'last day', the end of his world, and the final confrontation with Christ, who comes at all times like a thief, when men least expect him.

8. THE SEVENTH BOWL: THE WORLD IS NO MORE (16:17–21)

The seventh angel poured his bowl into the air, and a great voice came out of the temple, from the throne, saying, 'It is done!' [18] *And there were flashes of lightning, voices, peals of thunder, and a great earthquake such as had never been since men were on the earth, so great was that earthquake.*

[19] *The great city was split into three parts, and the cities of the nations fell, and God remembered great Babylon, to make her drain the cup of the fury of his wrath.*

[20] *And every island fled away, and no mountains were to be found;* [21] *and great hailstones, heavy as a hundredweight, dropped on men from heaven, till men cursed God for the plague of the hail, so fearful was that plague.*

Thunder and lightning, part of the overture to Scenes 2, 3, and 4, accompany the climax of Scene 5. Earthquakes also have occurred elsewhere, as signs of the presence of God (Seal 6, Trumpet 6). This one, stated to be the greatest ever known, is the subject of a prophecy of Haggai (2:6) which is taken up and explained in Hebrews 12:26, 27. 'He has promised, "Yet once more I will shake not only the earth but also the heaven." This phrase, "Yet once more," indicates the removal of what is shaken, as of what has been made, in order that what cannot be shaken may remain.' The pouring out of Bowl 7 sweeps away time and history, and replaces them by eternity. When that day comes, it is not only the islands and mountains of God's earth which will vanish. The cities, the civilization which is the achievement of man's demon-driven pride, will collapse also. The 'great city' is no doubt Babylon, the symbol of the whole Satanic structure. She will be remembered, she who now says in her heart, 'God has forgotten',[1] and under the storm of God's anger she will disintegrate: 'Hail will sweep away the refuge of lies' (Is. 28:17). With this the divine punishment 'is done' (verse 17). Bowl 6 brought wholesale destruction; Bowl 7 brings total erasure.

[1] Bede, quoting Ps. 10:11 (Swete, p. 211).

17:1–19:10

SCENE 6:
BABYLON THE WHORE:
seven Words of justice

THE IDENTIFYING OF SYMBOLS

SCENE 6 is at once one of the plainest and one of the most obscure parts of the whole book. The reader who has been hoping—on the whole, vainly—for identifications of its symbolic language is given more of them here than anywhere else: the kind of thing, that is, which we find in 17:15, 'the waters that you saw . . . are peoples and multitudes and nations and tongues.' But there is no denying that the way these identifications seem to be meant to tie in with the 'real world' provides further puzzles. Commentaries suggest, for example, that 'the seven heads are seven hills' (17:9) because the beast is the empire of Rome, the city of seven hills; and the seven kings which they also represent (17:10) are the Roman emperors from Augustus to Titus.[1] But there are reasons why suggestions of this kind, though undoubtedly true from one point of view, may be oddly unsatisfying. For they do not deal with certain questions which lurk unspoken, almost unformulated, at the back of one's mind.

a. Difficulties in John's method

Two such questions, which begin as mere impressions during the study of the earlier part of the book, come into focus here in Scene 6, and are confirmed when one re-reads with them specially in mind.

1. Why are the identifications so sporadic? Among the features of the vision of Christ in Scene 1 which the reader may have found puzzling at first sight are the seven lampstands and the seven

[1] See p. 156 f.

stars (1:12, 16). But he is not long left in doubt. They are forthwith identified by the angel who has first spoken to John: 'The seven stars are the angels of the seven churches, and the seven lampstands are the seven churches' (1:20). How helpful it would be, now, if an angelic running commentary were to give similar equations throughout the book. 'Tell us the parable of the tree of life, and the hidden manna, and the white stone, and the key of David, and the pillar in the temple'—and that is just Scene 1, and will be followed by requests for explanations of the elders, the living creatures, the sealed scroll, the riders, and the 144,000 in Scene 2, and so on and so on.

But in point of fact the next clear 'this = that' after the stars and lampstands of 1:20 is an isolated one in 4:5, 'Seven torches of fire, which are the seven spirits of God' (a definition which is itself an enigma); and thenceforward the identification parade straggles on in desultory fashion, with just one fairly numerous cluster here in Scene 6, as we have already noted.

Now this is a very unsatisfactory literary method. Either the author should decide that he is writing an allegory or myth, in which he will deliberately identify nothing, and leave the reader to guess his meaning throughout; or he should provide a comprehensive key, in the manner of the vocabulary at the back of a foreign language textbook. But not, surely, this haphazard procedure.

2. *Why is the allegory so inconsistent?* The first identification, that of the lampstands and stars with the churches and their angels, is the starting-point for another provoking train of thought. For granted that 'lampstand' means 'church', the one presumably being the symbol and the other the reality, why does the introductory vision of Scene 1 show us the symbol (1:12), while in the main action of the Scene Christ goes on to address the reality (3:22)? Bunyan knows better than to mix his categories like this; we do not find him describing Giant Pope as an ogre on one page and as a church on the next. Why is the principle ignored by John (or, still more, by the One who gives John the revelation; for the higher the view we take of the book's authorship, the more inexplicable does shoddy workmanship become)?

b. An approach to their solution

There are a number of optical illusions in which a single design can appear as either of two different objects, depending on the way you look at it. The symbols of Revelation can similarly be approached in more ways than one; it may be that some of the problems attaching to them arise simply because we are not looking at them quite as John meant us to. Let us be clear first of all what he means by the word 'mystery' (17:5), and we may then see more clearly what his so-called 'identifications' are intended to mean.

1. 'Mystery' A very cursory study of the New Testament use of the word 'mystery' shows that it does not there carry its usual modern sense of 'puzzle'. It is indeed something hidden, but not in such a way that you can follow a series of clues and eventually find it out; rather, it is a truth which you either know or do not know, depending on whether or not it has been revealed to you. To the initiate, it will never again be a secret; but so long as he was an outsider, it could never be anything else. The 'mysteries' of the New Testament are open secrets to every Christian. The 'mystery of Christ' spoken of in Ephesians 3:3–6 is a truth which was hidden from 'men in other generations', but 'has now been revealed to his holy apostles', and Paul in turn has 'written briefly' of it to the Ephesians; it is, in a sentence, that 'the Gentiles are . . . partakers of the promise in Christ Jesus' along with God's ancient people the Jews. To Paul and his readers this is no longer a secret.

Now it is easy to accept that the word has this special biblical meaning, different from the one which is familiar to us in detective fiction and newspaper reporting. But in studying this strange book of Revelation, in which 'mysteries' in our modern sense are to be found on every page, it is equally easy to forget that fact, and to read it as though when John says 'a mystery' he means 'a puzzle'. So although we know that John does not mean that, we tend—understandably—to read 1:20 as follows: 'As for the mystery (= the puzzle) of the seven lampstands, they are the seven churches (= the solution to the puzzle).'

This, though the RSV might seem to support it, is not what John meant. The older versions put a full stop half way through verse 20, and enable us to read it as two separate statements, which might be paraphrased like this: 'Here is the Mystery of the Seven Lampstands' (= neither the puzzle of the lampstands nor the puzzle's explanation, but the complex of divine truths which can be called by this title). 'I call it "the seven lampstands", although of course it could equally well be called "the seven churches", since both words refer to the same thing.'

2. *'Identification'* It will be seen that on this view 1:20b is not strictly an identification. If it were, John—or the angel—would be talking about a symbol, 'lampstand', which represents a reality, 'church'. This, we begin to see, may be a misunderstanding, based probably on the unspoken assumption (which we know is not correct) that 'mystery' in verse 20a means 'puzzle', and that 'lampstands = churches' in verse 20b is the answer to the puzzle. But what the angel is saying when he identifies 'lampstand' with 'church' is not that one is a symbol while the other is what the symbol 'really' means. He is saying that here are two things which correspond to each other, being *equally real from different points of view.*

What justification is there for such a suggestion? More than one might at first realize.

Chapter 21 proposes two other symbols for the church: ' "I will show you the Bride . . ." . . . And [he] showed me the holy city' (21:9, 10). But are they symbols? For the church really is a commonwealth of citizens: 'city' is surely something more than a mere symbol. Furthermore, a reading of Ephesians 5, where the relationship between husband and wife is likened to that between Christ and the church, makes one wonder which is 'archetype' and which is 'ectype', which the original and which the copy. And if the marriage of Christ and the church is the archetype, of which all human marriages are but blurred copies, who is to say that from a heavenly point of view 'bride' may not likewise be as much a reality, in a sense we cannot grasp, as 'city' or 'church'?

Turn then to chapter 11, which describes the other great city, the one where God's two witnesses preach and perish and rise again. It is 'allegorically called Sodom and Egypt', and is also

the place 'where their Lord was crucified' (11:8). Now what is
the reality behind those allegorical names? The view taken
earlier[1] is that they stand for the hostile world in general; but
they were also geographical places, each in its time the home of a
God-defying society. If we indicate symbols by inverted commas,
Revelation 11 tells us that 'Sodom' means the world; but Genesis
19 tells us that 'the world' means Sodom. Which is the truth, and
which the allegory?

A final clue is provided by the references in John's Gospel to
Christ as the true bread, the true vine, and so forth.[2] The word
'true' crystallizes the whole argument. For it means that Christ is
real bread, since only he can satisfy the *real* hunger of men. But
if you assent to that, what are you saying? Picture the Last
Supper: at the table sits Christ, on the table lies a loaf. Which is
allegorically bread, and which is *really* bread? The answer is
obvious, we might think. But the unexpected answer of John
6:32 is that the real bread is the person, not the thing! 'Bread-
ness', the quality of 'being bread', belongs in its purest essence
to Christ; it belongs to the loaf on the table only in a secondary,
derived sense. So it is with the marriage symbolism. If 'bride' is
a symbol, what does that imply? That the church is the true
bride, of whom every human bride is a picture or copy; and the
bride that John sees in Revelation 21 is the *real* bride, *and not the
symbol*. Similarly, if Sodom is a symbol of the world, what John
sees in 11:8 is the real Sodom. For the reality is not the ancient
city of the plain where Lot lived. That is merely the symbol. The
reality is the world-system, of which that Sodom is an illustration.

What then of our original identification? If lampstands
symbolize churches, what John saw was seven *real lampstands*—
that is, the heavenly archetypes of which all actual earthly
lampstands are mere copies.[3] It follows that in 1:20b, 'the

---

[1] See p. 106.
[2] Jn. 6:32 ff.; 15:1.
[3] *Cf.* R. C. Trench, on the symbolism of 'kingdom': 'The Lord is
King, not borrowing this title from the kings of the earth, but having
lent his own title to them—and not the name only, but having so
ordered, that all true rule and government upon earth, with its
righteous laws, its stable ordinances, its punishment and its grace, its
majesty and its terror, should tell of Him, and of his kingdom which
ruleth over all—so that "kingdom of God" is not a figurative ex-

lampstands are the churches', we have, not an explanation of a symbolic term by a real one, but a statement that these two terms, which are equally real, are simply interchangeable.

c. Solving the general difficulties

It will readily be seen how these suggestions help towards an understanding of the different features noted earlier.

So long as we regard verses such as 17:9–12, 15, and 18 as a kind of crib, explaining the real meaning of symbolic language, we shall wonder (1) why we are given half a dozen explanations here but hardly any in other passages which are just as obscure, and (2) why John serves up such a disparate mixture of realities and symbols, as if he were stirring together oil and water. But once we free ourselves from the notion that the world we live in is the touchstone of reality, and that the truths of the spiritual world, being less palpable, are therefore less real, we can see that John is giving not explanations, but equivalents. He is not concerned to tell us that 'lampstands', which we do not understand, means 'church', which we do. He is rather concerned to tell us things *about* the lampstands and the bride and the city and the church, the twenty-four elders and the 144,000 and the numberless multitude; their meaning we should know already from the rest of Scripture, and he merely reminds us in passing that all of these correspond to one another and are different descriptions of the same thing.

c. Solving the difficulties of Scene 6

If this interpretation is applied to the particular problems of Scene 6, many of them also evaporate.

Take as an example 'The seven heads are seven hills . . . They are also seven kings' (17:9, 10). This is commonly taken to mean that the heads of the beast on which the woman sits are a symbol for a geographical reality (easy: the seven hills of Rome), and also, as it happens, for a historical reality (not so easy, but by

---

pression, but most literal: it is rather the earthly kingdoms and the earthly kings that are figures and shadows of the true' (*Notes on the Parables of Our Lord* (Macmillan, 1877), pp. 14, 15).

dint of a little juggling we can list seven nearly consecutive Roman emperors who fit the required period).

But if our reasoning is right, this so-called identification should be interpreted in quite a different way. First, the seven-headed beast of 13:1 we have taken to be the godless world, and the seven-headed dragon of 12:3 is the prince of this world, the devil. One of these, or a combination of them, is presumably the beast which supports Babylon the whore, in 17:3. Next, we have proposed that 'seven-ness' means the essence of a thing, so that, to use a modern idiom, the sevenfold head is as it were 'The Head' with a capital H; and we have suggested that this Head is a symbol of strength.[1]

But then the second term of the equation (heads = *hills*) is just as striking an image for anyone who knows his Bible. We need go no further than the book of Psalms to see what it meant to the Hebrews. Strength again is what the mountains represent; God's holy mountain, the hill of Zion, supremely (2:1–6; 125:1, 2). They are both the symbol and the source of it (30:7; 121:1, 2). One way of expressing the greatness of God is to say that he is *even* greater than the mountains (76:4); when he marches forth, *even* the mountains tremble (18:7; 114:4–7).

On this principle, it is not going too far to say that the third term also (heads = hills = *kings*) is as likely to be 'real' in the sense described above, as in the more prosaic sense of a succession of actual Roman emperors. It could well be closer to the abstract idea 'kingship'—or Kingship, as it is sevenfold!—than to the concrete noun 'king'.

When John, then, is being shown the scarlet beast which supports the woman Babylon, the images brought to his mind are those of The Head, The Mountain, The King, all with a devilish or worldly colouring. There is of course more to be said about the actual hills of Rome and the emperors who reigned there, in the second section of this Scene. We are by no means breaking the traditional link between John's visions and these actualities; they are after all concrete embodiments of the Mountain-image and the King-image. But first, bearing in mind the foregoing discussion, we are to be shown the mystery of Babylon.

[1] See p. 117.

1. SCENE 6 OPENS: THE FIRST WORD ABOUT BABYLON (17:1-6)

Then one of the seven angels who had the seven bowls came and said to me, 'Come, I will show you the judgment of the great harlot who is seated upon many waters, ²with whom the kings of the earth have committed fornication, and with the wine of whose fornication the dwellers on earth have become drunk.'

³And he carried me away in the Spirit into a wilderness, and I saw a woman sitting on a scarlet beast which was full of blasphemous names, and it had seven heads and ten horns. ⁴The woman was arrayed in purple and scarlet, and bedecked with gold and jewels and pearls, holding in her hand a golden cup full of abominations and the impurities of her fornication; ⁵and on her forehead was written a name of mystery: 'Babylon the great, mother of harlots and of earth's abominations.' ⁶And I saw the woman, drunk with the blood of the saints and the blood of the martyrs of Jesus. When I saw her I marvelled greatly.

Babylon has appeared on two previous occasions, in 14:8 and 16:19. The first mention is in Scene 4, where the cosmic conflict is being described. There we saw the ideology of evil, which exalts the dragon's godless system to a position of supreme authority, opposed by the divine ideology, the everlasting gospel; and part of the gospel's function is, as Paul would put it, 'the pulling down of strongholds, casting down imaginations and every high thing that exalteth itself against the knowledge of God' (2 Cor. 10:4, 5, AV). That aspect of the gospel message is graphically summarized in the words 'Fallen, fallen is Babylon the great.'

The second mention is in Scene 5. As the outpouring of the bowls of God's anger reaches its climax, civilization ('the cities of the nations') begins to collapse, for the 'great city'—the archetypal city, the godless system itself—is breaking up. And there too we found the ominous name, for what is happening is described as 'God remembered great Babylon.' Already, therefore, we have not only seen the name, but also gained some inkling of what it stands for. But so important is 'Babylon' that an entire Scene of the drama is now to be devoted to her.

What is she? A figure of gaudy splendour. But underneath

all the glamour, she is simply 'the great harlot'. Names of blasphemy cover the beast on which she sits, but what she has written all over her is fornication, fornication, fornication. We are only too familiar with this word's Greek root, *porn-*; and five times John repeats it,[1] not as one relishing it but as one trying vainly to spit out a filthy taste.

We are not, of course, to imagine that Revelation is here condemning sexual immorality as the ultimate sin. In Scene 8 we shall find that the counterpart to Babylon the whore is Jerusalem the bride; and 'the wife of the Lamb' (21:9) is the church, the city of God. There, a faithful marriage-relationship is a picture of something far greater, the spiritual union between Christ and his people. By the same token, the fornication into which Babylon seduces the inhabitants of the earth is, as we saw in Scene 4, no mere sexual sin, but the worship of the dragon instead of God (13:11, 12). 'If any one loves the world, love for the Father is not in him' (1 Jn. 2:15).

As the first Letter of John goes on to say, 'that world is passing away' (1 Jn. 2:17, NEB). The 'world' in a spiritual sense, meaning human society organized independently of God, and represented in Scene 4 by the beasts and here in Scene 6 by Babylon and her beast, is as impermanent as anything in the physical 'world'. The first Word about Babylon, however,[2] shows her in her power and glory. See first how *influential* she is. The waters of Babylon were an actual geographical feature of that ancient city.[3] But here they are a symbol, whose meaning is given in verse 15. She is enthroned over all nations, and has the inhabitants of the earth and their kings in her power (verses 1, 2, 18). If men so numerous and so able are taken in by her wiles, how should weak individuals like ourselves beware of her! Then see how *evil* she is (verse 3). The power that supports her is a creature with the heads and horns of the dragon (12:3) and

---

[1] It is the root of 'harlot' as well as of 'fornication'.

[2] Here, as in Scene 4, John's revelations are both visual and aural. But that Scene is chiefly a series of Visions, while this one is almost entirely concerned with what John hears; hence what we shall call the 'seven Words'. One cannot claim to find in it an unmistakable sevenfold structure; but the analysis offered here nevertheless seems to yield good sense.

[3] Ps. 137:1.

of the beast from the sea (13:1). She is therefore to be hated as
well as respected. Yet see how *attractive* she is—for while John
describes first the evil that upholds her, and only then her glamour
(verse 4), the simple soul is likely to be dazzled by the Beauty
before he notices the Beast. For her attractiveness she must be
feared. But John shows us finally how *repulsive* she is; what has
made her drunk is her apparent victory over those who witness
to the Christian truth she hates (verse 6), and for that she will be
shunned by all who hold truth dear.

It would be foolish to underestimate her. Even John finds
himself marvelling, as the inhabitants of the earth marvelled at
the beast (13:3). But he has been taken into a wilderness in order
to witness this Scene, and the wilderness 'represents the per-
petual condition of Christian detachment from the affairs of
civilization . . . It is from the "desert" that the Christian
is able to view civilization clearly, as it really is.'[1] Happy the
servant of God who sees worldliness for what it is, applies the
wise man's words in Proverbs 5 and 7 to this loosest of 'loose
women', and learns to respect and to hate, to fear and to shun
Babylon the whore.

2. THE SECOND WORD: THE MYSTERY OF BABYLON (17:7–18)

*But the angel said to me, 'Why marvel? I will tell you the mystery of the
woman, and of the beast with seven heads and ten horns that carries her.*

[8] *The beast that you saw was, and is not, and is to ascend from the
bottomless pit and go to perdition; and the dwellers on earth whose
names have not been written in the book of life from the foundation of the
world, will marvel to behold the beast, because it was and is not and is to
come.*

[9] *This calls for a mind with wisdom: the seven heads are seven hills
on which the woman is seated;*

[10] *they are also seven kings, five of whom have fallen, one is, the other
has not yet come, and when he comes he must remain only a little while.*
[11] *As for the beast that was and is not, it is an eighth but it belongs to
the seven, and it goes to perdition.*

[12] *And the ten horns that you saw are ten kings who have not yet*

[1] Kiddle, p. 339. See our comment on 12:6, 14 (pp. 118 f., 120 f.).

received royal power, but they are to receive authority as kings for one hour, together with the beast. [13] *These are of one mind and give over their power and authority to the beast;* [14] *they will make war on the Lamb, and the Lamb will conquer them, for he is Lord of lords and King of kings, and those with him are called and chosen and faithful.'*

[15] *And he said to me, 'The waters that you saw, where the harlot is seated, are peoples and multitudes and nations and tongues.*

[16] *And the ten horns that you saw, they and the beast will hate the harlot; they will make her desolate and naked, and devour her flesh and burn her up with fire,* [17] *for God has put it into their hearts to carry out his purpose by being of one mind and giving over their royal power to the beast, until the words of God shall be fulfilled.*

[18] *And the woman that you saw is the great city which has dominion over the kings of the earth.'*

Remember that 'I will tell you the mystery' does not mean 'I will give you the key to the puzzle.'[1] What seems at first glance to be a sizeable bunch of keys—the 'definitions' of verses 9 to 18—turns out on closer inspection to be of little use in unlocking the enigma of Babylon. But then that is not what the angel says he intends to do. Rather, he will *exhibit the picture* of Babylon; that, as we have come to see, is the real meaning of his words.

It is the 'mystery', not mysteries, of the woman and the beast; they are combined in a single picture. Indeed, it is not easy to separate them, because there is an ambiguity in the Babylon of this chapter which comes to light when one attempts to define her in terms of other visions in the book.

Is she the equivalent of Scene 4's beast from the sea (13:1)? We have taken that beast to represent the 'world', in the sense of human society without God; and when that world is collapsing, at the end of Scene 5, we are told that 'Babylon' is being made to drain the cup of the fury of God's wrath (16:19). In addition, we shall find in due course (in Scene 8) that the whore is to be replaced by the bride, Babylon by Jerusalem; and since Jerusalem stands for God's society, the church, Babylon presumably stands for godless society, the world.

But she can also be compared with the second beast of Scene 4, the one from the earth (13:11), which we have taken to be

[1] See p. 153 f.

false religion. The first beast is the institution; the second is the message. In support of this comparison we may note the close resemblance between the first beast and the creature which carries the woman (13:1; 17:3), while the second beast's activity is very like the seductions and deceptions practised by the woman herself (13:12–17; 17:2, 4, 18).

Perhaps this kind of ambiguity is the reason why the woman and the scarlet beast form a single mystery. They are to be regarded as one composite truth, somehow combining both the beasts of Scene 4. John is to learn something of its meaning, not by having it explained to him, but by having his mind focused on it in several different ways. He is involved in the same kind of process as that which showed him the heavenly truth of Scene 2 at varying focal lengths, so that he saw at one time the four horsemen and at another time the four winds, and so on.[1]

First his attention is drawn to the scarlet beast: not its appearance, but its career (verse 8). Where have we come across this 'was—is not—is to come' sequence before? First in Scene 1, as a description of the progress of the Christ: 'I am . . . the living one; I died, and behold I am alive' (1:17, 18). Next, Satan's counterfeit of that, in Scene 4, where the beast from the sea appears, then is mortally wounded, then revives from its fatal injury (13:3). The third occurrence is here in Scene 6. There will be another in Scene 7, where we shall find a period during which Satan himself 'is not', in a manner of speaking (20:1–3). It is a moot point whether the beast here is out of action in the same sense that Satan is rendered powerless there. The closest parallel to the passage before us is 13:3, and perhaps the kind of life, death, and resurrection suggested as an explanation of that verse (see p. 124 f.) is the threefold pattern which here causes the inhabitants of the earth to marvel. They do not see the eternal dimension which makes it in fact a fourfold pattern: for just as Christ lived, died, rose again, *and now lives for evermore*, so the beast was, is not, will rise again from the pit, *and will go to perdition*. Those whose names are 'written in the book of life' are aware of this. They know that however well the powers of evil, like Pharaoh's magicians, succeed in aping the power of God, in the end he will be the victor.[2]

---

[1] See pp. 78 f., 81.
[2] Ex. 7:22; 8:7, 18, 19.

Next, attention is focused on the creature's sevenfold head: and behold, it is a sevenfold hill (verse 9). Both are symbols of strength, one in the sense of leadership and authority and the other in the sense of solidity and permanence.[1] On the interpretation we are following, this shift of focus simply reveals the power of the beast under another aspect. Both for the original readers and for us the reference to seven hills would naturally evoke the city of Rome. But whether this was intended to be its basic meaning is open to question. To look *through* the picture of seven heads *to* the seven hills of Rome is to stop short of the vision's innermost truth. A deeper insight would look beyond not only the Head (authority) but also the Hill (solidity), and see the ultimate reality (strength) which is embodied in different ways in both of them. The fact that Rome is an actual example of a city on seven hills need be no more than a coincidence. That does not mean it is irrelevant or insignificant. It does mean that if, since prehistoric times, hilltops have had obvious strategic value as sites for human settlement, and if the number seven is deeply rooted in human consciousness as a number with mystical values, then it is not surprising to find that the visionary city and the actual one are in this respect alike.

The third aspect of the beast (verses 10, 11) is often used to locate it historically, in the same way that verse 9 seems to locate it geographically. The seven kings are taken to be a succession of Roman emperors, and we should be able, incidentally, to date John's vision in the reign of the sixth of them—if only we could work out who was to head the list, and who was to be included in it! There is no agreement on this, and, as Caird points out, 'there is no reason to think that John's first-century readers would have been in any better case than we are' in identifying the seven; 'perhaps, then, we have been looking for the wrong sort of solution.'[2] An alternative suggestion harks back to the statue in Nebuchadnezzar's dream (Dn. 2) which represented four successive world empires from Babylon to Rome; if the list were

---

[1] For 'head', note the words we derive from its Latin equivalent *caput* (capital, captain, chieftain, *etc.*); for 'hill', see pp. 156 f., and compare the Old Testament phrase 'the everlasting hills' (Gn. 49:26; Dt. 33:15; Hab. 3:6).

[2] Caird, p. 128.

begun from the start of Israel's history, Egypt and Assyria would precede Babylon, and make Rome not the fourth, but the sixth, with Rome's successors (whatever they may be) as the seventh.[1]

Again, these historical facts may well, in the providence of God, coincide with the pattern the angel describes. But as always, the archetype is greater than its copy. If the Head means authority and the Mountain durability, the real meaning of the sevenfold King is political power. And Christians of *any* century have been able to look back over a succession of worldly governments ('five . . . have fallen'), have recognized another power in their own time ('one is'), and have normally expected the system to continue at least for a while longer (the seventh yet to come and remain for a little).[2]

Verse 11 then merges two symbols, and says that in regarding the beast's heads as kings, we have found an appropriate image for the beast itself also. It too is a king: 'it is an eighth but it belongs to the seven', *i.e.* it is another of the same kind. If they are empires, the beast is Empire with a capital E. The King symbol is useful here, because unlike the Head and the Mountain, seven kings can be listed by John in a sequence, to convey the variable fortunes and final doom of the beast.

Fourthly, John's attention is drawn to the horns, yet another biblical symbol of strength (verses 12–14). As the heads immediately turned into hills, so the horns at once become kings. The ten differ from the seven in being explicitly future, and in holding power for only one hour (a very brief period compared with the symbolic weeks, months, and years which abound in Revelation). Their unanimous support of the beast and their final defeat by the Lamb are other features which we shall take up again in connection with verses 16 and 17.

The grouping of these four points to form the first part of the angel's discourse, with three points still to come (yet another seven stitched unobtrusively into the fabric!), recalls similar groupings in earlier Scenes. The angel recommences with a fifth look at the mystery: the waters under the beast and the woman (verse 15). The identification of these as a multitude of

[1] So, for example, J. A. Seiss, quoted at length in Walvoord, pp. 251–254.
[2] The RSV's *'only* a little while' is incorrect.

nations, as in Isaiah 17:12, has been referred to already (see p. 159).

Sixthly, we have another look into the future (verses 16, 17), previewing a remarkable split in the ranks of evil. The beast's ten horns turn against the woman and destroy her. 'How can Satan cast out Satan?' How indeed? But our Lord's words go far to explain these verses; for 'if Satan has risen up against himself and is divided, he cannot stand, but is coming to an end' (Mk. 3:23–26). What would clarify them further would be teaching elsewhere in Scripture about a prophesied rising of evil powers, which for a short period (verse 12) will promote the beast's cause with such fanatical singlemindedness (verse 13) that even the historic alliance with false religion will be for-sworn (verse 16) as serving no further useful purpose: the iron hand is revealed, there is no more need for the velvet glove. As usually happens among revolutionaries, the men of high-minded theory will be replaced by the men of blood. The brief rule of the ten takes us up to the point when God's plan is completed (verse 17); in line with this, the description of the Lamb who defeats them is very like that of Christ in his ultimate victory (verse 14; *cf.* 19:11–16). We have in fact found allusions to an episode of this kind, in 11:7–13.[1] It is the time of the great rebellion, when Satan's power will be finally unmasked. The beast repudiates his former ally, the woman, discarding persuasion in order to rely on naked power. But as Christ says, in the words quoted above, things are at a desperate stage when dog begins to eat dog: 'If Satan has risen up against himself', he must be 'coming to an end.' That is one comfort; and the other is that even the rule of the ten is not outside the plan of God (verse 17).

Lastly the angel focuses on the woman herself (verse 18). In what sense is she the great world city? If she is to be identified with one of the beasts of Scene 4 rather than the other, the angel's exposition in this Scene has gradually established her identity with the second beast, false religion, while the first beast there corresponds to the scarlet beast here. The beast is the institution, the woman the ideology. Thus although the beast will in the end exist in its own right, without needing to justify itself by appealing to any ideology (verse 16), for most of human

[1] See pp. 106 f.

history the Satanic ideology of godlessness governs the powers of this world, and the powers in their turn dominate mankind. In the words of Revelation, the woman is enthroned on the beast, and the beast on many waters.

3. THE THIRD WORD: THE FALL OF BABYLON (18:1-3)

After this I saw another angel coming down from heaven, having great authority; and the earth was made bright with his splendour. ²And he called out with a mighty voice, 'Fallen, fallen is Babylon the great! It has become a dwelling place of demons, a haunt of every foul spirit, a haunt of every foul and hateful bird; ³for all nations have drunk the wine of her impure passion, and the kings of the earth have committed fornication with her, and the merchants of the earth have grown rich with the wealth of her wantonness.'

The first angel has confronted John with the mystery of Babylon, and has then made him face one aspect after another of the beast and the woman who comprise it. We may or may not reckon to have grasped the meaning of his long discourse (17:7-18), but have we grasped its menace? The reader who has not been frightened by it has not begun to understand it. The 'power of evil' in the Satanism of cheap fiction is a mere pantomime demon compared with this description of the real thing. The angel scours the dictionary of metaphor to find synonyms of power to apply to the beast. Neither dare we underestimate the persuasiveness of the woman. We may react to the glamour of 17:4 with a shudder—'How cheap, how tawdry!'—because that is what we think is expected of us. But in practice, in daily life, the pearls and the purple and the golden cup have an awful fascination. The world *is* powerful, its message *is* attractive, and we know what it is to be like the bird held by the glittering eye of the snake.

This is why the spell needs to be broken by a voice of even greater authority. The second angel comes from heaven, with a glory brighter and a voice more compelling than that of Babylon, to declare again that vital part of the divine message which assures us of her final downfall.[1] It is the message which the

[1] See 14:8.

finger of God once wrote over the actual historical Babylon: 'God has numbered the days of your kingdom and brought it to an end' (Dn. 5:26). Whether it is totalitarian repression or decadent capitalism which Christians have to cope with, they need to be reminded that neither the beast nor the woman is permanently in power, despite all the symbolism of the 'everlasting hills', and that one day their universal dominion will be in retrospect no more than a nightmare from which one has awakened.

4. THE FOURTH WORD: THE JUDGMENT OF BABYLON (18:4-20)

Then I heard another voice from heaven saying, 'Come out of her, my people, lest you take part in her sins, lest you share in her plagues; ⁵for her sins are heaped high as heaven, and God has remembered her iniquities. ⁶Render to her as she herself has rendered, and repay her double for her deeds; mix a double draught for her in the cup she mixed. ⁷As she glorified herself and played the wanton, so give her a like measure of torment and mourning. Since in her heart she says, "A queen I sit, I am no widow, mourning I shall never see," ⁸so shall her plagues come in a single day, pestilence and mourning and famine, and she shall be burned with fire; for mighty is the Lord God who judges her.'

⁹And the kings of the earth, who committed fornication and were wanton with her, will weep and wail over her when they see the smoke of her burning; ¹⁰they will stand far off, in fear of her torment, and say, 'Alas! alas! thou great city, thou mighty city, Babylon! In one hour has thy judgment come.'

¹¹And the merchants of the earth weep and mourn for her, since no one buys their cargo any more, ¹²cargo of gold, silver, jewels and pearls, fine linen, purple, silk and scarlet, all kinds of scented wood, all articles of ivory, all articles of costly wood, bronze, iron and marble, ¹³cinnamon, spice, incense, myrrh, frankincense, wine, oil, fine flour and wheat, cattle and sheep, horses and chariots, and slaves, that is, human souls. ¹⁴'The fruit for which thy soul longed has gone from thee, and all thy dainties and thy splendour are lost to thee, never to be found again!' ¹⁵The merchants of these wares, who gained wealth from her, will stand far off, in fear of her torment, weeping and mourning aloud, ¹⁶'Alas, alas, for the great city that was clothed in fine linen, in purple and scarlet, bedecked with *gold, with jewels, and with pearls! * [17] *In one hour all this wealth has been laid waste.'*

And all shipmasters and seafaring men, sailors and all whose trade is on the sea, stood far off [18] *and cried out as they saw the smoke of her burning, 'What city was like the great city?'* [19] *And they threw dust on their heads, as they wept and mourned, crying out, 'Alas, alas, for the great city where all who had ships at sea grew rich by her wealth! In one hour she has been laid waste.*

[20] *Rejoice over her, O heaven, O saints and apostles and prophets, for God has given judgment for you against her!'*

The fall of historical Babylon in 539 BC, marking the end of the Chaldean or neo-Babylonian Empire, is the subject of several Old Testament prophecies. The next heavenly voice echoes their language in this fourth Word about mystical Babylon. The parallel chapters are Isaiah 13, 14, 47, Jeremiah 50, 51, and Habakkuk 2. We find there many of the features of Revelation 18: Babylon's pride and luxury, the golden cup with which she intoxicates the nations, her wickedness and the punishment due to it; the suddenness of her fiery destruction, the total desolation that results, and the horror of those who have come to depend on her; and the warning to God's people not to be involved in her sin and its penalty.

A curious verse in one of these prophecies calls Babylon a 'destroying *mountain*' (Je. 51:25). It reminds us that we are in the realms of symbolism; for Babylonia was the flattest of flat lands, and its capital was situated, as Jeremiah says in the same chapter, 'by many waters' (51:13). The streams of the Euphrates, like Arnold's river Oxus 'shorn and parcell'd', aptly represent the many nations over which Babylon ruled. Rome, on the other hand, sat on seven hills, thereby indicating the strength and (apparent) durability of its empire. It should not surprise us therefore when Ezekiel 27 and 28, a further prophecy which shows many resemblances to Revelation 18, turns out to refer to yet another city—Tyre, the great port on the Mediterranean coast of Palestine. For the commercial empire of Tyre was particularly well suited to symbolize a third aspect of the 'world'—its affluence (verses 12, 13). The whore herself is greater than any of these cities. The hills of Rome, the streams of Babylon, the seas of Tyre, are all called in to illustrate different aspects of her. But she, the ethos of humanist society, is the reality behind all of them.

The merchandise of Tyre, the harlot's finery, is paraded daily before the eyes of men. The underprivileged desire it, the privileged desire more of it; it seduces all the nations. But God's people will see it in its context, in the total picture; they know that Tyre is Rome is Babylon, and as the summons of verse 4 brings to their minds yet another city of wickedness—the Sodom from which Lot was called out (Gn. 19:12 ff.)—they see in prospect 'the smoke of her burning' (verse 9). Unlike worldly Lot, they understand the issue clearly enough to 'come out of her', and to 'rejoice' over her judgment (verse 20).

5. THE FIFTH WORD: THE DEATH OF BABYLON (18:21–24)

Then a mighty angel took up a stone like a great millstone and threw it into the sea, saying, 'So shall Babylon the great city be thrown down with violence, and shall be found no more; [22]*and the sound of harpers and minstrels, of flute players and trumpeters, shall be heard in thee no more; and a craftsman of any craft shall be found in thee no more; and the sound of the millstone shall be heard in thee no more;* [23]*and the light of a lamp shall shine in thee no more; and the voice of bridegroom and bride shall be heard in thee no more; for thy merchants were the great men of the earth; and all nations were deceived by thy sorcery.* [24]*And in her was found the blood of prophets and of saints, and of all who have been slain on earth.'*

The tumult of the waters, as the great boulder is hurled into the sea, dies down to a flat calm. All the more impressive because of its rarity, in a book where destruction is normally accompanied by clamorous noise, is the silence which closes in on Babylon's death. As the lamps of the city go out, a fearful stillness descends: no more the sounds of leisure or industry or human relationship. The stone sinks beneath the surface, and civilization is as though it had never been.

The acted parable of the stone, the cessation of ordinary life, and the responsibility for the martyrs' blood, are all spoken of by

Jeremiah (51:63 f.; 25:10; 51:49), and the last two find additional echoes in the Gospels (Mt. 24:37-42; 23:29-39). The last one
is particularly meaningful. The murderer denounced by Jeremiah is Babylon. But when Jesus makes the same charge, the
name of the accused is Jerusalem. John reserves this name for the
whore's successor, the bride, God's city; he avoids using it here,
or in chapter 11, when speaking of the place where Christ was
crucified. But still that is the place—old Jerusalem—where lies
the responsibility for the death of God's servants. Thus a fifth
city, besides Babylon, Rome, Tyre, and Sodom, is assimilated
to the image of the whore, indicating yet once again that she
herself is a spiritual reality greater than any of them.

6. THE SIXTH WORD: THE DOOM SONG OF BABYLON (19:1-5)

*After this I heard what seemed to be the loud voice of a great multitude
in heaven, crying, 'Hallelujah! Salvation and glory and power belong to
our God,* ²*for his judgments are true and just; he has judged the great
harlot who corrupted the earth with her fornication, and he has avenged
on her the blood of his servants.'*

³*Once more they cried, 'Hallelujah! The smoke from her goes up for
ever and ever.'*

⁴*And the twenty-four elders and the four living creatures fell down and
worshipped God who is seated on the throne, saying, 'Amen. Hallelujah!'*
⁵*And from the throne came a voice crying, 'Praise our God, all you his
servants, you who fear him, small and great.'*

'What seemed to be the loud voice of a great multitude'—the
sound, contrasting with the silence of 18:22 f., comes indistinctly
across vast distances, for we are back again in the eternal perspectives of Scene 2. The vision of the fell horsemen in that
Scene (chapter 6) would have been intolerable, had John not been
given the proper setting in which to see it; so first he was shown
the divine order, the circles of heaven, within which such evils
take their appointed place to the glory of God (chapters 4, 5).
So here. Small and clear in the foreground we have seen Babylon
on the Euphrates, Jeremiah's Babylon, and looming behind it the
spiritual reality, John's Babylon, which for a century or two it

embodied. But now even spiritual Babylon is merely an actor on a stage, watched by the numberless multitudes of the heavenly world. What is taking place on the tiny stage, which is our world, elicits from that immense audience acclamations which rise to the throne of God.

Again the formality of a diagram may be useful. In the centre let us imagine God's earth, his original creation. Within it is his church, the new creation, the twice-born. These two are like concentric circles, one inside the other. From below reaches up the power of Satan to gain hold of them. It comes as a voice, a message, presenting evil as the serpent offered the fruit in Eden, 'good for food . . . a delight to the eyes . . . to be desired to make one wise' (Gn. 3:6); and the mouthpiece of this Satanic gospel is Babylon the whore. Through her he sets about his twofold project of destroying the servants of God, the inner circle, and corrupting the earth, the outer circle. But from above God reaches down, with salvation both for his church and for his world, and glory and power which more than equal Babylon's. His voice speaks judgment; Babylon the destroyer is finally herself destroyed; and church and world are safe for ever. No wonder praises go up from the throng of spectators, not least from the representatives of those who benefit from God's justice—the elders, standing for his church, and the living creatures, standing for his world.

7. THE SEVENTH WORD: THE SUCCESSOR OF BABYLON (19:6–8)

Then I heard what seemed to be the voice of a great multitude, like the sound of many waters and like the sound of mighty thunderpeals, crying, 'Hallelujah! For the Lord our God the Almighty reigns. ⁷Let us rejoice and exult and give him the glory, for the marriage of the Lamb has come, and his Bride has made herself ready; ⁸it was granted her to be clothed with fine linen, bright and pure'—for the fine linen is the righteous deeds of the saints.

The seventh division is like the corresponding section of almost every other Scene, in that it takes us beyond the end of history. This Scene has dealt exclusively with the godless world; but since by the time Word 7 is spoken that world is no more, what particular aspect of eternity might we expect it to deal with? The answer is Babylon's rival and successor. After the whore, the bride.

Where a distinction has had to be made between the whore and the beast she rides, it has seemed increasingly that the latter represents godless society as an institution, while the former symbolizes its ideology or message. The bride, however, seems to be a single figure uniting both concepts, since she represents nothing if not a society, and is thus the counterpart of the beast, as well as being obviously the counterpart of the whore, Jerusalem over against Babylon.

The last Word is at all events a shout of acclamation, on an even grander scale than Word 6, at the apotheosis of the bride. The final coming of the reign of God means the coming of the Lamb's wedding feast, and his bride is ready. See, as she comes at last on the scene, the contrast with what has gone before. For two whole distasteful chapters the complex magnificence of the whore has been detailed. But the wedding dress of the bride is utterly simple, and is described in half a verse: 'fine linen, bright and pure . . . the righteous deeds of the saints'. From one point of view she has made the dress herself; she has worked out her own salvation (verse 7; Phil. 2:12). From another, 'it was given unto her', for God has been at work in her (verse 8, RV; Phil. 2:13). The second is the deeper truth, and is the one dwelt on by Paul in the passage in Ephesians 5:25–27 where he speaks of the marriage between Christ and the church. All is the work of God: both the destruction of old Babylon, on which Scene 6 has concentrated, and the creation of new Jerusalem, which is to have the whole of a later Scene to itself.

8. THESE ARE TRUE WORDS OF GOD (19:9, 10)

And the angel said to me, 'Write this: Blessed are those who are invited to the marriage supper of the Lamb.'

And he said to me, 'These are true words of God.'

10 Then I fell down at his feet to worship him, but he said to me, 'You must not do that! I am a fellow servant with you and your brethren who hold the testimony of Jesus. Worship God.' For the testimony of Jesus is the spirit of prophecy.

John is now to write a postscript to his account of Scene 6. As the lengthy description of the whore has been followed by a very brief passage describing the bride (19:8), so the prolonged lament of the whore's devotees is contrasted with the briefest of statements about the blessing of those invited to the wedding of the bride and the Lamb.[1]

The rsv is no doubt right in assuming that 'he' who is now speaking to John (verse 9, av, rv), is the angel who first introduced the scene in 17:1. But the revelation has been overwhelming, and John so far forgets himself as to fall in worship at the feet of the speaker, mere angel though he be. This of course is quite improper, as the angel reminds him; but it is understandable. For let us recall what John has seen. Each revelation has been more awesome than the last, and in one way Scene 6 surpasses all earlier scenes. Five tremendous Words have described the pomp and power of Satan's activity in the world. But the Babylon they set before us is a city doomed to perish; and the viewpoint of the last two Words is that of a camera tracking backwards and upwards to heights from which Babylon's smoking ruin is first dwarfed by the host of heavenly spectators (Word 6) and then lost to sight altogether (Word 7). No wonder John is overcome with awe. The monstrous power of evil which tyrannizes the world—is that all it will come to?

> '. . . Dost thou lie so low?
> Are all thy conquests, glories, triumphs, spoils,
> Shrunk to this little measure?'[2]

Yes; and to see Babylon like this in its right perspective should affect the Christian's whole outlook. It should restore his sense of proportion, and therefore his assurance, his hope, his confidence, courage, and joy. It makes his problems *manageable*.

The headings we have used for this Scene (seven Words) were suggested by the fact that it does consist of utterances rather than visions, as the angel points out here in verse 9b. These words, says he, 'are true words of God'. John must have both

---

[1] With the distinction between the bride and the wedding guests, *cf.* the woman and her children in 12:17 (p. 122).

[2] Shakespeare, *Julius Caesar*, III i.

known and felt that what he heard spoken by 'the tongues of men and of angels' was no less than the word of the Almighty; that was why he fell at the angel's feet.

The meaning of the last sentence of verse 10, however, is not immediately clear. Does it mean, 'He who has the spirit of prophecy will witness to Jesus', or does it mean, 'He who has the witness of Jesus will prophesy'? The more acceptable meaning will be the one which fits in better with the general sense of the passage; and the view taken here is that the second interpretation is more likely, the sentence being part of the angel's reply (not a separate statement as in RSV). The angel will not let himself be worshipped, and wants John to realize that both of them stand on a level as servants of God. It is true that he has been uttering words which have struck John with awe. But John himself has 'the witness of Jesus'; therefore he too can prophesy, and has words to proclaim which are just as amazing.[1]

And those words are before us. Are *we* awestruck? Certainly, John must not worship the angel; neither do we dream of worshipping John, still less his book. But he who has never been tempted has no cause to be proud of his virtue. Most of us, to our shame, seldom come within hailing distance of such a temptation. To open ourselves to these mighty words with such abandon that their impact brings us to our knees in worship— that is something to be sought; once we get that far, we shall soon be put right if our disoriented praise happens to be aimed too low.

---

[1] 'John discourages angel-worship . . . not by abasing angels, but by exalting Christians' (Kiddle, p. 383).

19:11–21:8

SCENE 7:
THE DRAMA BEHIND HISTORY:
seven Visions of ultimate reality

THE MILLENNIUM

WE come in this Scene to one of the most difficult, or at any rate one of the most disputed, parts of the book. See what your commentator has to say about Revelation 20, and you will get a good idea of his approach to the rest. The millennium, the 'thousand years', is plain to behold in every verse from 20:2 to 20:7; but its place in the general scheme of Christian history is much less obvious. Interpreters generally divide three ways over the question. A cross-section of comment on the millennium, however, reveals more than the mere problem of where it fits in. For one thing, the issue is complicated by all sorts of subdivisions, which can be allotted little more than a passing reference here. For another, one's understanding of the millennium is not reached in isolation from one's study of the rest of the book, or indeed the rest of Scripture. In other words, the three interpretations of chapter 20 have both branches and roots; and it is to the latter that we shall be paying more attention.

Even shorn of extra complications, the problem cannot be stated without a good deal of detail. To simplify it too drastically is to miss it altogether. We note at the outset, therefore, the numerous items that have to be borne in mind.

a. The data of the problem

First, it is agreed that the parousia, the return of Christ in glory, has been described at least once before chapter 20 begins: many would say immediately before, in 19:11, 12, but even if not there it has appeared in other earlier chapters.

Secondly, chapter 21 begins with a description of the new age, in which the various evils of chapter 20 no longer exist.

Thirdly, between these are the events of chapter 20. Satan is seized, bound, thrown down and sealed in the bottomless pit; for a thousand years he will be unable to deceive the nations (verses 2, 3). For the same period, the martyred and/or faithful saints live and reign with Christ: this is described as the 'first resurrection' (verses 4, 5). At the end of it, Satan is released and mounts a final assault on the saints (verses 7–9). He is overthrown and destroyed (verses 9, 10); the rest of the dead rise and are judged (verses 5, 12, 13); and together with Satan, the beast, the false prophet, Death, and Hades, all whose names are not in the book of life are thrown into the lake of fire, which is the 'second death' (verses 10, 14, 15). There is a clear sequence here, for events are listed according to whether they take place before, during, or at the end of the millennium. To recapitulate, we have the binding of Satan, then the thousand-year reign of the saints, then Satan's last revolt and its defeat, then judgment and the elimination of all evil.

Fourthly, there are several other events spoken of elsewhere in the New Testament, some or all of which belong to the time of the end, and are therefore related in some way, one presumes, to the sequence of Revelation 20. They include the worldwide spread of the gospel, the salvation of Israel, the 'great apostasy' or falling away, the 'great tribulation', the coming of the 'man of lawlessness' or Antichrist, and the 'rapture', or the catching up of the saints 'to meet the Lord in the air' (1 Thes. 4:17).

The three different pictures which can be built up from these jigsaw pieces are known as the premillennialist, amillennialist, and postmillennialist views of Revelation. The reason for these names will become apparent as we consider each of them.

b. Premillennialism

Premillennialism is rooted in the belief that the truth of Revelation is basically a literal truth; and that in two respects. First, *description* is to be taken at its face value. This does not necessarily mean a crass literalism which would involve, for instance, imagining Satan to be physically bound (spirit being though he is) with an actual metal chain. But it may very well mean a literal thousand years; and it certainly does mean a binding of Satan and a reign of the saints such that his helplessness will be unmistakable, and their authority will be manifest, in a way which has never yet been known.

Secondly, *sequence* is to be taken as it stands. In the order of history, the binding of Satan will follow the parousia, because in the order of the book chapter 20 follows chapter 19. It is agreed that this chapter is the only place in Scripture where the idea of a millennium following the parousia seems to be clearly taught. But taking its order seriously means that this sequence of events, though unique, has just as much authority as the outline given, for example, in Matthew 24; therefore it is to be regarded not as a mere underlining of something already contained in our Lord's teaching in that place, but as the addition to it of extra truth which was there omitted. The teaching of the passage is 'extensive', not intensive.

The interpretation which grows from these roots is, in summary, as follows. Christ's return in power and glory will deprive Satan of all his power, raise the Christian dead, and set up the kingdom of the saints on earth. After a thousand years, Satan will re-emerge from his imprisonment, attempt once more to destroy the saints, fail, and be destroyed himself. Then will come the resurrection of the rest of the dead, the judgment of the great white throne, the final destruction of the wicked, and the making of a new heaven and earth. Events of the fourth group mentioned above (those found in other parts of the New Testament—the appearing of Antichrist, the tribulation, the rapture, and so forth) are usually held to have taken place before Christ's coming in victory, and that in turn comes before (*pre-*) the millennium: hence the name of this interpretation.

Because of its literal approach, premillennialism is open to two kinds of danger. Taking the descriptions of Revelation too naively has led in the past to the excesses of what is known as 'chiliasm',[1] an expectation of a thoroughly materialistic 'rule of the saints' which appeals to the worst instincts of men. Attempts

[1] From the Greek word for 'thousand'. For a detailed study of chiliasm in the Middle Ages, see Norman Cohn, *The Pursuit of the Millennium* (Secker & Warburg, 1957).

to take its sequence too pedantically, on the other hand, and to build them into a detailed time chart, can lead to excess of another kind: prolonged debate as to whether the tribulation precedes or follows the rapture, detailed calculations of the 'times of the Gentiles' or the length of the 'little season', a futurist view of the book which makes its practical contribution to Christian living little more than a vicarious thrill, or explorations of the wilder reaches of dispensationalism.[1] Where chiliasm promised to feed the hunger of the belly, such ingenuities feed the vanity of the mind.

But the positive value of present-day premillennialism is that it has refused to treat Revelation as a book shackled either to the personal mysticism of John or to the remote historical circumstances of the first century. It may overreact against the older liberal notions which did this, and thereby kept the book's immediate challenge at arm's length; but it does at least take Revelation seriously as a message from God for our own time, and the time to come.

c. Amillennialism

The view of the amillennialist arises from a different understanding of the sense in which Revelation is 'true'. He holds that neither descriptions nor sequences can be taken at their face value. So much description in the book is (indeed is actually stated to be) symbolic rather than literal, that he presumes this to be John's general rule, and non-metaphorical language to be the exception. The chain and the pit are not literal; probably, then, neither are the thousand years. He still has to decide, of course, which is symbol and which is not, and then how the symbols are to be explained. If he is wise, he will do so not by a subjective judgment but by a comparison with the rest of Scripture.

This, moreover, is the only way he can interpret the sequences

[1] Walvoord's comment on 19:9 (p. 273; our italics) well illustrates the theory that God 'dispenses' grace to men by different methods in different ages: 'The wife of the Lamb is distinguished from the attendants at the wedding, the wife apparently being *the church*, and the attendants at the wedding *the saints of past and future ages*. The *unfounded notion* that God treats all saints of all ages exactly alike is hard to displace in the theology of the church'—perhaps because the apostles cemented it in place too well!

of the book. The premillennialist believes in an actual millennium, which, though mentioned nowhere else, nevertheless stands in its own right on the basis of Revelation 20, and is therefore to be built on to the existing fabric of prophecy. The amillennialist, not believing this, has to find some other way of fitting in the thousand years, and (again if he is wise) will try to do so in terms of the rest of Scripture.

Let us see what grows from these roots. The New Testament knows of only one parousia, and that is the 'day of the Lord' which will end all things. If this 'end' is described in chapter 19, then the thousand years described in chapter 20, even though they follow it in the book, must precede it in actual history; in a word, 20:1-6 is a flashback. The binding of Satan, the first resurrection, and the millennium are all metaphors for the present situation in this world, covering the period between the first and second comings of Christ. There is still to come the last revolt of evil, which is held to be the setting for such other predicted events as the great tribulation and the appearing of the man of lawlessness. It will be ended by Satan's overthrow and the judgment, which are described not only in 20:9-15 but also in 19:11-21. On this view, Christ will return without (a-) any millennium of the kind envisaged in other interpretations, that is, a thousand years which are only one section of Christian history, distinguished from the greater part by its extremes of good and evil.

The danger of such an approach is that when particular symbols are 'explained away' as general truths, they tend to lose their force. The hard edges are blurred; the immediacy, the expectancy, is toned down. The amillennialist must remember that the the truths he claims to see beyond the metaphors are not vague spiritualizations, but demanding realities: not less, but more, solid than the stuff of his vision.

Indeed, this points up the special value of the amillennialist view. Which is more real, a 'spiritual' reign of the saints which is in fact the present church age, or an actual earthly reign of the saints after Christ's return? The latter is concrete and definite, and fosters Christian hope. But the former, by the very fact of being a generalization, challenges Christian experience not only yesterday and tomorrow, but *today*.

d. Postmillennialism

Suppose you do not feel able wholly to accept either of these views. As regards the sequence of events, the simplicity of the amillennialist time scheme, with its single 'day of the Lord' destroying evil and bringing history to an end, seems more in accordance with the plainer prophecies of the New Testament. You feel that the complexities of Revelation are less likely to be an extension to the basic scheme (extra pieces tacked on to a patchwork quilt) than to be a repetition of it in different words (the working-over in paint of a pencil sketch). So far as the description of the millennium is concerned, however, you side with the premillennialists, in hoping for a rather more effective 'binding of Satan' and 'reign of the saints' than most of the Christian centuries seem to have experienced. You would expect there to be, near the end of history, one period when the power of evil will be markedly less, and the authority of the church markedly greater, than at any previous time. You are a 'literalist' to the extent that you look to see Satan chained and the saints crowned, if not physically, yet still in a more obvious way than the vague 'spiritual' binding and crowning of which the amillennialists speak. If this is how you interpret Revelation 20, you are a 'postmillennialist'. You envisage a thousand years, which may or may not be a literal thousand years, but which is certainly a special period distinguished from the rest of history by the way good triumphs over evil in the course of it. Some have understood this in terms of social improvement; others, truer to the biblical emphasis, have looked for a great spiritual advance, with the conversion of Jewry on the largest scale (Rom. 11:12) and the gospel 'preached throughout the whole world, as a testimony to all nations; and then the end will come' (Mt. 24:14). There will be a single climax to history, the parousia; and it will come after (post-) the millennium.

Whatever his view of prophecy, every Christian is an optimist, because he knows that God is ultimately in control. But taking the third view could make him more optimistic than he really has a right to be, since it tends to concentrate on the promises of success for the church and to play down the equally numerous warnings of coming trouble. The danger of being too sure that

things are inevitably on the upgrade is of course that one becomes complacent about them, and misses the urgency of Christ's
summons to zeal and watchfulness. What may nevertheless be
said in favour of postmillennialism is that, at its best, it sets before
us an inspiring vision of the church as it might be, were all its
members to realize the challenge of worldwide evangelism.
There were Christians who thought they saw the golden age
dawning in the days of nineteenth-century colonialism, when the
opening up of 'dark continents' was followed by an unprecedented
spread of the twin benefits (as they seemed then) of civilization
and Christianity. There is a very postmillennial ring about many
of the missionary hymns we have inherited from the Victorians.
The gloom of our own century has made us take a rather more
realistic view of the difficulties of the task. But we should not give
up reaching after an ideal simply because we fail to grasp it.

e. Conclusion

Each interpretation of Revelation 20 can thus have spiritual
value. The question remains, which is the value that we are
actually intended to find in it? Having considered all three, which
one do we opt for? It is a matter once more of inspecting their
roots, and of asking ourselves not only which we should choose,
but why. In what sense do we understand both the general
outline and the descriptive phrases of chapter 20 to be 'true'?

In the matter of description, the view of this book is that the
practice of the rest of the New Testament must be normative;
and the conclusions of a detailed study (for which we have no
space here) would appear to show that the apostolic church would
have understood language like that of Revelation 20 to be highly
symbolic, and mostly timeless. What those first Christians would
have thought the symbols were meant to represent is suggested
in the comments on the text of this Scene. As regards those parts
of the chapter which they would not think to be timeless, but
which should be fitted somehow into a scheme or sequence of
events, there also Revelation should not stand on its own as an
independent framework, but should be taken as a repetition in
highly coloured language of the sequence already made sufficiently clear in the non-symbolic teaching of the Gospels and

Letters. The resulting interpretation is therefore along amillennialist lines; and it is hoped that enough is said in the course of this exposition to commend such a view as being neither odd nor unscriptural, and to bring out what it means in terms of applying the teaching of Revelation to the spiritual needs of today.

I. SCENE 7 OPENS: THE FIRST VISION: THE CAPTAIN OF THE ARMIES OF HEAVEN (19:11-16)

Then I saw heaven opened, and behold, a white horse! He who sat upon it is called Faithful and True, and in righteousness he judges and makes war. [12] *His eyes are like a flame of fire, and on his head are many diadems; and he has a name inscribed which no one knows but himself.* [13] *He is clad in a robe dipped in blood, and the name by which he is called is The Word of God.*

[14] *And the armies of heaven, arrayed in fine linen, white and pure, followed him on white horses.*

[15] *From his mouth issues a sharp sword with which to smite the nations, and he will rule them with a rod of iron; he will tread the wine press of the fury of the wrath of God the Almighty.* [16] *On his robe and on his thigh he has a name inscribed, King of kings and Lord of lords.*

'The heavens were opened', says the prophet Ezekiel in the first verse of his book, 'and I saw visions of God.' Practically every such opening of heaven mentioned in Scripture reveals such visions, and the beginning of Scene 7 of the Revelation is no exception. The superficial likeness between the rider on the white horse here and the one in Scene 2 (6:2) is belied not only by factors we noted when considering chapter 6, but by the differing settings of the two Scenes. There, the rider is as it were contained within the sealed book, and the book is in the hands of the Lamb, and the Lamb stands in the midst of a vast concourse of spectators. For all his awesomeness, that rider is cut down to size by the perspectives of his surroundings. This one, however, irrupts on to the stage of the drama and immediately fills it with his divine presence.

For his divinity is placarded before our eyes three times over, at beginning, middle, and end of the Vision. The title 'The Word' (verse 13) is found also in the opening verses of both the Gospel and the first Letter of John, and 'Faithful and True' (verse 11) and 'King of kings and Lords of lords' (verse 16) occur in previous chapters of Revelation, one in the earliest and the other in the latest Scene we have read (3:14, Scene 1; 17:14, Scene 6). All three names belong to Jesus Christ, and a comparison between this vision and the description of Christ in chapter 1 will show yet more points of similarity.

Besides the parallels which serve to identify the rider as Christ, there are other reminiscences too. His followers, his iron rule, and the treading of the wine press of God's anger, all reappear from Scene 4 (14:4; 12:5; 14:19, 20). The threads are being gathered together, to be tied into a memorable knot.

Much of this language is drawn from more remote sources. We can go back even beyond Ezekiel's sight of the opened heaven, to the descriptions in Isaiah 63:1–6 of one bloodstained from the trampling of the wine press, in Isaiah 11:3, 4 of one who judges in righteousness and smites the earth, and in Psalm 2:8, 9 of one who breaks the nations with a rod of iron. The whole is a picture of great sternness. Is there any prophecy more heartwarming than that which ends with Isaiah 11:9, 'They shall not hurt or destroy in all my holy mountain'? Yet is there not at the heart of even that vision of the Lord's goodness the plain statement that 'with the breath of his lips he shall slay the wicked' (verse 4)? The two sides of the divine character, 'the kindness and the severity of God' (Rom. 11:22), are equally plain to see when we look at Scene 1, and find that it is the Faithful and True who will both reward the church at Philadelphia (3:7 ff.) and reject the church at Laodicea (3:14 ff.).

If these chapters of Revelation are meant to have a time scheme into which this passage fits, it may be interpreted as the victorious Christ riding forth to his last battle. It should be pointed out, however, that the passage itself says nothing about a 'last' battle. Apart from the reference to Psalm 2 ('he will rule them'), there is not even a verb in the future tense anywhere in these verses. They describe not what Christ *is going to do* but what he *is*: conquering King, righteous Judge, Captain of the armies of heaven. It will only be at his parousia that 'every eye will *see* him' like that (1:7); but at no time, not even on the cross, has he ever *been* anything other than that. Many a scripture encourages

us to believe that his heavenly army, which includes us as well as
the angels, is being led out even today to fight with evil, and
that men are being brought even now to the 'judgment', or
krisis (which is the Greek word for it), of decision.[1]

2. THE SECOND VISION: HIS VICTORY IS SURE (19:17, 18)

*Then I saw an angel standing in the sun, and with a loud voice he called
to all the birds that fly in midheaven, 'Come, gather for the great supper
of God,* [18]*to eat the flesh of kings, the flesh of captains, the flesh of
mighty men, the flesh of horses and their riders, and the flesh of all men,
both free and slave, both small and great.'*

It is scarcely possible to meditate on Revelation without a
'silence for about half an hour' not only after the seventh Seal,
but at the end of every other Scene also. Each one builds to a
breathtaking climax, and leaves you wondering what more can
possibly be said. A few pages back we were engrossed in the
closing section of Scene 6, the stupendous seventh Word:
'the voice of a great multitude, like the sound of many waters and
like the sound of mighty thunderpeals, crying, "Hallelujah!
For the Lord our God the Almighty reigns." ' Handel's setting
of the text is but a faint echo of the heavenly music that resounds
in the mind which tries to imagine this.

Yet Scene 7 has truth still more concentrated, still more
powerfully drawn. Vision 1 superimposed on the outline of a
horseman images of Christ taken from all over Scripture; and
now Vision 2 reveals an angel, or rather *'one* angel' (RV mg.),
instead of the many who have acted as the divine mouthpiece
up to now. It is as though all of them are merged into one, and
that one stands 'in the sun', where all the light is focused in a
single burning spot. His message is that the birds of the air may
expect a feast of carrion when God's war comes to an end. What
that last battle means we shall consider in the next section; for the
present we may note that insofar as they refer to the final destruction of God's enemies, Visions 2 and 3 do contain a chronological
reference which (as we have seen) is not really to be found in

[1] Eph. 2:6; 6:12 ff.; Jn. 3:19.

Vision 1. That we shall take up later. But the clear message of the 'one angel' is that the result of the war has already been decided by God. He is giving a macabre parody of the invitation to his other banquet, the 'marriage feast for his son ... "I have made ready my dinner, my oxen and my fat calves are killed, and everything is ready; come"' (Mt. 22:2–4; *cf.* Rev. 19:9). God has made his preparations. There is no question about their outcome.

3. THE THIRD VISION: HIS ENEMIES ARE DOOMED (19:19–21)

And I saw the beast and the kings of the earth with their armies gathered to make war against him who sits upon the horse and against his army. 20 *And the beast was captured, and with it the false prophet who in its presence had worked the signs by which he deceived those who had received the mark of the beast and those who worshipped its image. These two were thrown alive into the lake of fire that burns with sulphur.* 21 *And the rest were slain by the sword of him who sits upon the horse, the sword that issues from his mouth; and all the birds were gorged with their flesh.*

Here is the climax of the war in which God's Champion, who rode forth in Vision 1, brings his campaign to its predetermined end, which was proclaimed in Vision 2.

Here, moreover, is the tying together of other themes from earlier parts of the book. As in the person of the 'Captain of the armies of heaven' there emerges once again the Christ we have seen frequently elsewhere, so as leaders of the rebel forces we see the familiar figures of the beast and the false prophet. We did not know them exactly by those names; but by comparing verse 20 with 13:11–18, we see that these two are none other than the beast from the sea and the beast from the earth, the two great evil powers in the cosmic conflict of Scene 4. We met them also in different guise in Scene 6, where the whore and her beast were shown by their activity to be another representation of the same 'world rulers of this present darkness' (Eph. 6:12). Scene 4 includes both a warning and a preview of the destruction of evil (14:8–11; 17–20); the same theme expands to fill most of

Scene 6; and it is taken up again here and concentrated into three verses.

Like so much prophecy, the picture in these verses is much foreshortened. Into a single sentence ('These two were thrown alive into the lake of fire . . .') are condensed the protracted death throes of Babylon, which occupied a whole chapter in Scene 6; and in the same statement are merged the two destructions which there were distinct—the whore destroyed by the beast (17:16) and the beast by the Lamb (17:14). But in one respect the foreshortening is unlike that of much Old Testament prediction. When the old prophets looked on to the coming day of the Lord, they could not always distinguish between the distant peaks and the nearer hills. Some of their predictions referred to the last judgment day, some to more immediate judgments which have since come true. The complex events of which John's Vision is a simplified statement are not, however, a combination of things remote and near; they belong entirely to the last day. For the beast and the false prophet are the very principles of evil at work in this world, and when they are thrown into the lake of fire that will be the end of history. It is 'at the close of the age', Jesus tells us, that his angels will take 'all causes of sin and all evildoers, and throw them into the furnace of fire' (Mt. 13:40–42).

Vision 3, then, refers to the future in a way that the previous Visions do not. The first is timeless: ever since the days of his incarnation Christ has been King and Judge and Lord of hosts. The second is ambivalent: at all times it has been true that every creature which opposes itself to God is bound to perish, though the invitation to the gruesome supper does refer particularly to the time of the end (see pp. 184 f.). But the third is placed firmly at the final point of history.

Verse 20 predicts the doom of the supernatural powers of evil; verse 21 the doom of 'the rest'. It would seem that this means the men, rather than the demons, who follow the beast and false prophet, for two reasons: they are the counterpart of the army of Christ, which as has been suggested is as likely to be the church militant as the angelic host; and they are destroyed by the sword of Christ's mouth, which we take to be his message (Eph. 6:17; Heb. 4:12)—and it is men, not spirit beings, to whom that message is primarily addressed. It promises them salvation if they repent—in which case they are of course enrolled in the heavenly army—but doom if they rebel. The carnage of the battlefield described here is no doubt as much a symbol as the sword which slays the rebels. But if that is a mere symbol, what will be the reality?

4. THE FOURTH VISION: THE DEVIL (20:1-3)

Then I saw an angel coming down from heaven, holding in his hand the key of the bottomless pit and a great chain.

²And he seized the dragon, that ancient serpent, who is the Devil and Satan, and bound him for a thousand years, ³and threw him into the pit, and shut it and sealed it over him, that he should deceive the nations no more, till the thousand years were ended.

After that he must be loosed for a little while.

The controversies which have raged around this passage have been referred to already in the introduction to this Scene. What we shall consider here is the meaning of Satan's thousand years of imprisonment when seen in the context of the rest of Scripture.

On the face of it, the millennium has certainly not arrived yet. Television, radio, and the papers remind us daily (though not in these words) that Satan is alive and well and living on planet earth. How can he be said to be bound and sealed in the bottomless pit? This fourth Vision must surely therefore depict an event which is still in the future, like the battle of Vision 3.

But what exactly is said here, and what does the rest of Scripture have to say about it?

First, the deed: Satan is seized and bound. Whatever interpretation may seem to be placed on this by the writings of commentators or by the state of the world around us, Christ's own words must carry the greatest weight; and it is there, in the teaching of Christ, that we find the only other biblical reference to the binding of Satan. All three synoptic Gospels relate the parable of the 'strong man, fully armed', who 'guards his own palace' so that 'his goods are in peace'.[1] The story goes on to

[1] Lk. 11:21; *cf.* Mk. 3:27; Mt. 12:29.

describe the coming of 'one stronger than he', whose object is to plunder the strong man's property. The newcomer 'assails him and overcomes him', says Luke, and 'binds' him, say Matthew and Mark. Now we know from the context that this story was told expressly to illustrate something which happened *to Satan*, and which happened to him *at the time of the incarnation*. With Christ's first coming, the kingdom of God had come, and he went about casting out evil spirits to demonstrate precisely this— that Satan, for all his strength, had been seized and bound. We may still question what was actually implied by his 'imprisonment', since he seems to have continued very much at liberty; but there is no escaping the fact that the same word and action, the 'binding', link Revelation 20:2 with Mark 3:27.

Secondly, the object: Satan is thrown bound into the pit in order 'that he should deceive the nations no more'. Here again, it may seem quite untrue to say that he is even now prevented from deceiving the nations, and indeed has been unable to do so ever since the time of Christ; surely he does still deceive them, and this also indicates that the millennium is yet to come?

But again, consider what is said about the nations in the rest of Scripture. Their blessing will come through the seed of Abraham, their light through the promised servant of the Lord; and when Christ is born, the aged Simeon recognizes that the baby in his arms is himself the Seed and the Servant, a light for revelation to the nations as well as glory for Israel.[1] During the earthly life of Jesus, the undeceiving of the nations is foreshadowed by the visit of the wise men, and exemplified by his contacts with a Roman centurion, a Canaanite woman, and a company of Greeks.[2] The same pattern is repeated in the life of the church: 'men from every nation under heaven' come to its cradle on the day of Pentecost, and its career is marked by the conversion of Samaritans, Romans, and Greeks.[3] Alongside Christ's prediction that the gospel will be preached to all nations, so often understood as something which will be achieved only shortly before his second coming, we have to place Paul's startling claim, that already, in the middle of the first century, it '*has been* preached to

[1] Gn. 22:18, RV; 49:6; Lk. 2:32.
[2] Mt. 2:1–12; 8:5–13; 15:21–28; Jn. 12:20 ff.
[3] Acts 2:5; 8:5 ff.; 10; 11:19 ff.

every creature under heaven'.[1] What do the apostle's words imply? Clearly, the worldwide evangelism of which he speaks cannot mean an actual preaching to each individual race, let alone to each individual person. But what has happened is that the gospel has been made *available* for the nations in general, instead of being restricted to the Jews. Since the time of Christ it has been a universal gospel, in a way that it never was before in 'the times of ignorance' (Acts 17:30).

It seems therefore to be quite in accord with Scripture to see in the millennium of Revelation 20:3 a period during which Satan is no longer able to keep in his custody the nations which, till Christ came to bind him and steal them away from him, were altogether in his power. With this would agree the links which Christ makes between the casting out of Satan and the visit of the Greek enquirers (Jn. 12:20–32), and between Satan's downfall and the early evangelistic campaign of Luke 10:17, 18. Every time we see a new convert added to the church, Satan's inability to deceive the nations is proclaimed afresh.

The 'thousand years', which on our view began with Christ's first coming, are thus still in progress, and are equivalent to the 'three and a half years' during which the witnesses of Scene 3 preach in the world and the woman of Scene 4 survives in the desert. But at the end of that period there will come a time, according to verse 3b, when 'for a little while' Satan will be freed from the restraints which the church age has placed upon him.

There are parallels to this end-of-millennium release which are readily to be found both in Revelation and elsewhere, and which support the interpretation we have been following. In Scene 3 God's two witnesses, who have preached unhindered for three and a half years, are then silenced for three and a half days (see pp. 105 f.). In Scene 4 we saw the beast from the sea revive after it had been fatally wounded; and though we have taken this to be a perennial characteristic of Satan's godless society (pp. 124 f.), we should not be surprised to find it is true also as the over-all pattern of Satan's own career. In Scene 6, the period of the seven heads, which to John is present, is followed by the period of the ten horns, which to him is future, and seems again to indicate a great resurgence of evil at the end of time (pp.

[1] Mt. 24:14; Mk. 13:10; Col. 1:23.

164 f.). So here in Scene 7. 'When the thousand years are ended, Satan will be loosed from his prison and will come out to deceive the nations' (verses 7, 8).

Paul describes in 2 Thessalonians 2 what will immediately precede the return of Christ: 'The rebellion comes first, and the man of lawlessness is revealed' (verse 3). For the present, a divine power 'is restraining him', though in some respects, of course, 'the mystery of lawlessness is already at work' (verses 6, 7). But when the restraints are off, the world will see again 'the activity of Satan . . . with *all* wicked deception' (verses 9, 10). Paul's non-symbolic predictions tally so remarkably with the symbolic prophecies of Revelation 20 that it is hard to see how the two passages could refer to different circumstances.

If the Thessalonians passage describing the end of the church age is indeed parallel to the Revelation one describing the end of the millennium, it settles the relationship between millennium and parousia; for in it we are told that it is the glorious second coming of Christ—'the epiphany of his parousia' (as the phrase in 2 Thessalonians 2:8 could be translated)—which will put an end to the last outbreak of evil, which in its turn (according to the chapter before us) will have brought to an end the thousand years' restriction on Satan's activity.

It will again be obvious that the order in which John receives his Visions is not the order of the events of history. Vision 3 takes us on to the end of the age, then Vision 4 takes us back to the beginning. The fact that John saw the beast destroyed before he saw Satan bound has nothing to do with the order in which these things actually happen. That must be determined by what each Vision is found to mean in the light of the rest of Scripture. Compare, for example, the millennium of Visions 4 and 5 with the chapters in Ezekiel to which it is linked by the use of the names Gog and Magog (20:8). The sequence of events in Revelation 20 is the defeat of Satan, the resurrection of the saints to a thousand-year reign, the rebellion of Gog when Satan returns, and the last battle, followed in 21 by the establishment of the new Jerusalem. The last chapters of Ezekiel show a remarkable parallel: the defeat of Edom and the resurrection of Israel to prolonged peace (35–37), then the rebellion and defeat of Gog (38, 39), followed by the vision of the new Jerusalem

(40–48). The interesting thing is that the invitation to the birds, which formed Vision 2 (way back in 19:17 f., apparently 'before' the downfall of Satan and the millennium), is, according to Ezekiel, an invitation to *pick the bones of Gog* (39:17 ff.), *after* the last rebellion of Vision 5. John (or Ezekiel, or both) is less concerned with chronology than some of his commentators are.

5. THE FIFTH VISION: THE CHURCH (20:4-10)

Then I saw thrones, and seated on them were those to whom judgment was committed. Also I saw the souls of those who had been beheaded for their testimony to Jesus and for the word of God, and who had not worshipped the beast or its image and had not received its mark on their foreheads or their hands. They came to life, and reigned with Christ a thousand years.

5 The rest of the dead did not come to life until the thousand years were ended.

This is the first resurrection. 6 Blessed and holy is he who shares in the first resurrection! Over such the second death has no power, but they shall be priests of God and of Christ, and they shall reign with him a thousand years.

7 And when the thousand years are ended, Satan will be loosed from his prison 8 and will come out to deceive the nations which are at the four corners of the earth, that is, Gog and Magog, to gather them for battle; their number is like the sand of the sea.

9 And they marched up over the broad earth and surrounded the camp of the saints and the beloved city;

but fire came down from heaven and consumed them, 10 and the devil who had deceived them was thrown into the lake of fire and sulphur where the beast and the false prophet were, and they will be tormented day and night for ever and ever.

In verse 4, the RV is closer to John's original words than the RSV, which reads as though he is distinguishing between two groups, 'those to whom judgment was committed' and 'also . . . those who had been beheaded . . . and who had not worshipped the beast'. But in the Greek there is no full stop, and no 'also I saw', and what John wrote was more like this: 'And I saw thrones (and they sat on them, and judgment was given them), and the souls of the beheaded, and such as had not worshipped the beast; and they lived and reigned.' From this it seems more likely that the thrones of judgment are occupied by a single group, the living, reigning saints who have suffered execution and/or refused worship to the beast.[1]

Even with that clarification, the millennial reign of the saints here in Vision 5 is, at a first reading, as mysterious as the millennial binding of Satan in Vision 4. It begins with the 'first resurrection'. It involves those who have been beheaded for Christ's sake, so its setting is presumably a world beyond death. In it they appear as 'judges', which brings to mind the church's authority over men and angels spoken of in 1 Corinthians 6:2, 3; and that, in whatever world it is set, is certainly a thing of the future. Yet all this takes place before the general resurrection of verse 5a. Looked at in this way, the reign of the saints, though still apparently a part of time, not eternity, does indeed seem to be far removed from the here and now.

On the other hand, Vision 4 seemed to show that the millennium is yet another symbol of the present church age. And when we ask if the description of it in verses 4 to 6 *necessarily* places it a world away from our present experience, the answer is No. It is quite possible to understand it in terms of this world. Here, in this age, God's people already reign as kings and priests: John told us so in 1:6. Paul makes his statement about the church's future authority (1 Cor. 6:2, 3) precisely in order to show that she is already competent 'to judge . . . matters pertaining to this life'. The 'first resurrection' is a perfectly understandable way of referring to what the New Testament in many places describes as a passing from death to life, namely a man's rebirth as a Christian.[2] The saints are all who enjoy this new life; perhaps in verse 4 John is distinguishing between those who have and those who have not yet gone through physical death, but even so they all live and reign with Christ.[3] Verse 5 can be taken in the same sense; if God has not 'made us alive together with

[1] Dn. 7:22, RV.

[2] Jn. 5:24; Eph. 2:5; 1 Jn. 5:11, 12. On the other hand, many amillennialists take the phrase to mean the Christian's passing from this life to the next at the moment of death; the enthroned saints are those who have died. See Walvoord, p. 284.

[3] Again RSV is misleading, with its 'they came to life'—even, in some editions, 'they came to life again'. Follow RV: 'they *lived* and reigned'.

Christ', we shall remain 'dead through our trespasses' for the rest of this age, till the day when even the wicked rise—though not to eternal life—at the voice of the Son of man.[1] The second death we shall consider later, under verse 14.

With verse 7, Visions 4 and 5 converge. The thousand years, during which the saints have reigned and the devil has been held in check, end in a cataclysmic war. Names and places are different, but there can only ever be one battle which is both so universal and so final as this one. It must be the same as the Armageddon of Scene 5, where 'the kings of the whole world' are assembled for 'the great day of God the Almighty' (16:14 ff.); it must be the clash between the ten horn-kings and the Lamb who is King of kings, in Scene 6 (17:14); it must be the war already described in the third Vision of this present Scene, where the beast gathers 'the kings of the earth with their armies' to fight against the Rider on the white horse, and perishes with all his host (19:19–21). In each case the rout is too complete for these passages to be anything other than varied descriptions of the same event—the last battle of history. Whatever actual enemy went by the name of 'Gog, of the land of Magog' in Ezekiel's prophecy (38:2), in Revelation he cannot be any particular power, or even bloc of powers: the scale of the conflict makes it impossible. For note the breadth of vision, which sees gathered beneath the banner of Gog not merely 'the kings of the whole world', but 'the nations which are at the four corners of the earth . . . like the sand of the sea'. Note the depth of meaning when two powerful images are merged in one to describe the church—at once the heavenly *city* which has foundations, and the *camp* of those who are strangers and exiles on the earth (Heb. 11:9, 10, 13). Note the height from which the enemy's destruction falls, when God himself intervenes, and 'the Lord Jesus is revealed from heaven with his mighty angels in flaming fire' (2 Thes. 1:7); and note the length of the punishment which follows the ultimate downfall of Satan, 'tormented day and night for ever and ever'.

For these are the ultimate realities. The name of Ezekiel's Gog is extended to cover all 'who do not know God and . . . who do not obey the gospel of our Lord Jesus' (2 Thes. 1:8). This is how things are in the last analysis. In the end there is

[1] Eph. 2:5; Jn. 5:28, 29.

only Christ or Satan: Christ who lives for ever, and those with him, and Satan who dies for ever, and those with him; between whom men are choosing daily—while they may.

6. THE SIXTH VISION: THE LAST JUDGMENT (20:11-15)

Then I saw a great white throne and him who sat upon it; from his presence earth and sky fled away, and no place was found for them.

[12] And I saw the dead, great and small, standing before the throne, and books were opened. Also another book was opened, which is the book of life. And the dead were judged by what was written in the books, by what they had done. [13] And the sea gave up the dead in it, Death and Hades gave up the dead in them, and all were judged by what they had done.

[14] Then Death and Hades were thrown into the lake of fire. This is the second death, the lake of fire; [15] and if any one's name was not found written in the book of life, he was thrown into the lake of fire.

So far we have understood this Scene to be showing us underlying realities, at an even deeper level than Scene 4. That Scene depicted 'the drama of history', the forces of good and evil and the cosmic conflict in which they are engaged. It was geared to the historical process because the conflict is caused by the old age, in which Satan the usurper is 'ruler of this world', colliding with and overlapping the new age, the age of the kingdom of God; and the new began with Christ's first coming, while the old will end with his second coming, both of them datable points in history. This Scene depicts the same drama, and the beginning and end of the 'thousand years' here coincide with the beginning and end of the 'three and a half years' there. But everything is simplified. The historical setting of Christ's incarnation in chapter 12 and the complex struggle of chapters 13 and 14 are reduced to the most starkly drawn outline yet. The first five Visions of this 'drama behind history' show simply Christ and his victory, Satan and his defeat, and the church, in whose life the war between them is fought out. Such is the character of Scene 7; and it agrees well with our earlier conclusions about the meaning of the number seven, that the seventh scene of Revelation should deal with such matters.[1]

[1] See pp. 62 f.

Its sixth section is like the corresponding section of almost every other Scene, in that most of them have a sense of finality. Seal 6 shows the world's death throes, Trumpet 6 God's last warning, Vision 6 of the fourth Scene the appearance of the last plagues, Bowl 6 God's last punishment, and Word 6 the last mention of Babylon.

We may plot the meeting-point of two lines of thought, therefore, and expect that here in 20:11-15 we shall see what is in two senses the ultimate: fundamental reality, as in the rest of Scene 7; and a termination of some kind, as in the rest of the sixth sections. And so it proves to be. It is the end of the created order (verse 11), the end of all whose names are not in the book of life (verse 15), and the end of the power of death, 'the last enemy to be destroyed' (verse 14; 1 Cor. 15:26). The last great reality is, basically and necessarily, judgment: the payment of all accounts, the righting of all wrongs.

This may throw light on the question of who exactly are 'the dead' who appear before the great white throne.

They could be simply the spiritually dead, who, according to our interpretation of Vision 5, are to rise again at the end of the thousand years (20:5). Christ teaches in John 5:24-29 that a man 'has passed from death to life' when he receives the gospel. That whole passage forms an illuminating commentary on Visions 5 and 6. The present hearing of Christ's voice, which gives eternal life to the spiritually dead (verses 24, 25), could thus be the 'first resurrection'. The future hearing of it will awaken *all* who are dead (verses 28, 29): those who have already received spiritual life but have since died physically will be brought to life a second time (the resurrection of life), and those who have never risen from spiritual death will be awakened for the first and only time, simply to receive their condemnation (the resurrection of judgment). Either of these might be the 'second resurrection' which is implied as a counterpart to the first one. As the saints are exempted from judgment (verse 24), they may not even have to stand before the great white throne, let alone be judged there; in which case the dead of Vision 6 and those of Vision 5 are identical, namely the wicked, the spiritually dead.

Alternatively, Vision 6 may depict all the dead, saints and sinners alike, appearing before the judgment of the throne. This is the plain sense of the words, if read independently of Vision 5; it accommodates the statements of Paul, that we must all appear before the divine judgment (Rom. 14:10; 2 Cor. 5:10); yet it allows that the saints will not 'come into judgment' in the sense of John 5:24, since the appearance of their names in the book of life will countermand the accusations found against them in the books of human responsibility.

There are possible objections to the second view;[1] but it would be supported by what has been said earlier about the position of this passage in the over-all plan of the book. What it describes is fundamental, being a part of Scene 7; and terminal, being the sixth section of that scene. In two words, it portrays *judgment*, and more precisely the *last* judgment. In doing so, one would expect it to use the broadest of brush-strokes and the boldest of colours; so that the plainer interpretation would be preferable to the more complicated one. We may even be off the mark in enquiring too closely into who 'the dead' are; perhaps John is simply being shown the stark truth that after death comes judgment (Heb. 9:27).

The only additional factor, but one of prime importance, is the basis on which the judgment is made. First the books of accountability are opened, and men are 'judged by what was written in the books, by what they had done' (verse 12). According to the strict rule established far back in Scene 1, Christ says, 'I will give to each of you as your works deserve.'[2] Yet it is not on this alone that the eternal destiny of man depends; for there is also the book of life to be opened, and whether or not a human soul is consigned to the lake of fire turns on whether or not his name is found in that book. But there is no evasion of divine justice. The judgment is still according to works; the question is, whose works? The book of life belongs to the Lamb (13:8), and all whose names are in it belong to him; his obedience covers their sin, and his power within them produces holiness. They are therefore accounted righteous because of his righteousness, both

[1] It may be disputed whether this meaning of 'the dead' would in fact be the obvious one to John's mind; whether the judgment of Christians might not be a separate affair from the judgment of the great white throne; and whether 20:15 necessarily implies that any of 'the dead' *are* found written in the book of life.

[2] 2:23; see p. 51.

imputed and imparted to them. Those however who have not accepted the shame of sin and the glory of salvation, and have never had their names written in the book of life, have nothing to plead but their own righteousness; and that is woefully inadequate to exempt them from the 'second death', the death of the soul. John's statement in 20:6 implies that there is a 'first death', which does have power over the saints, and which is presumably the death of the body; the two deaths are no doubt what Christ has in mind when he says, 'Do not fear those who kill the body but cannot kill the soul; rather fear him who can destroy both soul and body in hell' (Mt. 10:28).

7. THE SEVENTH VISION: THE NEW AGE (21:1-8)

Then I saw a new heaven and a new earth; for the first heaven and the first earth had passed away, and the sea was no more.

²And I saw the holy city, new Jerusalem, coming down out of heaven from God, prepared as a bride adorned for her husband;

³and I heard a great voice from the throne saying, 'Behold, the dwelling of God is with men. He will dwell with them, and they shall be his people, and God himself will be with them;

⁴he will wipe away every tear from their eyes, and death shall be no more, neither shall there be mourning nor crying nor pain any more, for the former things have passed away.' ⁵And he who sat upon the throne said, 'Behold, I make all things new.'

Also he said, 'Write this, for these words are trustworthy and true.'

⁶And he said to me, 'It is done! I am the Alpha and the Omega, the beginning and the end.

To the thirsty I will give from the fountain of the water of life without payment. ⁷He who conquers shall have this heritage, and I will be his God and he shall be my son.

⁸But as for the cowardly, the faithless, the polluted, as for murderers, fornicators, sorcerers, idolaters, and all liars, their lot shall be in the lake that burns with fire and sulphur, which is the second death.'

As most of the sixth sections seem to deal with some sort of finality, so most of the seventh sections seem to look past the 'end' to what lies beyond. Scene 3 (the Trumpets), Scene 4 (the Visions of cosmic conflict), and Scene 6 (the Words about

Babylon), all close with glimpses of eternity, and with the sounds of the heavenly multitudes praising God for his finished work. In Scene 5, which is concerned with the punishments poured out on the world of men, and therefore has little to do with eternity, the final ruin of Bowl 7 is still accompanied by a voice from God's throne saying, 'It is done!' Even in Scene 2, where a silence follows the breaking open of Seal 7, the same principle holds good; for if every seventh section looks into eternity, and Scene 2 deals with the troubles of this life only, naturally there is nothing more to be said once the six Seals of history have been opened.

Scene 7 follows suit. It has described the whole drama of sin and redemption in the most basic terms, and now in its seventh section looks forward into the distances of eternity. Here is the new world. It is recognizably a 'world' still, for John can describe it in terms of a heaven and an earth—we shall not find ourselves in an entirely alien order of being. But it is radically renewed, and the 'sea', all that chafed and fretted under the dominion of God, represented in the ancient mythologies by the chaos-monster Tiamat, is done away altogether.

In thus looking ahead, Vision 7 provides a remarkable example of the process we have noticed already, by which the parts of Revelation are bound together as a whole, and themes are developed and expanded from Scene to Scene.[1] For, as we shall discover, Scene 8 takes up the seventh sections of nearly all the previous Scenes, and blends them into a single but complex picture of the life of the world to come. It is as if we have passed through a series of seven-sided rooms, in each of which one window has looked out on to eternity; and in a moment we shall step out of the seventh room and find ourselves in the open air.

We are not there yet, for Scene 8 does not begin till 21:9. But looking ahead, we cannot help noticing the remarkable feature mentioned above. Compare Scene 8 with the seventh Trumpet or the seventh Word, and you can see the likeness; they are as it were depictions of the same subject. But compare Scene 8 with the seventh Vision of the present scene, and what you see is not likeness. It is identity. They are not just the same subject; they are the same picture. In other words, the passage before us is a

[1] See pp. 139 ff.

preview, both in detail and in order, of the last Scene of the drama, which is shortly to open.

. Meditation on the links between the two makes it difficult to agree with Morris's statement that 'John rounds off his book with a series of somewhat miscellaneous observations', with 'connections . . . so loose indeed that some commentators feel that John did not revise this last section and put it into final shape'.[1] What will, on the contrary, prove to be one of Revelation's most closely organized passages will be considered at length when we reach Scene 8; for the moment it is sufficient to notice the correspondence between what we see here and what we shall see there:

21:2 = 21:10-21—the first Revelation: God's city;

21:3 = 21:22-27—the second Revelation: God's dwelling;

21:4, 5a = 22:1-5—the third Revelation: God's world renewed;

21:5b = 22:6-10—the fourth Revelation: God's word validated;

21:6a = 22:11-15—the fifth Revelation: God's work completed;

21:6b, 7 = 22:16, 17—the sixth Revelation: God's final blessing;

21:8 = 22:18, 19—the seventh Revelation: God's final curse.

[1] Morris, p. 257.

21:9–22:19

SCENE 8:
JERUSALEM THE BRIDE:
seven final Revelations

1. SCENE 8 OPENS (21:9)

IN keeping with the difference between Scene 8 and the rest, this introduction also differs slightly from those of earlier Scenes; an extended comment on its first verse seems preferable to a separate short essay.

Then came one of the seven angels who had the seven bowls full of the seven last plagues, and spoke to me, saying, 'Come, I will show you the Bride, the wife of the Lamb.'

A brief enough text. But by this time we are aware of the wealth of meaning that may be contained within the simplest statements of Revelation. Reflect on the two persons mentioned here, and you begin to discern a picture which is both magnificent and moving.

a. The angel

We have already noticed the Bowl-angels as one of the threads which bind Revelation into a unity. Their earliest appearance was in the sixth Vision of Scene 4. That was a preview of Scene 5, which when it came was devoted entirely to them. Next, one of them took John to a wilderness to show him the whore of Scene 6; and now another (or perhaps the same one) takes him to a mountain top to show him the bride, and thus to introduce Scene 8.

The same question arises with the Bowl-angels here as with the living creatures in Scene 2 (6:1–8). Does the author make use of them as a 'chorus' introducing Scenes 6 and 8 merely because they happen to be on hand? Or is there some reason why a Bowl-angel rather than anyone else should be judged an appropriate spokesman in each of these places?

A clue to a possible reason can be found in 15:1, where they first appear. The plagues they will bring are there called 'the last, for with them the wrath of God is *ended*'. This is a turning-point in the drama. The Letters of Scene 1 open up the condition of the church in the world; Scene 2 is a literal opening, the breaking of the Seals, to reveal the troubles that affect church and world alike; the Trumpets fill Scene 3 with warnings, which we can describe as open-ended, since they offer men a choice of either repentance or doom; and the Visions of Scene 4 open out before us the spiritual drama of history. There is, in fact, in all these four Scenes a sense of 'opening out'. From Scene 5 onwards, however, this is replaced by a feeling of 'closing in'. The first verse of chapter 15, a window looking from Scene 4 into Scene 5, reveals the angels by whose work the wrath of God is to be 'ended'; and so it proves to be. While earlier Scenes showed a quarter of the earth destroyed in the ordinary course of history (Scene 2) then a third destroyed by way of divine warning (Scene 3), in Scene 5, which concerns unrepentant humanity, it is the whole earth which ends in disaster. Likewise Scene 6 describes the total end of the world-principle, and Scene 7, looking even deeper, the end of Satan himself. In these three Scenes we find no longer warning, but punishment; not openings, but closings; not beginnings, but endings.

So far, the over-all structure of the drama shows a marked correspondence with the structure of most of its individual Scenes. Four sections are grouped together, two more follow, and then a seventh which in most cases is not climactic so much as *transcendent*, the point at which the engine reaches its maximum revolutions and shifts into a higher gear. Thus Scene 7 takes up the drama which in the first six Scenes has been played out on the stage of history, and at last takes us behind history. In keeping with what seems to be the meaning of the number seven, it finally reveals things as they really are. When all's said, there is only either Christ or Satan; and the one will triumph, while the other is doomed.

But we are then left with a puzzling question. If this analysis

is correct, *why is there an eighth Scene*? Would we not have expected
Revelation to reach a fitting end with the seventh Vision of the
seventh Scene? Have we now to find some mystic meaning in the
number eight, of which the only previous example John has given
us is the unlikely one of 17:11 (the beast as an eighth king)?

Yes; there is an outstanding 'eighth' in Scripture, which fails
to spring to our minds only because we do not normally think
of it as an eighth. But we know it very well. Call to mind the most
obvious seven of all, in its Old Testament form: the week of six
working days crowned with a sabbath day of rest. Back in the
first chapters of the Bible we find it as a pattern established by
God himself in his work of creation (Gn. 1:1—2:3). But it is
also to be found at the centre of the biblical revelation, for he has
ratified it in his work of redemption. It is on Good Friday, the
sixth day of the week, that the redeeming work of Christ reaches
its climax: 'It is finished' (Jn. 19:30), not at the empty tomb, but
at the cross; and the Saturday is the day of rest, the seventh day,
which crowns the 'week' of that mighty labour of love. In the
Jewish calendar 'that sabbath was a high day' (Jn. 19:31)—and
indeed it was! Only because the disciples did not foresee Christ's
rising was it a sad day for them (Lk. 24:17); they should have
rejoiced, for by then the work was done.

But of course there was something else to follow. The seventh
day proclaimed the end of the law, the end of the entire Old
Testament system based upon it, and the end of the reign of sin
which drew its strength from it. But the Sunday, the *eighth* day,
did more. It proclaimed Christ to be 'Son of God in power . . .
by his resurrection from the dead' (Rom. 1:4). The first day of a
new week was in fact the first day of a new age. Small wonder,
then, that the pattern laid down in creation and amplified in
redemption should reappear in the last chapters of the Bible, in
connection with what Christ calls the 'new world' (Mt. 19:28—
literally, the 'new genesis').

Scripture goes even further in providing blueprints to explain
the last Scene of Revelation. For up to 21:8 we have had not
only seven Scenes, but seven Scenes with seven sections each—
forty-nine visions. And no Jew could doubt for a moment the
significance of 'forty-nine', and what should follow it. 'You shall
count seven weeks of years, seven times seven years, so that the

time of the seven weeks of years shall be to you forty-nine years. Then you shall send abroad the loud trumpet . . . And you shall hallow the fiftieth year, and proclaim liberty throughout the land to all its inhabitants; it shall be a jubilee for you' (Lv. 25:8–10). With the year of jubilee comes the release of every slave, the reunion of every family, the restitution of all wrongs. The eighth which follows the seven, and the fiftieth which follows the seven times seven, are alike symbolic of a glorious new beginning.

With variations here and there, but basically unchanging in their outline, the Scenes of Revelation have brought us to the world's end at each sixth section, and at each seventh section have shown us the triumph of Christ. To what purpose then serves an eighth Scene? Adapting a comment of Caird's,[1] when we ask, 'What on earth can its meaning be?' the answer is precisely that it has no meaning *on earth*: it deals entirely with heaven. To repeat an illustration used earlier, from nearly every room one window has looked out into the garden; and on leaving the seventh room we find ourselves actually in the open air—in the garden of God, which is Paradise. 'The old has passed away . . . the new has come' (2 Cor. 5:17). It is altogether appropriate, therefore, that Scene 8 should be introduced by one of the angels whose Bowls brought to an end the wrath of God.

Few commentaries bring out the meaning of the eighth Scene better than the final paragraph of C. S. Lewis's classic story *The Last Battle*.

'The things that began to happen after that were so great and beautiful that I cannot write them. And for us this is the end of all the stories, and we can most truly say that they all lived happily ever after. But for them it was only the beginning of the real story. All their life in this world and all their adventures in Narnia had only been the cover and the title page: now at last they were beginning Chapter One of the Great Story which no one on earth has read: which goes on for ever: in which every chapter is better than the one before.'[2]

[1] Caird, p. 1, concerning the heavenly symbols of the book as a whole.
[2] C. S. Lewis, *The Last Battle* (Lane, 1956), p. 165.

b. The bride

Even that is not the best of it. The angel introduces the bliss of
heaven; the bride tells of those fortunate souls who are to enjoy
it.

We heard of *her*, in an indirect way, some time before we first
saw *him*. The Bowl-angels do not appear till half way through the
book, whereas in the case of the bride, both the symbol and the
thing symbolized are to be found right back in Scene 1.

The concept of the 'bride of Christ' forms the background of
the Letter to Thyatira, where Christ accuses the false teacher
Jezebel of 'beguiling my servants to practise immorality' (2:20).
That, as we have seen, could well have meant sexual sin. But
when applied to Jezebel herself, the term 'immorality' (2:21, 22)
is a metaphor for spiritual sin. We looked briefly at its long
biblical pedigree in studying chapter 2. When in the Old Testament Israel is accused of adultery, it is because she is bound in a
marriage relationship to her God ('Your Maker is your husband', Is. 54:5), and all sin can be described as unfaithfulness to
him. Now there can be no adultery where there is no marriage;
so if there was unfaithfulness in the church at Thyatira, it implies
that there were marriage vows to be unfaithful to. The Christians
there had been wedded to Christ. In other words, the Lord's
bride, in Old Testament times Israel, is nowadays the church, as
many a New Testament reference makes plain;[1] not of course
that he has two wives, but that 'Israel' and 'the church' are two
interchangeable names for the same bride. She is, in short, the
people of God in all ages, and another aspect of the 'mother'
figure of 12:1–6.

While the symbol of the bride is thus implicit in Scene 1, the
earthly reality which she symbolizes is quite explicit there, for the
state of the church (represented by the seven actual churches) is
the theme of that Scene. We thought at the time, no doubt, that
in the seven Letters the divine Physician was diagnosing the
church's 'real' condition. And on one level, that of the Christian
community's day to day life in the actual world, the Letters were
indeed an exhaustive diagnosis. But that was drama in black and
white on the flat small screen, compared with the full-colour,

[1] Mk. 2:19; Mt. 22:2 ff.; Jn. 3:29; 2 Cor. 11:2; Eph. 5:25 ff.

three-dimensional, wide-screen epic that has unrolled since. Our minds have been stretched to take in something of what the apostle calls 'the breadth and length and height and depth'; our vision has been enlarged to see, as the prophet puts it, 'a land of far distances' (Eph. 3:18; Is. 33:17, RV mg.) It is true that every one of these revelations has had practical lessons to teach. Nevertheless, there is no denying that the humdrum daily round, the nuts and bolts of Christian living, have receded from view while the immense drama has unfolded. The poor old Christian church, with her problems and faults, has been rather left in the shadow as beasts and angels have stolen the limelight. And there is a sense in which it is good for us to have our attention turned more and more away from our own mundane affairs and concentrated on events in the heavenlies, and on the warfare of the Christ: he must increase, and we must decrease, till in the end he will be all in all.

So much the more remarkable, then, is this introduction to Scene 8. We have passed beyond the bounds of space and time into regions of eternal light, unshadowed by the slightest imperfection, not to say evil; where the eyes of every created thing are fixed in adoration upon the Lamb alone. *Yet he is not alone.* For sharing the Scene with him—indeed, taking its very title role—is a radiant stranger whose features, as we consider them, are nonetheless familiar. Can it be . . .?

It is 'the Bride, the wife of the Lamb'. It is the church of Christ. *It is you: it is I.* Whatever other metaphors we may use to describe our relationship with Christ, the last Scene of the Bible shows us ourselves married to him, 'cleansed . . . by the washing of water with the word', presented before him 'in splendour, without spot or wrinkle or any such thing' (Eph. 5:26, 27). Well would it be for the church in her present unlovely state if she could recapture first a sense of awe appropriate to a vision of such splendour; then a sense of amazement that she, unworthy as she is, should be raised to the place of honour by her beloved Husband in the wedding feast of heaven; and finally a sense of determination that so far as in her lies, she *will* be worthy. Since she thus hopes in him, she will purify herself as he is pure (1 Jn. 3:3).

2. THE FIRST REVELATION: GOD'S CITY (21:10-21)

And in the Spirit he carried me away to a great, high mountain, and showed me the holy city Jerusalem coming down out of heaven from God, ¹¹*having the glory of God, its radiance like a most rare jewel, like a jasper, clear as crystal.*

¹²*It had a great, high wall, with twelve gates, and at the gates twelve angels, and on the gates the names of the twelve tribes of the sons of Israel were inscribed;* ¹³*on the east three gates, on the north three gates, on the south three gates, and on the west three gates.* ¹⁴*And the wall of the city had twelve foundations, and on them the twelve names of the twelve apostles of the Lamb.*

¹⁵*And he who talked to me had a measuring rod of gold to measure the city and its gates and walls.* ¹⁶*The city lies foursquare, its length the same as its breadth; and he measured the city with his rod, twelve thousand stadia; its length and breadth and height are equal.* ¹⁷*He also measured its wall, a hundred and forty-four cubits by a man's measure, that is, an angel's.*

¹⁸*The wall was built of jasper, while the city was pure gold, clear as glass.* ¹⁹*The foundations of the wall of the city were adorned with every jewel; the first was jasper, the second sapphire, the third agate, the fourth emerald,* ²⁰*the fifth onyx, the sixth carnelian, the seventh chrysolite, the eighth beryl, the ninth topaz, the tenth chrysoprase, the eleventh jacinth, the twelfth amethyst.* ²¹*And the twelve gates were twelve pearls, each of the gates made of a single pearl, and the street of the city was pure gold, transparent as glass.*

John's experience is very like Ezekiel's, carried away 'in the visions of God into the land of Israel, and set ... down upon a very high mountain, on which was a structure like a city' (40:2). Less closely related at this point, but becoming much more so in the next part of the Scene, is Isaiah's vision of the new Jerusalem (Is. 60). There is also, we may presume, a link between the precious stones which adorn John's city and the gems listed in Ezekiel 28:13 (the lost glories of the king of Tyre), Isaiah 54:11 f. (the rebuilding of Zion), and Exodus 28:17 ff. (the stones in the high priest's breastplate, engraved with the names of the tribes of Israel). The composite picture which John sees, including elements from all these other passages, shows him in turn the light of the city; its walls and gates; its measurements, and its beauty.

The commentaries take up at length these biblical parallels, and the details of John's description. For our purpose, perhaps the most fruitful question we can ask concerns the vision's object. What is it about the city that John is meant to notice in particular, and why? The answer is surely that he has to understand *how* God builds it—its structure; and this is of a piece with the preview of Scene 8 which he was given at the end of Scene 7, 'the holy city . . . *prepared* as a bride adorned for her husband' (21:2). The preparing of the bride is more easily described if the alternative symbol, the city, is used. And that is the object of this first Revelation of Scene 8: to reveal how God prepares her for the marriage feast.

Again Christian readers must remind themselves that the bride, the city, is none other than the church of Christ. The churches of John's day, the churches of our own day, all of us are looking into a mirror in these verses. We are not merely spectators—we are ourselves the spectacle: it is we who are 'God's building' (1 Cor. 3:9). The city shown to us here is what we shall be in the age to come, what in a sense we already are, on the level of 'the heavenlies', and what in our earthly experience God is presently making of us.

First he gives the city light. The word which the RSV translates as 'radiance' normally means a light-giving body, such as a star or a lamp.[1] Perhaps the RSV (along with most other modern versions) opts for an abstract noun rather than a concrete one because it is hard to visualize the city lit by a single enormous lamp 'like a most rare jewel, like a jasper'. We shall, however, see odder things than this (verses 16, 21), and certainly there is one particular light which is brought to mind by the lamps, stars, and torches of the first two Scenes: that is the Spirit of God, who indwells and illuminates the whole structure (1 Cor. 2:9–13; 3:9–17). The first characteristic of the eternal city is that 'God', by his Spirit, 'is in the midst of her' (Ps. 46:5); in the same way, Ezekiel's final word concerning the glorious Jerusalem of his vision is that her name henceforth shall be 'The Lord is there' (48:35).

[1] As in its only other New Testament occurrence, Phil. 2:15.

Next we see the gates and walls of the city. The reference to its 'twelve *foundations*' (verse 14) is rather misleading, and makes it unnecessarily hard to imagine. Perhaps John saw something like what the builders of a later age produced, in erecting the west front of the cathedral at Wells: each of its six great buttresses rises from an immense plinth, and they alternate with doorways which are scarcely higher than this row of 'foundations' or bases. The walls and gates of John's Jerusalem were likewise apparently set up in such a way that, when looking at any one of the four sides of the city, he would have seen, in order, corner-base—*gate*—base—*gate*—base—*gate*—corner-base.

Furthermore, each gate bears the name of a Jewish tribe, and each base the name of a Christian apostle. The entire twelve-plus-twelve, a number we have seen long ago reflected in the twenty-four elders of Scene 2 (they too encircled one who shone 'like jasper', 4:3), represent a group of related ideas. The gates and walls presumably stand for the city's security, the means of access to it, and the limits of it. The gates on every side of the city stand open, and 'men will come from east and west, and from north and south' to join Abraham and Isaac and Jacob there, Gentiles and Jews united in the heavenly Jerusalem (Lk. 13:28, 29). There is eternal safety for him who enters 'Israel', and who bases his faith on apostolic truth (Eph. 2:19–22). There is none outside those limits.

The city is then measured, as the temple was in Scene 3 (11:1), to show, no doubt, that every inch of it is accounted for, and known to God. The measuring reveals a shape quite odd enough to enable us to accept the oddity of the jewel-like lamp of verse 11, for the city turns out to be not only square, but cubic—and a cube, moreover, of 1,500 miles each way! It is presumably then the thickness, not the height, of its colossal wall which is given as 'a hundred and forty-four cubits'. These figures are necessarily human, or angelic, measurements (verse 17), because they express in human terms things which are in fact spiritual, or more accurately multi-dimensional, and therefore incapable of actual computation as we would understand it.[1] But they present no

[1] See p. 130. Hidden in the angel's arithmetic is another significant figure, for if he measured all the edges of the cube, the total measurement would have been 12 × 12,000 stadia = 144,000!

problem to John's guide, whose rod of gold can reckon with equal ease the feet and inches of the wall's thickness and the hundreds of miles of its length. 'You examine me and know me . . . you read my thoughts from far away . . . you know every detail of my conduct' (Ps. 139:1-3, JB).

Lastly the beauty of new Jerusalem is portrayed: walls encrusted with precious stones, every gate a single pearl, the buildings and open spaces of the city made of an inconceivable crystal-clear gold. With this glittering splendour God completes his preparation of 'the Bride, the wife of the Lamb'. The light of his Spirit illuminates her from within; she unites in one body all who belong to the twelve tribes and are built upon the teaching of the twelve apostles; she is known to him in every last detail; and he clothes her in matchless beauty. For whatever of this preparation we may see in the church as we know her today, we may thank God: it is his doing, and 'whatever God does endures for ever' (Ec. 3:14). Conversely, whatever is no part of this permanent work should have no place among us. If it will not enhance the bride's beauty then, when she comes to share her Bridegroom's place at the marriage feast, it has no business to sully her now.

3. THE SECOND REVELATION: GOD'S DWELLING (21:22-27)

And I saw no temple in the city, for its temple is the Lord God the Almighty and the Lamb.

23 And the city has no need of sun or moon to shine upon it, for the glory of God is its light, and its lamp is the Lamb.

24 By its light shall the nations walk; and the kings of the earth shall bring their glory into it, 25 and its gates shall never be shut by day—and there shall be no night there; 26 they shall bring into it the glory and the honour of the nations.

27 But nothing unclean shall enter it, nor any one who practises abomination or falsehood, but only those who are written in the Lamb's book of life.

It was Isaiah who declared, 'You shall call your walls Salvation, and your gates Praise' (60:18). John's vision of the new Jeru salem, at first so similar to Ezekiel's, becomes more and more like Isaiah's; the links between the passage before us and the glorious sixtieth chapter of Isaiah are remarkable.[1]

But as before, we must ask what is the purpose of these verses. What we are meant to see in them is not only a network of Scripture references, but a powerful statement of biblical doctrine. If the first of these Revelations in Scene 8 sums up the church, the second of them sums up the gospel. So the synopsis at the end of Scene 7 made clear; for the gospel is the divine message which brings men back into relationship with God, and that is the heading given there to the Revelation which is seen here—the promise that 'he will dwell with them, and they shall be his people' (21:3).

That is why this second Revelation concerns a temple, or rather the lack of one. The Jewish Temple, like its predecessor the Tabernacle, was the place where God had said he would meet his people, and be known to be dwelling among them (1 Ki. 6:11-13; Ex. 25:22). In the heavenly Jerusalem there is no need of a temple, because merely to be in the city is to be with him. His glory pervades every nook and cranny of it; we have already seen that even the gold of which it is built is 'transparent as glass' (verse 21); and not only is the glory itself seen everywhere, but everything else is seen in the light of it. Such total interpenetration between man and his God—the light in the city, the city in the light—is the aim and object of the gospel.

It is the gospel not simply of God, but of Christ. In one of those unobtrusive pointers to the deity of Christ with which Scripture abounds, the verse which speaks of the replacing of sun and moon by the divine light goes on to say (in Is. 60:19) that 'the Lord will be your everlasting light, and your God will be your glory.' But when John uses the same turn of phrase concerning the city, he says that 'the glory of God is its light, and its lamp is *the Lamb*.' The Lord and the Lamb are one and the same; Jehovah (despite what his so-called 'Witnesses' say!) is Jesus; only he is 'the light of the world', and only the man who follows him 'will have the light of life' (Jn. 8:12).

The phrase 'the light of the world' implies a third great truth

[1] With verses 23-26, cf. Is. 60:19, 3, 11. Compare also verse 27 and Is. 52:1.

about the gospel: 'By its light shall *the nations* walk' (verse 24)—the Gentiles as well as the Jews, for it is a universal message. As we have seen, its gates are open to all, regardless of race, or (we may add) wealth, brains, power, or influence.

Fourthly, it is a glorious gospel. 'The glory and the honour of the nations' contribute to the magnificence of the city; all that is truly good and beautiful in this world will reappear there, purified and enhanced in the perfect setting its Maker intended for it; nothing of real value is lost.

Lastly, it is a gospel of holiness, and a gospel of salvation. The only thing which disqualifies a man from entering the presence of God is sin; the only thing which will qualify him to enter is to have his name written in the book of life of the slain Lamb. These are two sides of the same coin. Either he trusts in the crucified Christ for the forgiveness of his sins, or he is excluded from the Presence. 'If you do not believe that I am he you will die in your sins' (Jn. 8:24, JB).

Such is the gospel proclaimed from one end of the Scriptures to the other, and crystallized here in the Revelation to John.

4. THE THIRD REVELATION: GOD'S WORLD RENEWED (22:1-5)

Then he showed me the river of the water of life, bright as crystal, flowing from the throne of God and of the Lamb ²through the middle of the street of the city; also, on either side of the river, the tree of life with its twelve kinds of fruit, yielding its fruit each month; and the leaves of the tree were for the healing of the nations.

³There shall no more be anything accursed, but the throne of God and of the Lamb shall be in it, and his servants shall worship him; ⁴they shall see his face, and his name shall be on their foreheads. ⁵And night shall be no more; they need no light of lamp or sun, for the Lord God will be their light, and they shall reign for ever and ever.

Reminiscences of the rest of the Bible are now coming thick and fast. The springing of the water of life was foreseen by three of the prophets of Israel, Joel before the exile (3:18), Ezekiel during it (47:1-9), and Zechariah after it (14:8). The miraculous river flows, in fact, through the length of Scripture. It nourishes the godly life of the Old Testament saints (Ps. 1:1–3; Jer. 17:7, 8), and is explained by our Lord as the life-giving Spirit who is to be received only from him (Jn. 4:14; 7:37–39). Ezekiel's vision, indeed, resembles John's in some detail, and includes tree as well as river: 'On the banks, on both sides of the river, there will grow all kinds of trees for food. Their leaves will not wither nor their fruit fail, but they will bear fresh fruit every month, because the water for them flows from the sanctuary. Their fruit will be for food, and their leaves for healing' (47:12).

But the most significant parallel is with the opening chapters of Genesis. This tie-rod, running from end to end of the sixty-six books, shows that the third Revelation of heaven here in Scene 8 is a summary of the biblical doctrine of creation. The heading given to it at the end of Scene 7 was: ' "The former things have passed away . . . Behold, I make all things new" ' (21:4, 5). It concerns what Christ called 'the new world' (Mt. 19:28), literally 'the new genesis'. The first chapter of the Bible describes how God made the world; the last one shows how he will remake it. The creation as it was, and as it will be, is an immense organism alive with the life of God, for the stream flows 'from the throne of God and of the Lamb', and thence 'through the middle of the street of the city'. Notice here that the Spirit proceeds from the Father *and the Son*, and the Son's power not only creates but also sustains the whole thing: 'He is before all things, and in him all things hold together' (Col: 1:17). Thus the rivers and trees of Genesis reappear as living water and continual fruitfulness (verses 1, 2).

Two elements have been added to the pristine simplicity of the Genesis picture by the experience of human history. Instead of a garden only, there is now the developed structure of a garden city: Eve, 'the mother of all living' (Gn. 3:20), has in the plan of God become the ancestress of a great society of nations. The other difference is that the plans of Satan have been maturing also. A curse has come upon the human race, and the nations need healing. That is why the original creation has had to be remade.

But with the curse removed by Christ, the new creation will eventually be what it was meant to be: the throne at the centre of all, and the people of God seeing him, serving him, sealed by his name, and reigning with him in everlasting day.

5. THE FOURTH REVELATION: GOD'S WORD VALIDATED (22:6-10)

And he said to me, 'These words are trustworthy and true. And the Lord, the God of the spirits of the prophets, has sent his angel to show his servants what must soon take place. ⁷ And behold, I am coming soon.' Blessed is he who keeps the words of the prophecy of this book.

⁸ I John am he who heard and saw these things. And when I heard and saw them, I fell down to worship at the feet of the angel who showed them to me; ⁹ but he said to me, 'You must not do that! I am a fellow servant with you and your brethren the prophets, and with those who keep the words of this book. Worship God.'

¹⁰ And he said to me, 'Do not seal up the words of the prophecy of this book, for the time is near.'

The English title for the whole book is Revelation; we are using the same word to describe each of the seven sections of this last Scene of it; and now the subject of the present passage, the fourth of those sections, is itself 'revelation'—that is, the doctrine of how God makes himself known to man. In a nutshell, the doctrine was stated thus at the end of Scene 7: 'Write this, for these words are trustworthy and true' (21:5b). Here it is filled out, and we may learn much from it concerning the method and the matter, the value and the validity, of God's revelation of himself.

His method has always been to convey messages about himself through certain chosen men—supremely, of course, through his Son (Heb. 1:2), but before the brief years of the Son's incarnation it was the 'goodly fellowship of the prophets', and afterwards it was 'the glorious company of the apostles', who were his messengers. This self-revealing Lord is named (verse 6 makes no bones about it) as 'the God of the spirits' of these men, wielding divine authority over their minds and hearts. The free play of their literary skill or human temperament is in no way denied. What is asserted is that the message they pass on represents precisely the truths which the God who is dealing with their spirits requires to be passed on.

Its matter is 'what must soon take place'. Here is another link with the beginning of the book, where we saw that 'soon' meant the bringing into our immediate view of things which in the time of Daniel had still been far future.[1] But throughout Scripture, even with Daniel's prophecies, the real message of God always concerns what must *soon*—indeed, *now*—take place, for the words John uses for 'soon' may signify either 'in a short time' or 'quickly, at once, without delay' (AG). It speaks to me, about what I shall be doing and thinking today, and what I am planning for tomorrow. 'Behold, now is the acceptable time; behold, now is the day of salvation' (2 Cor. 6:2). This divine immediacy is again centred on the Son: as he was the supreme example of God's method of revelation through chosen messageners, so he is also himself the heart of the matter. What will *soon* happen is that the Son will *soon* come. One of the oldest prayers of the Christian church, found in 1 Corinthians 16:22, is 'Maranatha' (AV), 'Our Lord, come!'; and it expects two kinds of answer—the bodily return of Christ to this earth, and also his coming as Saviour and Lord into our experience 'soon': today, this very hour.

This in itself shows the value of God's self-revealing. The knowledge of him which comes to us through 'the prophecy of this book', and by extension through the Bible as a whole, cannot help but bring a blessing, and the blessing is the knowledge of God in Christ given to those who 'keep' the words of it. The term used here for 'keep' is frequent in John's Gospel, and means to 'observe, fulfill, pay attention to' laws or teachings (AG). The attentive, obedient study of Scripture, therefore, and of this last book which sums it up, produces not a mind stuffed with knowledge, but a spirit quickened into life.

The validity of the message is testified by a strange feature of John's experience as related here. Once more we put ourselves in his place, and hear a voice—apparently the same voice throughout—saying, ' "I am coming soon . . . You must not [worship me]! I am a fellow servant with you . . . I am coming soon . . . I Jesus' (verses 7, 9, 12, 16). Is it the angel, since he refuses John's worship? Or is it the divine Christ, who accepts such worship? Scene 8 contains the most striking of all John's shifts of focus. We have noticed them in a number of places before, but here, as we might expect in the Scene which reveals

[1] See p. 32.

the last concentration of the light of God, it is very hard indeed
to discern which of its dazzling personages is speaking at any
one time. What that means in relation to the Word of God is that
though the angel and the Christ are distinct persons, yet their
messages are indistinguishable. It is brought home to us in this
highly dramatic way that the book is, as we were told in its
opening verses, a Revelation given by God to Christ, by Christ
to the angel, by the angel to John, and by John to us, without at
any stage losing its divine authority; so that what John says is
what God has said. Such indeed is the classical doctrine of the
inspiration of Scripture as a whole, underlining the belief that
John's book is intended as a summary of, rather than an addition
to, the rest.

6. THE FIFTH REVELATION: GOD'S WORK COMPLETED (22:11-15)

'*Let the evildoer still do evil, and the filthy still be filthy, and the righteous
still do right, and the holy still be holy.*' *12'Behold, I am coming soon,
bringing my recompense, to repay every one for what he has done. 13 I am
the Alpha and the Omega, the first and the last, the beginning and the
end.' 14 Blessed are those who wash their robes, that they may have the
right to the tree of life and that they may enter the city by the gates. 15 Outside are the dogs and sorcerers and fornicators and murderers and idolaters
and every one who loves and practises falsehood.*

Scene 7's heading to this section is the knot at the far end of yet
another thread running right through Scripture. In Eden the
work of creation was finished (Gn. 2:1, 2); at Calvary the work
of redemption was finished (Jn. 19:30); in Paradise the voice of
God will finally say, concerning the whole of his work, 'It is
done!' (21:6). The verses before us sum up the biblical doctrine of eschatology, the 'last things'; their subject is the final
state of God's creation. This will be brought about by Christ,
who once again indicates his deity by taking the titles Alpha and
Omega,[1] the beginning and the end, which in 21:6 belong to
God.

Verse 11 is a summary of human destiny. The force of the

[1] See p. 35.

words is not clear in the English, which could mean three different things. The verse sounds like an exhortation ('Be bad', 'Be good'), or a permission ('You are allowed to be bad', or 'to be good'); but in fact we come closest to John's Greek when we understand it as a declaration. At this point also, Revelation 22 corresponds to Genesis 1, and is illuminated by it, for the verbs which God utters are of the same kind in both places.[1] As at the beginning the divine Word said, 'Let there be light', and there was light, so at the end the same Word will declare, magisterially and definitively, 'Let this man be evil, and that man holy'; and it will be so, thenceforth and for evermore. The words 'indicate the fixity of the state' in which both good and evil will find themselves; there will have come 'a time when change will be impossible—when no further opportunity will be given for repentance on the one hand or for apostasy on the other'.[2] If therefore 'it is appointed for men to die once, and after that comes judgment' (Heb. 9:27), and if the judgment is the end, and ushers in this final state of permanent righteousness or unrighteousness, it follows that on the one hand we have no grounds for hope in any kind of second chance, or reincarnation, and must take seriously this present life as the only opportunity for a change of heart; and on the other hand we need have no fears that heaven, once attained, will ever be lost again.

Verse 12 emphasizes these last points, and shows on what the outcome depends. The final state is directly related to this present life: it will be a repayment to every man for what he has done here. And it is Christ's recompense, since 'what he has done' means really 'what he has done with Christ' and 'what he has allowed Christ to do through him'. That criterion, forgotten or ignored by millions, will be re-established on the day of judgment, for he is the last as well as the first, the end as well as the beginning.

---

[1] Aorist imperatives (referring of course to the Greek version of Genesis). The NEB, and still more JB ('Meanwhile let the sinner go on sinning, and the unclean continue to be unclean', etc.), translate as if the Greek verbs were present imperatives, and show how a preconceived idea of what the passage means can blind a translator to what the text actually says.

[2] Swete, p. 305.

Verses 14 and 15 make plain who it is who belongs in the city, and who will be left outside. Those whose character and practice are evil ('dogs', the pariahs of an eastern city's slums, symbolize all who are unclean) are on that account barred from the city of God. But those who are admitted do not get in on account of their goodness. The blessing is theirs solely because they have washed their robes—'made them white', as John was told in 7:14, 'in the blood of the Lamb'. Knowing themselves to be cleansed by the crucified Christ, they have 'the right to the tree of life'. What was forbidden to the first man is now available to the new men, and sums up what was said above concerning verse 11: 'Take also of the tree of life, and eat, and live for ever' (Gn. 3:22).

7. THE SIXTH REVELATION: GOD'S FINAL BLESSING (22:16, 17)

'I Jesus have sent my angel to you with this testimony for the churches. I am the root and the offspring of David, the bright morning star.' [17] *The Spirit and the Bride say, 'Come.' And let him who hears say, 'Come.' And let him who is thirsty come, let him who desires take the water of life without price.*

The first five sections of this Scene have summarized the doctrines of the church, the gospel, creation, revelation, and the last things. The end of the book is, as Glasson says, 'a kind of triumphant finale to the Bible; it reminds us of a composer gathering up the themes of his symphony in a closing burst of glorious music.'[1] And now, in the sixth section, all the revealed truth of God is crystallized in two verses. David, Israel's greatest king, stands for the glory of the whole Israelite economy; but Jesus is much more. He is not only 'great David's greater Son', Lord and King of the new Israel. He is also David's Lord; he is Isaiah's 'everlasting Father'; before Abraham was, he is; indeed he is before all things (Mt. 22:41 ff.; Is. 9:6; Jn. 8:58; Col. 1:17). He is, in two words, both 'the *root* and the *offspring* of David', both his ancestor and his descendant, adding another all-

[1] Glasson, p. 6.

inclusive pair of titles to those of verse 13. He encompasses the whole of history.

Then, as the 'bright morning star', he heralds the dawn of eternity, telling us that this life is only the prelude to the real life of the world to come; and by sending his angel with this testimony, he shows the love, power, and wisdom of the God who wants to reveal these things to his creatures.

Nor does the scheme of divine truth, embracing time and eternity and announcing itself to men, fail of its effect, for all whose ears are opened to it respond, and welcome the coming Christ. That is, the bride—the church—welcomes her Bridegroom, because the Spirit who teaches her to pray (Rom. 8:26 f.) is praying in the same terms.

Is the reader thirsty for such blessing? Does he desire to be included in this glorious scheme of salvation? It is the water of life, there for the taking, if he for his part is prepared to meet Christ's coming by coming himself to receive the blessing.

8. THE SEVENTH REVELATION: GOD'S FINAL CURSE (22:18, 19)

I warn every one who hears the words of the prophecy of this book: if any one adds to them, God will add to him the plagues described in this book, [19] *and if any one takes away from the words of the book of this prophecy, God will take away his share in the tree of life and in the holy city, which are described in this book.*

The stretching of one's mind and heart which results from prayerful study of Revelation should ensure that one does not take these verses at their surface value. Tampering with the text of the last book of the Bible is a minor matter compared with the sin they really condemn. For if (as our reading has seemed to show) the whole biblical revelation is summed up in this book, and particularly in this last Scene of the book, and in the most concentrated form of all in verses 16 and 17, then of course we dare not add to it or take from it. It is the gospel itself that we should be obscuring or impairing. And the threat of plagues added, and life taken away, with which God reacts to such cavalier treatment of his message, is not mere bombast, but a statement of sober fact.

For if we believe that what God has said in his book is not sufficient for salvation, but that we need to make certain additions of our own if we are to be saved; or if we believe that some of the demands of God's book are superfluous, and we can get by without observing them; then we are not only saying that we know better than him—we are (which is much worse) acting as if that were true. Rudeness he can forgive; but blind wilfulness is the sin against the Holy Spirit. Of the curse that comes upon those who alter the gospel to suit themselves, it will be said, with the most terrible truth, that they have asked for it.

22:20, 21

THE EPILOGUE

THE BOOK WE COULD DO WITHOUT

'TO the end that we should alway remember the exceeding
great love of our Master, and only Saviour, Jesus Christ,
thus dying for us, and the innumerable benefits which by his
precious blood-shedding he hath obtained to us; he hath
instituted and ordained holy mysteries, as *pledges of his love*, and
for a continual remembrance of his death, to our great and end-
less comfort.'

So speaks the Book of Common Prayer, concerning the communion; and so also Christ instituted baptism as a similar pledge,
this to be a sign and seal of the beginning of the Christian life,
as that is of the continuing of it.

We practise both sacraments at Christ's command, for the
church must observe what her Lord says. Yet we are well aware
that this 'must' is not of the same kind as the word in John 3:7,
'You must be born anew.' The new birth is a *sine qua non*; without
it we perish. No such threat attaches to non-observance of the
sacraments, for Christ is quite clear that eternal life is a matter of
coming *to him*, not to his sacrament—coming, hearing, repenting,
believing. But though it is by the inward state of the soul that its
destiny stands or falls, yet still the outward observances are the
subject of a divine command. To repentance and faith belongs a
'must' of necessity; to baptism and communion, a 'must' of
obligation.

A *pledge of his love*—we could apply the same beautiful words, in
the same sense, to the book of Revelation. In many places our
interpretation of the book has suggested that there is nothing
new in it, no extra truth which is not available elsewhere in
Scripture. This is borne out by a phrase here, in the second to last
verse of the last chapter. 'He who testifies to these things' is, as
the context makes plain, Jesus Christ the corresponding phrase

in the second verse of the first chapter, the 'testimony of Jesus', is thus vouched for as a subjective genitive—that is, the word 'of' means the witness which Jesus himself bears, and not someone else's witness to him. The things of which Jesus bears witness are the truths of Revelation. We have been given to understand that the whole book is a message given by the Father to the Son, for him to make known, through his angel, to John, so that John can in turn pass it on to the church (1:1, 2; 22:6). But as we saw in studying the Prologue,[1] the Word of God and the Witness of Jesus were not only the great drama which John was to be shown on Patmos (1:2). The cause of his being on the island at all was his loyalty to the Word and the Witness; for he had already received them. Indeed, as early as the time of the passion Jesus could say concerning his apostles, in his prayer to his Father, 'I *have given* them the words which thou gavest me' (Jn. 17:8), and what they learnt from him after his resurrection and from the Holy Spirit after Pentecost was no more than an exposition of what was already theirs in embryo (Lk. 24:44–48; Jn. 14:26). There is no indication in the New Testament that the gospel being preached all over the Roman world by the middle of the first century was in any way defective—that the Word and the Witness already known to John before he went to Patmos had certain gaps in them which his Revelation was intended to fill.

No; from that point of view the book of Revelation is quite superfluous. The sixty-five books from Genesis to Jude contain sufficient gospel to save the world. To what purpose then serves the sixty-sixth?

The same phrase, the Word and the Witness, tells us the answer. For that was what John already knew; but it was also what he was then shown, all over again, in the drama of Patmos. His great vision was the last and grandest repeat of the patterns. There come to mind, incongruous yet remarkably apt, the claims of the makers of modern patent foods—nothing added, nothing taken away, just pure concentrated goodness! And when we ask why the already-completed revelation of God should need this final restatement, the answer to that question may be found in the comparison with which we began. We *know* we have been

[1] See p. 31.

washed from our sins, we *know* that the cross avails to cleanse us daily; we must of necessity know these things if we are to have eternal life. There is no similar 'must' about the sacraments—we can be saved without them. But who would want to disregard these 'pledges of his love', by which he makes real to us, in living, dramatic form, the truths we already know?

And Revelation is a 'pledge of his love'. We could do without it; it tells us nothing we could not learn elsewhere in Scripture. But Jesus has given it to us as a sacrament of the imagination, to quicken the pulse and set the soul aflame over the gospel which all too often we take for granted.

THE AUTHOR'S LAST WORD (22:20, 21)

*He who testifies to these things says, 'Surely I am coming soon.' Amen. Come, Lord Jesus! * [21] *The grace of the Lord Jesus be with all the saints. Amen.*

To all the saints, God's people everywhere, the closing greeting is addressed, leaving in our mind's eye as we close the book (not just Revelation, but the whole volume of Scripture) one final picture of the Lord Jesus. It is threefold, reminding us that he is 'the same yesterday and today and forever' (Heb. 13:8).

First, he is the 'faithful witness' (1:5; 3:14), testifying to the truth of what John has been shown, and thereby, as we have seen, authenticating the entire message—based in the Old Testament and crowned with the New, its far side in the shadow of law and its near side bright with gospel: to all 'these things' he has borne witness. Thus with John's Revelation the canon of Scripture closes and stands complete, the Word of God and the Witness of Jesus.

He is also the coming one: he promises it, the church responds to the promise with gladness. He who declared the message of salvation in those far-off days will soon return to complete the work, and take his ransomed saints home to heaven.

In the meantime, he is the giver of grace, who cheers and strengthens his expectant people by bringing home to them the living power both of the message to which they look back and of the hope to which they look forward. That grace, a tonic for hard times, is available to every man who is prepared to take to his heart not only these twenty-two chapters, but all 'the revelation of Jesus Christ, which God gave him to show to his servants . . . Blessed is he who reads' (1:1, 3).